COASTAL FORCES
AT WAR

Haynes Publishing

COASTAL FORCES
AT WAR

THE ROYAL NAVY'S 'LITTLE SHIPS' IN THE NARROW SEAS 1939-45

DAVID JEFFERSON

SECOND EDITION

First published in 1996 by Patrick Stephens Limited,
an imprint of Haynes Publishing

This 2nd Edition published in 2008 by
Haynes Publishing

British Library Cataloguing-in-Publication Data:
A catalogue record for this book is available from the
British Library.

ISBN 978 1 84425 562 7

Library of Congress catalog card number 2008926347

Haynes Publishing,
Sparkford, Yeovil, Somerset, BA22 7JJ

Printed and bound in Great Britain

Jacket illustrations.
Front, top: MGB Flotilla manoeuvring at sea;
bottom: British Power Boats of 6th MGB Flotilla.
Back, top: Officers and crew of MTB *459* (National
Archives of Canada PA108024);
bottom: HMS Hornet, Gosport (IWM A25146)

Contents

Foreword

Commander Christopher W.S. Dreyer DSO, DSC AND BAR, RN (RTD)

I joined MTBs early in January 1940, and then spent nearly seven years either in the boats or on the staff or in the Admiralty, doing jobs connected with Coastal Forces. After I was invalided out of the Royal Navy in 1956, I spent more than 20 years working for Vosper, one of the major designers and builders of small, fast warships. So I have been involved with Coastal Forces for much of my working life, and I have, naturally, a special affection for these warships, and some knowledge of them and their history.

For a naval officer, the main attraction of small ships is the marvellous opportunity which they give for command at a young age. For both officers and men there is also the sense of belonging to a team, living in close company, and with everyone playing an important part. A worked-up, efficient Coastal Force craft in wartime was a really very special team of shipmates and friends.

Since Peter Scott wrote his excellent *Battle of the Narrow Seas* in 1945, there have been a number of books published describing the boats, the people, and the battles. Some have been good, and some less so – but every accurate history is valuable in helping to keep the record straight for the future.

David Jefferson has written an excellent and well-researched record, which is specially valuable in that it includes a number of pieces of the story which have been little reported elsewhere, in particular regarding the landing of agents and small raiding units in Brittany and other places, mainly by the 15th MGB Flotilla, and the story of the return of the 1st MTB Flotilla from Malta to the UK through the canals of France late in 1939.

I commend this book to everyone who is interested in the story of Coastal Forces.

Author's Note

Christopher Dreyer died on 24 June 2003.

Acknowledgements

I should like to acknowledge the following: the late Commander Christopher Dreyer, DSO, DSC*, RN (Rtd) who read the manuscript for the first edition and made helpful corrections and suggestions; Douglas Hunt DSC for putting me in touch with many of those listed below; Geoffrey Hudson, the Honorary Historian of the former Coastal Forces Veterans' Association (officially disbanded in 2007) for his guidance, particularly with the content of Chapter 3.

I am particularly grateful to those who allowed me access to personal war diaries and documents, including: Charles Coles OBE, VRD; Antony Hichens; Captain Denis Jermain, DSC*; Captain H.L. Lloyd, CBE, DSC; Vice-Admiral D.H. Mason, CB, CVO; Harold Pickles, DSM; L.C. Reynolds, OBE, DSC; R.E. Seddon, DSC; and A.M. Turner of the Lowestoft Archaeological and Local History Society.

For photographs from private collections: Frederick Bourne, DSC; R.G.R. Haggard; Grahame Nicholls; the Coastal Forces Heritage Trust; and MTB *102* Trust.

For their individual contributions: Rear Admiral Courtney Anderson, CB; J.R. Bone; Frederick Bourne, DSC; Arthur Coleman; Lt-Cdr Jack Collings; Cdr Sir John Eardley-Wilmot, MVO, DSC, RN; Michel Guillou; R.G.R. Haggard; Norman Kaufmann; R.C. Lawrence; R.A. Merritt; The Rt Hon Lord Newborough, DSC; James Shadbolt, MBE; Andrew Smith, DSC; Ian Trelawny, OBE, DSC; Lt-Cdr Ben Warlow, RN; Captain Roger Webber, RN; Peter Williams, DSC; and R.G. Woods, DSC.

From the Allied navies: J. Czarnota; Per Danielsen, DSC; Finn-Christian M. Stumoen; Marcel Ollivier; and Captain Johan Schreuder, DSC.

Mrs Janet Stuart, for French translations.

Reed Consumer Books, for permission to quote from Peter Scott's *Battle of the Narrow Seas*. Harold Pickles for permission to quote from *Untold Stories of Small Boats at War*.

10, Downing Street,
Whitehall.

30 May, 1943

I have noted with admiration the work of the
light coastal forces in the North Sea, in the Channel and
more recently in the Mediterranean.

Both in offence and in defence the fighting
zeal and the professional skill of officers and men have
maintained the great tradition built up by many generations
of British seamen.

As our strategy becomes more strongly offensive,
the task allotted to the coastal forces will increase in
importance, and the area of their operations will widen.

I wish to express my heartfelt congratulations
to you all on what you have done in the past, and complete
confidence that you will maintain the same high standards
until complete victory has been gained over all our
enemies.

Winston, Churchill

Introduction

Called the 'Little Ships' of the Royal Navy, Coastal Forces played an important part in Second World War. Although *Coastal Forces at War* is about those boats which operated in the North Sea and English Channel, it should be remembered that the Royal Navy's motor torpedo boats, motor gunboats and motor launches also achieved very considerable success in the Mediterranean, Aegean, and Adriatic, and were active on the Arakan coast of Burma.

The book covers the growth of Coastal Forces from a mere handful of boats to a formidable number of flotillas, capable of taking on the might of the German Navy. The roles of Coastal Forces were varied, ranging from escorting convoys through the Narrow Seas to minelaying within sight of the enemy coastline. As the war progressed, these 'Little Ships' were used increasingly in offensive roles, lying in wait to intercept enemy convoys and their escorts. With their small crews, shallow draught and low profiles, they were particularly suited to this work, being capable of operating in enemy waters where larger warships could not go.

Worldwide, Coastal Forces was involved in over a thousand actions and was credited with sinking 500 enemy ships. The motor torpedo boats fired 1,169 torpedoes, and achieved a proportionally greater success rate than any other torpedo carrier.

Operating in the North Sea and English Channel, the 'Little Ships' had none of the comforts of today's Royal Navy. The gun crews could be 'closed up' for long periods, with no protection from the elements. Those in the engine room had to endure heat, fumes, and noise, as well as the dreadful motion of a boat charging into head seas.

Most of those who served in the boats were 'hostilities only' personnel, from all walks of life and a wide variety of peacetime occupations. Much of the success of Coastal Forces can be attributed to the manner in which these individuals adapted to working together as operational crews. The actions would almost always be fought at close quarters, and the skill and bravery of many of those who served in Coastal Forces were recognised with decorations and Mentions in Despatches.

This book traces the development of the boats and crews, and some of the great battles fought by the 'Little Ships'. A chapter is also devoted to clandestine operations, another task to which the boats' speed and low silhouette were admirably suited, and there is some account of those Commonwealth and Allied Coastal Forces which made their own contributions to the war in the Narrow Seas.

Chapter One

Recall of the 1st MTB Flotilla

The months before the outbreak of the Second World War were halcyon days for many of those who had been posted to Malta to serve in the 1st MTB Flotilla. Based in Msida Creek, Grand Harbour, the flotilla was made up of twelve 60ft powerboats. With the exception of the flotilla leader, each boat was commanded by a young RN lieutenant. They went to sea regularly to practise torpedo attacks, sometimes using their depot ship as the target; they played the role of the enemy, testing the operational capability of the Mediterranean Fleet.

Life aboard these high-speed boats offered little in the way of home comforts. The crew, who lived on board, was made up of commanding officer, coxswain, seaman torpedo man, gunner, telegraphist, trained man (able seaman), leading stoker and stoker. Later, first lieutenants were appointed and then an engine room artificer (ERA) or motor mechanic. The boats had an enclosed wheelhouse with two clear-view screens. The helmsman worked the three throttle controls. The officer on watch would sit up outside, above the wheelhouse, with his legs hanging down through a manhole and his feet just behind the helmsman's head. Alternatively, the watch-keeper could stand on a ledge inside the wheelhouse with his head protruding out of the manhole, which gave him more protection from the elements but considerably less visibility.

LEFT: The badge designed for the 1st MTB Flotilla in 1937 by the wife of Lt-Cdr G.B. Sayer, Senior Officer of the flotilla (later Admiral Sir Guy Sayer). It depicts a flying fish with a scorpion's tail and was accompanied by the motto *'Caudae Spiculum Cave'* – 'beware the sting in the tail'.

They were not particularly good sea-going boats even in moderate conditions, when their hard-chine hulls would thump into head seas, drenching anyone on deck or on the bridge. On night exercises, even in the Mediterranean, there were occasions when any amount of extra clothing failed to keep out the cold. At other times they were driven at around 30 knots over Mediterranean blue seas beneath a cloudless sky, with each CO relishing the sheer exhilaration of working in close formation and manoeuvring at high speed. Where else in the Royal Navy could they have their own command at such a young age? And such an exciting command, too!

For a fortnight, the flotilla would embark on its summer cruise, independent of the disciplinary constraints imposed on it when working with the Mediterranean Fleet. Some of the flotilla visited the Greek Islands, stopping off at harbours and anchorages which were much too small to be attempted by any craft larger than a 60ft powerboat. This was idyllic cruising amongst totally unspoiled islands, before they were transformed by post-war tourism. The only other visiting boats at that time would have been those belonging to the exceptionally wealthy.

Although they were worked hard both around their shore base and at sea, the officers still had plenty of time to socialise ashore. Those who were unmarried were much in demand to attend grand dances at Government House. There were swimming parties at Tigne, polo at the Marsa, picnics, tennis, and sailing.

Towards the end of August 1939 all those on leave were suddenly recalled. For some time rumours had been rife about the possibility of war in Europe. Sitting round the radio in HMS *Vulcan* (the ex-trawler *Aston Villa* that acted as the flotilla's depot ship) listening to the news bulletins, it seemed depressingly inevitable, and it would then only be a matter of time before Italy entered the war (there were reports that 500 bombers had already assembled in Sicily).

Around this time, twelve Royal Naval Volunteer Reserve officers arrived to serve as first lieutenants aboard the boats. They would take over the navigation from their COs and organise victualling, refuelling, and routine maintenance. They were mostly experienced yachtsmen and boating enthusiasts who had been accountants and solicitors, brewers and ex-Bank of England.

Exercises were intensified, testing the defences of the military harbour. The Senior Officer organised more night operations. Then came the news of the invasion of Poland. All leave was again cancelled. Having proceeded to Valletta to take on war torpedoes and depth-charges, and topped up with fuel from their tanker *Patrella*, the boats were on five minutes' notice.

At 1100hrs the following day, 3 September 1939, personnel from the 1st MTB Flotilla were again huddled round radios aboard *Vulcan*, or ashore in the Union Club, to hear Prime Minister Chamberlain's sad, short speech and declaration of war. Not all those present shared the captain of HMS *Vulcan*'s optimism that it would be all over in 18 months. At 1230hrs a 'most immediate' Admiralty signal was received by the flotilla. 'Commence hostilities at once with Germany.'

Over the next eight weeks little positive news about the war in Europe filtered through to those in the 1st Flotilla. The Italians, as had been anticipated, showed no enthusiasm for entering the war at this stage. Malta became accustomed to observing the new blackout and curfew regulations.

MTB 01 setting out from Portsmouth on 22 June 1937, bound for the Mediterranean.

MTB 02 in Malta.

There was some speculation as to how and where the 1st MTB Flotilla would be deployed. Its high-speed craft represented a new form of naval warfare. A total of 18 had been built to a Hubert Scott-Paine design by his British Power Boat Company in a flourishing boat yard at Hythe, on Southampton water. Nos. *01–06*, built in 1935, were the original 1st MTB Flotilla. Nos. *07–12* formed the 2nd Flotilla based in Hong Kong. In spring 1939, Nos. *14–19* (there was no unlucky 13) were shipped to Malta to join the 1st Flotilla.

The boats, capable of 33 knots, were powered by three 500bhp Napier Lion aero engines. These could be handled by one man with his left hand controlling the port engine and the right hand operating the starboard engine. To handle the centre engine he would hook his left leg over the gear lever. The engines were reasonably reliable and, with three fuel tanks situated side by side beneath the wheelhouse and an extra fuel tank on deck, the boats could cruise for extended periods at 29 knots. Experience showed later that they

were underpowered, and manoeuvring was difficult as the reverse gear would burn out if operated spasmodically for a total duration of more than two minutes. The weak astern power was particularly noticeable when manoeuvring in harbour. The first design of astern gear used hand-operated phosphor bronze bands, which clamped the flywheels so that the epicyclic gear (as on the old Model T Ford) could engage astern. Subsequent designs used cast-iron bands, but astern power remained weak in this class.

Secondary armament of the original six boats in the 1st MTB Flotilla (*01–06*) and the Hong Kong-based 2nd Flotilla (*07–12*) consisted of twin Lewis guns mounted on monopods before and aft of the wheelhouse. The original 3rd MTB Flotilla (*14–19*) had a turret on either side of the wheelhouse each mounting quad Lewis guns. These 0.303in guns were relics of the First World War, when they had not proved entirely satisfactory. On the first six boats the guns were mounted over hatches forward and aft. The newer boats had them either side of the bridge, controlled with a double manual grip. By mounting the bottom pair of guns upside down, so that the magazines could rotate freely, all four guns could be worked simultaneously, but this arrangement made them less reliable.

The main armament was two 18-inch aircraft torpedoes or depth-charges (weight factors prohibiting the boats from putting to sea with both). Although the torpedo firing mechanism worked reasonably well, it was an extraordinary design and it was not incorporated in the new classes of MTBs being developed in the UK. The design had only been accepted by the Admiralty because it was all that was on offer at the time (1936). HMS *Vernon*, the torpedo school, hated the arrangement, as did the crews of the 1st MTB Flotilla.

Jack Collings, who was *MTB 14*'s ERA after her return to England from Malta, described what was involved in releasing a torpedo through the transom of these early boats:

The 18-inch torpedoes were mounted on rails in the engine room, one above the port engine the other over the starboard engine. The torpedoes had belly straps with grooved brass wheels which rested on the rails. The rails extended the length of the engine room to pass through the after bulkhead and across the tiller flat to end at the transom. Aft, hinged on the upper deck, were contraptions called outriggers. These were of a lattice work construction with a sloping top rail.

Firing the torpedoes was a time consuming affair. First a seaman, usually the torpedo man, would go over the stern to hang by his finger nails on one hand whilst using the other hand to release the catches that secured the transom port covers in place. The covers were then passed to someone on deck who would swing the outriggers outboard, thus making further extensions to the rails.

The torpedo man would then enter the engine room to prime the torpedoes. Once the target was lined up with the bows of the boat, a signal would be given for firing. The boat's speed would be reduced to dead slow. Stops were withdrawn from in front of the belly straps wheels. The boat speed was then increased to full ahead. This sudden acceleration gave the bows the required lift to cause the necessary incline to the rails and with a push from the torpedo man and one of the engine room ratings, the torpedo would glide down the rails to exit through the stern onto the outriggers to drop into the water. The boat would immediately turn out of the way of the following torpedo.

The main disadvantages of this method were the time taken to set the operation in progress, so much practice was needed to cut the time to an absolute minimum, and once the ports in the transom were open the boat could not go astern, otherwise the sea would flood the tiller flat and the engine room. Positioning the torpedoes in the engine room hampered maintenance of both the port and starboard engines.

The outriggers on deck were particularly vulnerable and prone to distortion, which led to release problems. The whole system was crude in the extreme, as indeed was the torpedo 'aiming off sight' in the wheelhouse. When what remained of the 1st MTB Flotilla finally reached their home base at Felixstowe, the Senior Officer there (Cdr R.H. McBean, DSC, who had served in Coastal Forces in the First World War) reckoned that this new generation of boats was actually a retrograde step, and that the Coastal Motor Boats (CMBs) in use at the end of the First World War were considerably superior, at least from the torpedo discharge aspect.

After the declaration of war, there was a sense of frustration amongst the crews of the 1st MTB Flotilla. There were reports that German submarines were operating in the Mediterranean, so the torpedoes were hastily exchanged for depth-charges. Most of the Mediterranean Fleet had left Malta, and the crews witnessed the final departure of the submarines from Grand Harbour to their secret destinations. Orders eventually came through that the C-in-C Mediterranean required the flotilla at Alexandria for patrol duties, replacing some of the destroyers which had by then moved away from the Mediterranean. The MTB crews were on stand-by for several days before the order was cancelled.

On 10 November, Lt-Cdr Monty Donner, the flotilla's Senior Officer, received the signal that his crews had all been waiting for. Within the next 24 hours, they were to prepare the boats for returning to England. The Admiralty had concluded that the Italians were not going to attack Malta and consequently the 1st MTB Flotilla would not be required in a defensive role against Italian assault craft. By contrast, back in Britain there was growing concern for the safety of merchant ships at sea off the East Coast; there were inadequate defences to prevent the Germans laying mines in these busy shipping routes, and the merchant ships were easy targets for German E-boats.

The first plan was to ship the flotilla back to Britain as deck cargo. However, there was deck-space for only two boats, so the Admiralty decided that the remaining ten should return via the French canals. They estimated that these boats could cross France in a matter of days. No one could have foreseen the problems that were to beset the flotilla on this unique journey.

The departure of the boats was supposed to have been secret. Frantic activity, however, could not be disguised, and over the next 24 hours many of the local trades people turned up with outstanding accounts to be settled. The boats were slipped for last minute checking and minor repairs. Torpedoes were loaded and fuel and fresh water tanks topped up. It was decided that *MTB 02*, not ready for the prolonged sea passage, should be shipped as deck cargo direct to Marseilles, where she would join up with the rest of the flotilla. The remaining nine boats sailed from Grand Harbour at midnight on 11 November.

The weather was fair and the crews optimistic of a fast passage to Bizerta. This first leg, however, was not without incident. *05* lost the use of a salt water pump and, with no suitable spares, she returned to Malta in company with *17*. These two boats would join *02* as deck cargo to Marseilles. One of the remaining boats (*15*) was finding it extremely difficult to keep in station, which resulted in further delays.

By dawn, the flotilla was many hours behind the planned schedule but still able to maintain 1,800 revs with a following sea. Then the weather started to deteriorate dramatically, and for safety the flotilla was forced to throttle right down. Lt D.H. Mason's boat (*14*) put her nose down into seas, which ripped off the mess deck cowls and washed overboard several other light pieces of deck equipment. Worse was to follow. She took another

wave green, momentarily burying the wheelhouse beneath the seas. When she emerged the whole front of the wheelhouse had caved in, the glass was shattered, and the few instruments had been rendered useless. Every time the hull hit a wave, the spray drenched the helmsman in the wheelhouse.

When the wet and weary crews of the seven boats arrived at Bizerta, they proceeded straight up the harbour to a long fuelling jetty at the French Air Force base. Engineers viewed *14*'s battered wheelhouse with some dismay, as the plan was still to sail the next day, leaving no time for a decent repair job. The officers were invited to a formal dinner in the French submariners' mess, and by the early hours of the morning all were riotously singing French and English songs. (Among the many exchanges, the French taught the British 'Auprès de ma blonde', which was still being sung at Felixstowe several months later; the British introduced the French to Gilbert and Sullivan, and in particular *HMS Pinafore*'s 'I am the ruler of the King's navee'.)

Fortunately for *MTB 14*, the planned departure the next day was cancelled because of the weather. The temporary repairs were ripped off and the French dockyard built a solid protective shield round the wheelhouse. However, the unsettled weather was the cause of some concern because, as was to be graphically demonstrated, the boats were simply not built to withstand the heavy seas which were not uncommon during winter in the Mediterranean. Lt-Cdr Donner conferred at length with the local meteorological officer and with the CO of the destroyer *Dainty*, which was to escort them. An easterly gale was predicted. The plan, therefore, was to make for Sardinia, and be in the lee of the island by the time the gale arrived.

When the boats were leaving harbour, a south gale warning cone was flying, but at least this would be behind them. Unfortunately, the weather forecast and the warning were hopelessly inaccurate. Instead of coming round to the east, the wind freshened from the west and the boats were soon butting into short head seas which meant constantly having to reduce the engine revs, thereby prolonging the time at sea.

The boats were soon facing a full gale from the north-west. Attempts were made to communicate with each other by Aldis lamp but replies were

HMS *Dainty* with the flooded *MTB 06* alongside before she was sunk. *Charles Coles*

invariably lost as the bows pitched into seas which cascaded over bridge and wheelhouse. A lighthouse to starboard initially gave some sense of security but it remained almost on the same bearing throughout the night, evidencing the flotilla's lamentably slow progress. In some of the boats, those off duty huddled in the wardroom or wheelhouse, for the motion made the mess decks virtually uninhabitable.

The boats had to be handled with considerable skill to cope with mounting seas. Between them, the officer on watch and the man at the wheel had to throttle up as the small hull climbed to the crest of a huge wave; at the top, back came the throttles with the boat stopping momentarily before plunging down into the black hole below.

Aboard the leading boat (*01*), the First Lieutenant was Sub-Lt Charles Coles. He was responsible for the flotilla's navigation. Apart from the occasional plot on a soggy chart, this involved keeping station on the starboard quarter of the escort ship and making certain that the rest of the flotilla kept up. On several occasions *01* had to slow down for stragglers who were signalled to increase speed. In this situation, *01* was in danger of losing *Dainty*.

At three in the morning, Sub-Lt Coles flashed up the boats astern on the Aldis, but received no reply. Soon afterwards *Dainty* switched on her navigation lights and turned to assist the missing MTBs. *06* flashed a distress signal to *Dainty*, indicating that she was severely waterlogged, with the sea nearly up to her motors, and was in danger of sinking.

When dawn came, the flotilla was only making about 9kt. *MTB 06* had dropped astern and *Dainty* went over to give assistance. The rest of the boats (except *MTB 04*, which was now missing) were ordered to heave to while the Senior Officer in *MTB 01* went over to investigate. *MTB 06* was low in the stern, with seas breaking over her. She was flying a red flag; the crew had assembled on the upper deck, looking tired and haggard and wearing

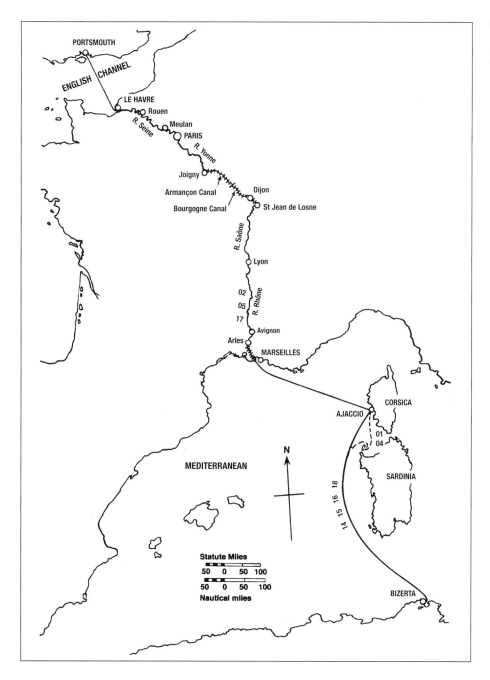

The 1st MTB Flotilla's return to the UK via the French waterways.

lifebelts. The CO, Lt Lloyd, shouted over through a megaphone that they had battled all night until the seas had finally defeated them, flooding into the engine room until the water was above the engines.

When passage-making, the boats carried additional equipment, including a fuel tank secured to the upper deck. This extra weight, together with the weight of the torpedoes aft, was simply too much for *06*'s old hull, and the punishing seas had opened up several seams. *Dainty* made a lee for *MTB 06* so that she could be lightened and her

crew transferred. This was no easy task, particularly lifting out *06*'s torpedoes. Her First Lieutenant is reputed to have changed into collar and tie and his Number 1 uniform before abandoning *06*. Lt Lloyd stepped off his boat clutching the wardroom clock, which had been a gift from Hubert Scott-Paine.

While the transfer was being made, the missing boat (*04*), also leaking badly, had managed to catch up with the rest of the flotilla. In spite of the seas, *Dainty* was able to get a tow-rope aboard *06*, and for the next two hours the boats continued their slow progress towards Ajaccio, Corsica. They had covered about 200 miles with another 120 still to go.

MTB 01's leading stoker came up onto the bridge to report that the after compartments were flooded and the water level was rising in the engine room. It was now *01*'s turn to fly the red flag. They hove to and donned lifebelts. After consultation with the other boats by megaphone, the SO decided to send the four relatively seaworthy boats on ahead to try to reach Ajaccio before dark. Meanwhile *01* and *04* attempted to close *Dainty* to lighten ship, but by then the swell made it unsafe to attempt a transfer. For several more hours, *Dainty*, with *06* in tow, steamed on very slowly towards Ajaccio. *01* and *04* followed astern. On *01*, one engine had failed and the crew were continuously pumping and bailing.

MTBs *14*, *15*, *16*, and *18*, now well ahead of *Dainty*, enjoyed a temporary respite in the weather and were able to increase revs to 1,400 – a speed sufficient to work the self-bailers. By the time they were safely moored up in Ajaccio, the weather was starting to break again. At 1900hrs *Vulcan*, which had sailed independently from Malta to Ajaccio, was called up to assist the boats still at sea. Sub-Lt Coles calculated that she would be with them at about 2230hrs, when she would be able to stand by in case *01* and *04* required salvaging (the CO of *Dainty* already had his hands full, with *06* in tow).

Dainty realised that *01* and *04* could never make Ajaccio in the worsening weather, so it was decided that they should seek shelter in the lee of Asinara Island, off Sardinia. Progress was now desperately slow, with crews pumping continuously to keep the water below the level of the engines. Up top on *01*, in their second night in gale-force winds, both Senior Officer and First Lieutenant were suffering from sickness and exhaustion. Charles Coles recalls falling asleep on his feet several times, only to be woken seconds later as the edge of the cockpit collided with his chin. The SO from time to time would hallucinate, seeing imaginary cliffs and jagged rocks ahead and yelling at his navigator to take immediate evasive action.

Some time after midnight, *01* and *04* became separated. At about two in the morning, *01* was close enough to the shore to identify her position from a lighthouse. Sub-Lt Coles navigated the boat into a small bay, taking soundings to get as close

inshore as was safe. Once they were at anchor, hot tea and beans were served up – the crew's first food for 48 hours. Before turning in, Coles looked into the mirror, hardly recognizing the bloodshot eyes, the salt-packed skin from which a beard was emerging, and the hair hanging down like rats' tails.

Battling against worsening weather and increasing seas, *Dainty* was struck by a violent squall during the night, and the towline to *06* parted. HMS *Dainty*'s captain (Cdr Walton) considered it too risky to attempt to re-connect the tow, and was left with no option but to sink the crippled boat. Consequently *MTB 06* was unceremoniously rammed, and broke into two pieces. Weighted down by its engines, the after portion sank quickly; the forward section, however, had to be rammed again. The wreckage was then churned up so that little evidence remained for examination by the Italians.

The next day, Sub-Lt Coles was able to take in his surroundings. *04* had managed to find her way into the bay and was anchored close by. On the land above the anchorage were the grim buildings of a penal settlement, where they could make out guards and prisoners. Two Italian officials visited them and announced that, though they were belligerents in a neutral country, the crews were not going to be interned. There was concern at that time that Italy might have already joined forces with Hitler, but the Italians did not formally enter the war until June 1940. Despite what the Italian officials had said *Dainty*'s CO felt it necessary to stay in neutral waters, 25 miles out at sea. She was virtually hove-to and battened down for the next 36 hours in one of the Golfe du Lion's worst winter gales. All those who had served in *MTB 06* were absorbed into *Dainty*'s watchbill. Lt Lloyd and his First Lieutenant, Ian Quarrie, were accommodated in the CO's after cabin, which they shared with his two Bedlington terriers.

Dainty kept in touch with *01* by radio, advising the SO that they would have to wait at least 24 hours for an improvement in the weather. This gave Lt-Cdr Donner and *04*'s CO, Lt A.J.R. Foster, the opportunity of surveying the state of their boats. The hull of *01* had taken such a serious battering that water was still seeping into the engine room and after compartment. The wireless mast was smashed and one engine was out of action. The leaks on 04 were even more serious, keeping the crew bailing every two hours. One of the engines had been flooded and the other two required urgent attention. They were unable to transmit or receive wireless and their fresh water tanks had emptied.

For three days the crews lived mostly on their iron rations of tinned beef and ship's biscuits. There was a shortage of fuel, so they had no heating arrangements and no means of drying out their clothing or the sodden interiors. Landing was strictly prohibited.

At the end of their enforced stay off the penal settlement, *01* and *04* put to sea, again accompanied by *Dainty*. When they were still many miles from Ajaccio they met more bad weather in the shape of the Mediterranean mistral – a sudden rising of the wind, usually in the late afternoon, which at that time of the year occurs two out of every three days. *Vulcan* was again called out from Ajaccio to provide an additional escort. Her First Lieutenant, Percy Odell, recalled the experience years later. He had to assume command when *Vulcan*'s CO went down with a violent stomach ulcer. His highly experienced coxswain, CPO Arnold, was continually struggling to keep *Vulcan*'s head to sea. However, any attempt to get her onto a course suitable for intercepting the boats resulted in such violent rolling that there was concern for the ship's safety. Reluctantly, he decided to head back to Ajaccio. Apart from Hong Kong typhoons, Percy Odell could not recall a worse passage in 30 years at sea.

Vulcan's coxswain expressed serious doubts that MTBs *01* and *04* would survive the passage. It was therefore with some relief that several officers from the other boats witnessed the eventual arrival of *01* and *04* from the *Vulcan*'s bridge. What a contrast between these, in their spotless uniforms with white cap covers, and the salt-caked, exhausted crews of the battered boats below them.

While repairs were undertaken to *01* and *04* at Ajaccio, there was time to dry out the boats and relax as guests of the French Navy. Of the original twelve-boat flotilla there were now only six left to make ready for the passage from Corsica to Marseilles: two had been shipped back to the UK, *06* had been sunk, and three had been transported direct from Malta to Marseilles as deck cargo. These last three boats (*02*, *05*, and *17*) were by now

starting their eventful journey across France. *Vulcan* too had already departed for the UK.

Ten days after leaving Malta, the remaining six boats left Marseilles in line ahead, with a pilot on *01*, making for the entrance to the Rhône River. In the stretch of canal that joined the lock basin to the sea, the crews got their first experience of the difficulties involved in navigating these high-speed craft in such narrow waterways: the leading boat failed to reduce speed in time, creating a wash that bounced back off the sides of the canal and hit the boat immediately astern, causing her to zigzag wildly, with no response from the rudder, so that she only just managed to avoid collision with the sides of the canal. This loss of control was repeated down the line to the last boat. Punts and small dinghies moored close to the canal banks were literally lifted right out of the water, some finishing up ashore. The friendly waves from spectators on the tow-path soon turned to the angry shaking of fists.

The Rhône, near its mouth, was broad and comparatively slow, flowing through wooded countryside. After Arles, their first night-stop, it narrowed and the rate of flow increased to about 6kt. The pilot was so concerned about the state of the river, which was exceptionally high, that he was reluctant to continue unless each boat had its own pilot; eventually a compromise was reached, and they continued up-river with one pilot for every two boats.

They made good progress up the Rhône, passing through attractive, hilly countryside. There was the occasional riverside village, large country house, and grand château. The sightseeing might have been more relaxing if it had not been for some of the low bridges that had to be negotiated. The first of these was what remained of the famous Pont d'Avignon. The Roman bridge, with its western spans missing, stretches only three-quarters of the breadth of the river. The existing arches were too low and narrow to pass through. With the propellers churning up the river-bed in the shallows, each boat therefore staggered, almost out of control, through the gap between the shore and the standing portion of the Pont d'Avignon, each in turn being caught in a ferocious eddy that swept it right across the river and tried to deposit it on the river bank where it curved round towards the ancient bridge.

1st MTB Flotilla on the French waterways. French pilot and the Senior Officer on the Rhône. *Charles Coles*

They soon developed a technique for negotiating the bridges; this involved positioning the boat and then shooting the bridge at full throttle into the current, which reputedly could reach 10kt. On the whole the technique worked well, though there were one or two exceptions, particularly at Lyon, where a difficult crabbing manoeuvre had to be performed to get through the city's narrow bridges with their low arches.

When the boats reached the Saône one of the pilots departed, as this river was reckoned to be easier due to ingenious sluices which made the current considerably less dramatic than that of the Rhône. But there were different problems – notably bits of sluice gate in mid-stream, and great concrete blocks strategically placed on the riverbed. Normally there was several feet of concrete revealed above the water, but, like the Rhône, the Saône was exceptionally high in November 1939, rising above some of the blocks and causing a considerable hazard to navigation. The other problem was that the vast expanse of flat land either side of the river was flooded, and without a pilot it would have been all too easy to stray from the river's true course and finish up in the middle of a meadow. The pilot on one of the boats joked *'Nous sommes dans les prés'*, for, apart from the occasional tree or hedge, they might just as well have been at sea.

The other pilots departed at St Jean de Losne as the boats left the Saône River and entered the canal system that crosses Burgundy. Ahead of them were nearly 200 locks to be negotiated in order to reach the tidal Seine at Rouen, and the northern coast of France. The flotilla was feeling pleased with its progress, having crossed almost half of France in three days. Little did they know that this second stage of their journey back to England would take at

Negotiating one of the many locks on the Burgogne canal. *Charles Coles*

least three weeks, and that the crews of boats with seriously damaged hulls or major mechanical problems would not make it home in time for Christmas.

There was no question of motoring along the Canal de Bourgogne under their own power, as the boats' engines were not suitable for running over extended periods at slow speeds, and the wash caused at normal cruising speed would do considerable damage to the sides of the canals. The plan was to tow the boats in pairs, using army tractors. After some altercation with the French Army captain in charge of the towing operation, who was insisting that the tractors should be positioned on the lee bank, the convoy set off at 20-minute intervals. This would give time for each pair to pass through the lock ahead and for the water level then to be lowered again by the lock-keeper, ready to receive the next pair.

The crews spent much of the time ashore, man-handling the boats into the locks and helping with the sluices. The canal banks were not vertical, and had sizeable stones at the base, so the shore parties were also kept busy prodding at the sterns of the boats when the wind pushed them into the shallows. This happened all too frequently, accompanied by the audible scraping of the propellers along the bottom. In addition manoeuvring the boats was made more difficult by the military tractors being apparently incapable of going at anything less than 18mph. The tow line would be slipped whenever they approached a lock, and each CO would then have to rely on the shore party to take the way off his boat. Any attempts to communicate in French with the drivers to get them to slow down apparently had the opposite affect; on more than one occasion it needed the rich native language of a stoker or coxswain to make them take notice.

They found the lock keepers particularly friendly. It was cold, and on many occasions there would be an invitation to visit the lock keeper's house for a glass of *marc*. This was the first distillation of the grape, which had been collected in jars to be sampled six months later. Each lock keeper had his own distinctive distillation, having added, in varying quantities, fruits such as cherries and peaches. This pure white liquid taken in congenial surroundings did much to bolster *entente cordiale* along the waterways of Burgundy.

After three days on the canals, the boats reached the summit and a 3km subterranean tunnel. The plan was for the tractors to be replaced by electrically operated towing boats, which went through the tunnel twice daily at 0900 and 1400hrs. *MTB 14* had fallen behind the other boats, so her CO, Lt Dennis Mason, decided on a 0400hrs start to catch up with the convoy in time for the 0900 tow. They arrived on time, only to find that the power supply for the towing boats had failed, so the MTBs would have to go through under their own power.

With restricted headroom, it was necessary to remove the compass, radio mast, and the barbettes on each side of the bridge; even the spray-screens had to be folded flat, as the tunnel was just 14ft high and 20ft wide. There were no lights in the tunnel, and the COs had been warned that the cables running along the roof were live and had no insulation.

The boats went through at 20-minute intervals, but even this time lapse did not prevent the tunnel from filling with exhaust fumes, which were too much for its few ventilation shafts. On *14*, with its replacement metal shield round the wheelhouse, the coxswain had a severely restricted view, and was unable to follow the roof of the tunnel, illuminated only by the boat's Aldis lamp. This meant the CO had to con the boat for the full length of the tunnel with only a foot or two to spare either side.

Progress through the waterways had been so slow that the Senior Officer had changed his uniform for casual flannels, shirt, walking boots, and beret, preferring to make the journey on foot. At the tunnel, he positioned himself above one of the ventilation shafts and, as the noise of a boat's engines approached, he would shout down for the crew to identify themselves.

After the tunnel, the locks came thick and fast. It took them another four days to reach the end of the canal system. Beyond the final lock on the Armançon canal, they would at last be under their own power along the River Yonne, with a river pilot to guide them. The Senior Officer requested that the boats' engines should be tested in the last section of the canal. The results were worrying – all the boats had, at one time or another, dragged their propellers along the bed of the canal, and all COs reported alarming vibration.

In contrast to the Rhône and Saône, the water level of the Yonne was only moderately high. It was decided that *01*, which had earlier collided with a barge, and *04*, should stay behind to locate an engineer and a carpenter to carry out basic repairs. The remaining four boats, with several of their propeller shafts well out of alignment, and encountering yet more locks (to pass the river's various weirs), made only modest progress. Having covered no more than a few miles the previous day, the pilot on *14*, anxious to make better time, pronounced that the water level was high enough for the boat to clear the top of the submerged weirs, thereby bypassing the locks and saving valuable time. This worked fine for the first two weirs, but when they attempted the third they discovered that there was simply not enough water, and the hull dropped violently on the other side, where the centre propeller hit the bottom. The damage, which could have been much worse, was restricted to a stopped engine and a more pronounced bend of the prop shaft. *14* was still able to keep up with the other boats and, by nightfall, reach Montereau, where the Yonne meets the Seine.

The boats refuelled on the outskirts of Paris and then, to be safely berthed in the centre of the city before dark, engine revs were increased, with the bows of the boats rising up out of the water for the first time for three weeks. The resultant wash was not well received by either the bargees with their heavily laden craft, or by the owners of the many houseboats that lined the banks. There was much angry shouting and waving of fists, and it was later learnt that the Admiralty had to pay out substantial sums of money to meet the cost of repairs.

The flotilla was making for the Quai d'Orsay (normally used by visiting heads of state) on the left bank, between the Pont Alexandre III and the Pont de la Concorde. With *01* and *04* left behind for necessary repairs, Lt Hilary Gamble was acting Senior Officer. On arrival at the Quai d'Orsay as light faded, Lt Gamble jumped ashore to report to the naval attaché. Simultaneously, one of the other boats, manoeuvring in the fast-running Seine, was swept downstream and collided with the Seine's oldest and most famous bridge, the Pont Neuf. The CO then had to come sheepishly alongside the Quai d'Orsay with much of his boat's bows stove in.

While they were in Paris, they learnt from the naval attaché about the experiences of the three boats in the advance party. By now, these boats were west of Paris, slipped in the Lorraine shipyard at Meulan. Two of them had been holed below the waterline in their after compartments. In both cases this was due to bent shafts and broken P-brackets (the supports for the shafts beneath the hulls), with the unsupported propellers cutting through the wooden hulls.

The late Sir John Eardly-Wilmot, then in command of *MTB 02*, recalled vividly the drama on his boat. She had struck something very solid on the river-bed, which broke one of the P-brackets. The still rotating propeller then cut a neat hole in the hull, and water quickly flooded the after compartment, upon which Eardly-Wilmot deliberately drove the boat into the bank. After he and the crew had made a rapid assessment of the damage, *02* was manhandled into the nearby lock. The local fire brigade was summoned to have pumping equipment at the ready and to provide two lengths of 6in manila rope. *Les pompiers* responded quickly to the call, and the manila ropes were soon in position fore and aft to make a cradle. The pumps were not actually required, for the sluices were opened up to empty the lock and reveal the extent of the damage. A large tingle was then positioned over the hole, and in due course *02* was able to proceed down-river to the Meulan boatyard for more permanent repairs.

The crews of the four boats in Paris spent three days alongside the Quai de la Concorde as guests of the naval attaché. By now the list of repairs needed to make the boats mechanically sound and seaworthy was so extensive that the SO decided all the boats should come out of the water at Meulan. When *14* was slipped, Lt Mason discovered that his boat's port P-bracket had parted, and the port

propeller, with a bent shaft, had cut about a third of the way through the wooden hull. It was decided to straighten only two of the propeller shafts, removing the port shaft altogether as there were no spare brackets.

Most of the boats spent about a week at Meulan. When they were on the slips, their crews were accommodated ashore. The officers virtually took over the Pinchon Hotel, where they were made very welcome. There was a *service militaire* concessionary rail fare to Paris, where several evenings were spent wining and dining, with a visit to the Casino de Paris to see Maurice Chevalier and Josephine Baker. In fact hospitality abounded ashore, where Lt Eardley-Wilmot was often found to be in the company of the mayor and the chief of police, playing, for modest stakes, the card game *manille*. There was only one brush with officialdom during this time, when it was insisted that, while the boats were on the slips, the torpedo warheads must be removed.

Crews of boats with major repair work being undertaken would spend Christmas at Meulan. Those boats considered sound enough for the Channel crossing underwent trials, and then left Meulan at first light on 15 December, arriving at Rouen in the late afternoon. Here, with no more locks or low bridges between them and the sea, they were able to raise their masts and assemble their armaments. Once more they had the appearance of a small flotilla of warships.

Those crews who would be home for Christmas were now anxious to get back as soon as possible, but they had another frustrating delay at Le Havre in the Seine estuary. In view of the fragile state of the boats, there was talk of providing them with a destroyer escort for the Channel crossing. They waited two days, and then, at very short notice, it was decided that the boats would slip at midnight and cross the Channel unaccompanied.

It was a dark and bitterly cold night. Imaginations ran riot with the expectation that, at first light, they would be pounced on by a squadron of Stukas. The passage home was, however, without incident, and the boats arrived in Portsmouth harbour in the afternoon. They made for Dolphin Creek, Gosport, where their depot ship *Vulcan* was waiting for them, along with the boats that had been shipped from the Mediterranean as deck cargo.

The prototype of the First World War 40ft torpedo boat (with single trough), built by Thornycroft. *IWM 47655*

Chapter Two

A Lesson Not Learned

The recall of the 1st MTB Flotilla ten weeks after the outbreak of the Second World War was a desperate move by the Admiralty to start the build-up of a pool of small ships, which could be deployed to provide escorts for the East Coast convoys.

In the course of the war, the German E-boats and submarines would wreak havoc in the North Sea, the English Channel and the Atlantic. Especially in 1940–1 the enemy came very close to achieving a blockade of the British Isles by stifling the water-borne transport of essential supplies.

It seems astonishing that Britain was so ill-prepared. The tonnage sunk and loss of life in the Merchant Marine was tragic. Later called the 'forgotten heroes', one in every four merchant seamen would not survive the war, and a large proportion of these losses occurred in the first two years of conflict. The reason why there was so little protection for merchant ships against the marauding German *Schnellboote* and submarines, particularly off the East Coast, calls for some explanation.

Between the wars, there had been a gradual run-down of the fleet of coastal motor boats and motor launches which had been so successfully deployed towards the end of the First World War. Although the pre-war MTB flotilla at Malta had been highly trained and had worked on many occasions with the Mediterranean Fleet, those responsible had little idea how to use such light coastal craft. Reports received at the Admiralty from the C-in-C Mediterranean were less than enthusiastic about these small boats, and the conviction remained that the strength of the Royal Navy in any future war would lie in its heavily armed battleships, cruisers, and destroyers.

Consequently, faced with severe cutbacks in capital expenditure between the wars, the Admiralty had decided against building up flotillas of armed coastal craft. Some development work was being undertaken (mostly for other navies), and it was felt that it would be a mistake to commit capital to building large numbers of small ships which might very quickly become obsolete. Naval ships of this kind could be built quickly, should the need arise, and the defence budgets were better invested in long-term shipbuilding projects that would increase the numbers of cruisers and destroyers. The Admiralty had also decided that the cost of operating a large number of peacetime coastal craft was prohibitive, both in terms of manpower and maintenance, particularly as the boats had, structurally and mechanically, relatively short lives.

This lack of commitment towards coastal craft in 1938–9 was an all-too-familiar situation to those whose memories went back to the First World War. Britain declared war on Germany on 4 August 1914. Published statistics show that at that time the British Fleet was, numerically, far superior. Britain's battleships numbered 62 compared with Germany's 43; the Admiralty had, for some years, given priority to the building of cruisers and could line up 118 against Germany's 55. British destroyers numbered 228 compared with Germany's 152. The relative strengths of submarines told the same story – 76 British against only 30 German. These figures, however, have to be qualified, for much of the Royal Navy was deployed in the Mediterranean and the Far East, protecting Britain's huge colonial interests.

The German submarines soon demonstrated their effectiveness when, on 23 September, they sank three Royal Navy cruisers off the Dutch coast. Several other major Royal Navy warships struck mines, which Britain claimed had been laid indiscriminately by the Germans, whereas Britain was still opposed to minelaying, believing that the seas should remain open to neutral shipping. Thus, in spite of having a numerically smaller fleet, Germany effectively challenged British naval supremacy in the first year of the First World War.

It soon became apparent that British merchant ships were an easy target for German submarines. This shipping carried food and other vital supplies for the war effort. By closing these supply routes, Germany believed that the British Isles could be successfully blockaded. Consequently they warned that all vessels, of any nationality, operating in British waters would be prey to German submarines, believing that this would deter neutral shipping from entering the war zone. The United States' warning to Germany to allow the free passage of its cargo ships was ignored.

The Admiralty had been firmly of the opinion that Germany's submarines could never represent a real threat to the outcome of the war by effectively blockading the British Isles; however, even with a numerical superiority in warships, it was clear that Britain had no real answer to the terrible losses being inflicted by the German U-boats.

About this time, the Royal Naval Boat Reserve became active. This consisted of many small privately-owned motor boats. Manned by enthusiastic volunteer crews, and ill-equipped for any major wartime role, these boats were used mainly for patrol work. The Admiralty, meanwhile, was at last coming round to the view that a fleet of fast surface craft, armed with torpedoes, depth-charges and guns, should be built without delay to take on the German U-boats. The specification drawn up by the Admiralty was for a 40ft craft with a displacement of $4\frac{1}{2}$ tons. Each boat should be armed with an 18in torpedo, and be able to reach a minimum speed of 30kt when fully loaded. The boats should also have a long range so that they could operate independently as far afield as the waters off Norway.

The only firm in Britain that was developing this type of craft was the family shipbuilding firm of John I. Thornycroft, which had launched the first torpedo boat back in 1874. At the outbreak of war,

the firm was fully occupied in building much larger craft for the Royal Navy. Sir John Thornycroft allocated some of the firm's resources, and hand picked small quality boatbuilders to construct a totally new concept in naval craft known as the CMB (Coastal Motor Boat). With their stepped hulls, these could reach a top speed of over 40kt, powered by petrol engines developing around 500bhp. The hulls would be light, but strong enough to take a pounding by the sea.

Thornycroft's designers had to come up with a method of launching the $\frac{3}{4}$-ton torpedo which would add very little overall weight to these small craft. Their solution was to launch tail first through the transom. The torpedo would be fired with the boat travelling at speed in the direction of the target. Immediately the torpedo hit the water, the boat would turn sharply to avoid the track of the missile. Tested by the experts at HMS *Vernon*, the design was approved with the one qualification that the craft must be able to maintain a minimum speed of 30kt when firing. This somewhat crude firing system was similar to that adopted by the 1st MTB Flotilla between the wars, as described in the previous chapter.

The Admiralty ordered twelve of the 40ft CMBs, which were built in great secrecy by Thornycroft at its Hampton yard. The first of them proved so successful that a further twelve were ordered. Thornycroft was then commissioned to design a larger boat without the $4\frac{1}{2}$-ton weight restriction. These 55ft twin-screw CMBs would be powered by a variety of engines, giving them speeds of between 32kt and 40kt. A single engine was started either by compressed air or a small petrol engine. Once one engine was working, the second engine would be turned over, and started by the movement through the water of the trailing screw. In all Thornycroft and its subcontractors built 123 CMBs in the First World War.

Although the Admiralty was, therefore, at last commissioning high-speed coastal craft capable of intercepting German torpedo boats and larger enemy ships, there was also an immediate requirement for a substantial number of all-purpose motor launches. With no boatbuilders in the UK capable of mass production, a senior government official was sent over to New York with authority to purchase any light craft that could be easily

First World War 55ft *Coastal Motor Boat (CMB)*
65A carrying depth-charges. *IWM Q20636*

converted into small warships and transported back to the UK as deck cargo. If nothing was available, then shipyards had to be found which could rapidly build such boats. At first the mission seemed hopeless, but then the official met up with Henry R. Sutphen, who was building sleek, fast motor boats for the leisure market. His designs were built at the Elco Shipyard at Bayonne, New Jersey.

The two men did their sums. The Elco yard under normal conditions built about four quality boats similar to the Admiralty's requirements in a single year. Mr Sutphen thought that by introducing a mass-production programme at his yard he might possibly meet the Admiralty's order for 50 craft within the following 12 months. The two men shook hands on the deal, and the Admiralty contract was signed on 9 April 1915.

On 8 May, the Cunard luxury liner *Lusitania*, on her return voyage from New York to Liverpool, was torpedoed off the Irish coast by a German submarine, Cunard having believed that the *Lusitania*'s impressive speed was sufficient to protect it from prowling submarines. Holed with two torpedoes, the great liner sank within 20 minutes with a loss of 1,198 lives. Among those drowned were many Americans, and outrage spread across the United States.

The Elco boats were to be manufactured in parts at the Bayonne Yard, New Jersey. The parts would then be transported over the border to a Montreal yard established by Henry Sutphen, where they would be assembled and shipped to Britain. Within three weeks of the signing of the contract, the prototype mouldings of a 75ft motor launch had been set up. The building programme was impressive by any standards, for within weeks the Admiralty was seeking from Sutphen an additional 500 craft to meet what was becoming a major crisis. The Royal Navy, with its conventional fleets of large ships, was no match for the U-boats. It was unable to provide cover to the merchant ships, which at this time were still sailing through the war zones in ones and twos, with little communication between the Admiralty and their owners.

Sutphen's target was to build and ship 550 boats by 15 November 1916, the equivalent of a boat a day. The original 50 would be 75-footers and the balance of 500 would be 80-footers. It was boatbuilding on a scale never before undertaken. Sutphen acquired a second yard in Ottowa, which, along with the Montreal yard, would assemble all the boats. From these two points the boats would be transported to Halifax by rail, for their journey across the Atlantic by freighter. There would be a total of 130 shipments, all of which arrived safely and on schedule.

The new boats would form the Royal Navy's first fleet of purpose-built motor launches (MLs, as they were called in both world wars). They were a totally different concept to the Thornycroft CMBs, which were designed for high-speed attack with torpedoes. The maximum speed reached by an ML, with its two 220bhp petrol engines, was 19kt. The MLs would be armed with combinations of 3in AA guns and Lewis or other machine guns. The smaller 75ft boats would have a crew of eight, the larger craft eight or nine. They could carry 1,650 gallons of fuel, giving them a range of 1,000 nautical miles at a cruising speed of 15kt. They would also carry depth-charges and had equipment to make smoke. Towards the end of the First World War, some of these craft were also fitted with a crude form of hydrophone which, when dropped over the side, could sometimes detect the sound of a vessel's propellers within a two-mile range.

When the boats first started arriving in Britain early in 1916 they were treated with great scepticism by both the Admiralty and those who were to serve on them. There were grave doubts about how such vessels, hastily built without the benefit of extended trials, would cope with the gale-swept seas around the British Isles. It was the first time that warships would be deployed with engines that could use up full tanks of fuel in just 48 hours, compared with other escort-type craft such as sea-going tugs, which could stay out at sea a week or more without having to return to base for refuelling. To placate some of the critics, more time and money had to be spent to improve the first batch of 75-footers when the shipment arrived in Britain. The first crews found them distinctly wet and uncomfortable. There was also concern about the noise level of the engines' exhausts, which would be picked up by an enemy several miles away.

Germany, meanwhile, was remorseless in its battle to control the seas around Britain, and the defenceless merchant ships were still suffering appalling losses. In May 1917 alone over a hundred British merchant ships were torpedoed. The Admiralty then introduced the concept of convoys, and, under the protection of warships, a large fleet of merchantmen arrived safely from Gibraltar. But the wrangling in the War Cabinet and at the Admiralty continued, with one side arguing for more RN protection for the Merchant Navy, while the other claimed that there were insufficient warships to provide convoy escorts.

In this environment the MLs and the CMBs, even with their late entry into the First World War, were quick to prove their worth. MLs provided the essential convoy escorts for merchant ships in coastal waters, and were also used as submarine hunters, inshore raiders, minelayers, and mine-sweepers, while the CMBs, arriving on the scene somewhat later, were to be involved in some spectacular engagements with submarines and larger German ships.

When MLs and CMBs were first introduced there was scepticism about the decision that the majority of their officers and crews would be 'hostilities only' personnel. Many questioned the wisdom of using reservists in the front line, as they would not have the traditional naval discipline. Time would prove such views to be a serious misjudgement, for the reservists would display both bravery and skill in the performance of an invaluable service.

Sadly, the salutary lessons in the wartime use of coastal craft were all too quickly forgotten between the wars. With the nation once again ill-prepared, the organisational skills required to build up Coastal Forces in the Second World War would be monumental.

Chapter Three

The Race to Build Boats

The arrival of the 1st MTB Flotilla from Malta added a mere handful of offensive high-speed craft to the few already in home waters. Some of the older boats (built in 1936), having been nursed all the way from the Mediterranean, would soon be disarmed and used as motor attendant craft (MACs) for assorted work, including some air/sea rescue; others would finish their days being driven at high speed over booms to test the defences of Portsmouth harbour. The experience of the newly arrived officers and crews would, however, prove invaluable in the urgent build-up of Coastal Forces both at home and overseas.

At the outbreak of the Second World War, apart from two surviving First World War coastal motor boats (CMBs *103* and *104*) there were only nine home-based boats which would be designated Coastal Forces. There was an experimental Vosper 68ft MTB and three new 1939 70ft MTBs (a Vosper and two Thornycrofts, which would form part of the 4th Flotilla). There were also five British Power Boat 60ft motor anti-submarine boats. These 25kt MA/SBs, completed in 1938–9, had been ordered for use against enemy submarines, which the Admiralty was convinced would be penetrating the coastal waters around the British Isles. Within a few months they would change their minds about MA/SBs. The German submarines rarely came close inshore, and there were serious doubts about the effectiveness of these submarine-chasers, due to the

Hubert Scott-Paine at HMS *Vernon*, Portsmouth Harbour, in June 1936, after the handing over of the first MTBs to the Royal Navy. From left to right: Scott-Paine, Lt-Cdr Sayer (Senior Officer, 1st MTB Flotilla), Capt Willis, and Engineer Cdr Meggs of HMS *Vernon*. *Southampton City Heritage Services*

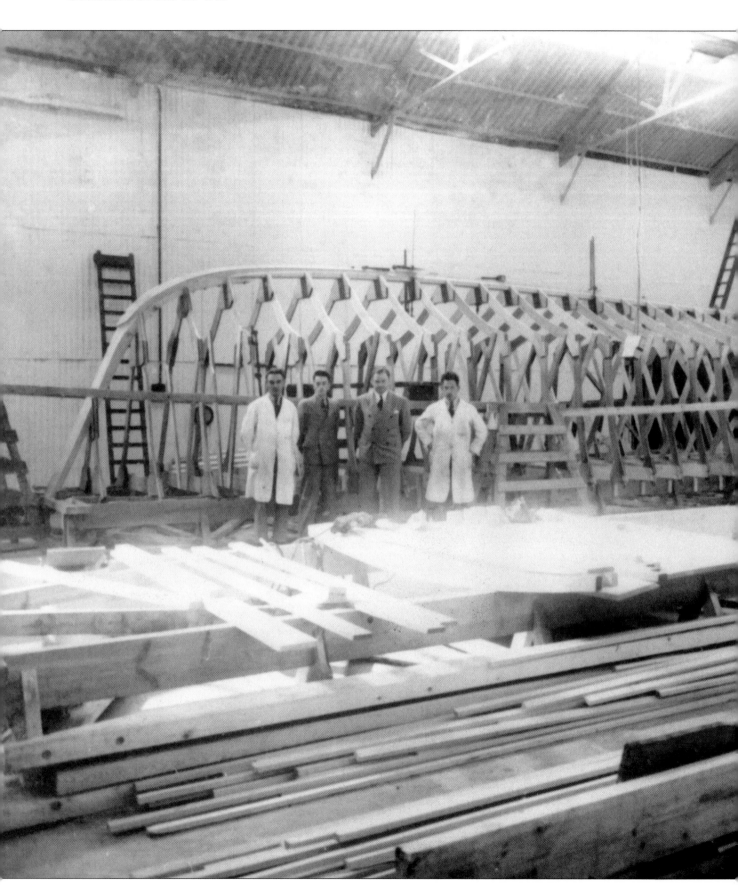

lack of suitable small-craft submarine detection equipment (ASDIC). Being under-powered for conversion to MTBs, two would be shipped to the Mediterranean and the remaining three used for air/sea rescue or target-towing.

There were no motor gunboats (MGBs) at the beginning of the war, and no general-purpose motor launches (MLs). Compare this with the strength of Coastal Forces four years later, on 1 January 1944:

Operational Craft, Home Waters

Harbour defence motor launches (HDMLs)	70
Rescue motor launches (RMLs)	50
Motor launches (MLs)	162
Short motor torpedo boats (MTBs)	92
Long MTBs/MGBs (D-boats)	67
Long MGBs (C-boats)	21
Short motor gunboats (MGBs)	35
Steam gunboats (SGBs)	6
Motor anti-submarine boats (MA/SBs)	17

The above formed 66 flotillas, operating out of 21 different locations in home waters. Coastal Forces by then had its own staff division and material departments at the Admiralty, and operational controllers attached to the various C-in-Cs' staffs around the British Isles. The flotillas had their own specialist maintenance staff, and there was a training establishment exclusively for Coastal Forces (HMS *St Christopher*, Fort William), with anti-submarine schools at Ardrishaig and Larne, and a working-up base at Holyhead (HMS *Bee*). The build-up of Coastal Forces craft between 1939 and 1944 is a remarkable story of brilliant design combined with boatbuilding on a scale never before seen in Britain.

By the end of 1939, the German Navy already had a highly formidable force of 21 torpedo boats (*Schnellboote*) and 40 motor launches (*Raumboote*). German naval command believed that supremacy in the Channel and North Sea would be quickly established, and did not have long to wait before Germany held every port between Bergen in Norway and Bordeaux in the Bay of Biscay.

Construction of the hull of the first 60ft British Power Boat MTB at the Hythe yard in 1935.
Southampton City Heritage Services

MTB 28 was one of three 72ft Thornycroft MTBs built for the Royal Navy between 1938 and 1940. *IWM FL25666*

The Royal Navy had only limited resources to provide protection to the merchant ships carrying essential war supplies. The Germans also knew that there were too few MTBs operating along the East Coast to offer any serious threat to their own convoys. They doubted that the Admiralty would be able to commission the building of large numbers of coastal craft, starting from such a weak base.

Germany would hold the upper hand in the war in the North Sea and the English Channel from mid-1940 through 1941, as evidenced by the appalling losses of merchant ships to E-boats and U-boats. Germany not only had numerical superiority in light coastal craft at the beginning of the war, it also had highly-trained crews and boats that had been thoroughly tested in all kinds of weather. Based on experience gained between the wars, the German Navy opted for the round bilge hull-form which was

to prove so successful when travelling at speed into head seas. The Germans also had well-tried Daimler-Benz diesel engines – marinised versions of the engine designed originally for Zeppelins.

Faced with this critical situation, the Admiralty was in the hands of three firms of boatbuilders with experience in designing and building fast, light coastal craft. They were Thornycroft, British Power Boat, and Vosper.

CMBs and MTBs from Thornycroft

The family shipbuilding firm of J.I. Thornycroft had a long association with the Admiralty and with torpedo boats dating back to 1874, when they designed and built HMS *Lightning* (*TB No 1*), the Royal Navy's first torpedo boat. Forty years later, Thornycroft was building 40ft and 55ft coastal motorboats (CMBs). This remarkable design, based on their racing hydroplane *Miranda IV*, scored a number of wartime successes in the First World War. With stepped hulls, some were capable of 40kt. After the First World War, Thornycroft designed and built *Miss England III*, which captured the world speed record on Loch Lomond in 1932, with runs averaging 119.81kt.

The distinctive stepped-hydroplane CMBs, although phased out by the Admiralty between the wars, continued to be manufactured, with improved engines, for foreign navies, right up until 1941. Some of these later orders, totalling fourteen 55ft CMBs, were taken over by the Royal Navy as they reached completion. Two previously decommissioned Thornycroft CMBs were also pressed back into service.

Rear Admiral Courtney Anderson, a young lieutenant in May 1940, recalls commissioning MTBs *67* and *68* that had been ordered from Thornycroft by Finland and were about to be shipped from Blyth, Northumberland, loaded as deck cargo aboard a merchant vessel. When they were commandeered by the Admiralty, Lt Anderson had to deal with a reluctant master who was only willing to part with the craft after he had been given a receipt from Anderson on a piece of paper torn from a signal pad. These 55ft MTBs were very similar to the Thornycroft First World War CMBs, carrying their 18in torpedoes in stern chutes. They had a stepped-hydroplane hull with a round bilge and had clocked up an impressive 53.4kt during trials over a measured mile.

Thornycroft had completed four experimental MTBs, Nos *104-107*, which were effectively shortened versions (40ft and 45ft) of their CMBs. Two had stepped-hydroplane hulls and two hard-chine hulls. Trials of these experimental boats had failed to prove conclusively which was the better hull-form. It was thought that these shorter craft might be suitable for carrying on deck in cruisers, but this idea was never adopted by the Admiralty which had, by that time, decided that 70ft was the ideal length for the short MTBs. Several other fast CMB-type MTBs were built at Thornycroft's Hampton works and used on special operations.

MTB 105 remained an experimental craft and, with her stepped-hydroplane hull and speed, was seriously considered for boom-jumping in the Rade de Brest to torpedo one of the German battle-cruisers in harbour there during 1941-2. Towards the end of May 1940 the Thornycroft MTBs *104*, *106* and *107* joined MTBs *67* and *68* to form the 10th MTB Flotilla. They sailed together for the first

Boats and crews of the 10th MTB Flotilla.
Magnum

time on 25 May from Gosport to Dover en route to Felixstowe. They were referred to affectionately as 'The Wobbly Tenth'. Lt Anderson was the 10th Flotilla's first SO. He remembers these craft as being virtually open motorboats, very wet, and with none of the comforts of the new breed of lengthier MTBs coming into service with their galleys, living accommodation and superior navigation equipment. The tiny open bridge had to accommodate the CO, first lieutenant, coxswain, signalman and a gunner with his 0.303in machine guns on twin AA mounts (see photo above). They were not good sea boats and their crews, exposed to the elements, suffered from exhaustion.

After Dunkirk, the 10th Flotilla attempted patrols off the Dutch and Belgian coast, but the boats proved unsuitable for this operation being mechanically unreliable. For a time they were deployed on anti-invasion patrols, and then moved round to Sheerness for air/sea rescue duties in the Thames Estuary. They were also used as 'human minesweepers' to set off acoustic mines parachuted down by the enemy into the Thames Estuary and off the East Coast. RN minesweepers at that time were ill-equipped to tackle this new type of mine. It was decided that MTBs could be driven at full speed over a reported drop area in the hope that the vibrations from the MTB's propellers would cause the mines to detonate, but the speed of the craft would take it safely beyond the explosion. After the loss of two boats – *MTB 106* (10th Flotilla) and *MTB 16* (1st Flotilla) this unconventional and highly dangerous method of minesweeping was abandoned.

MTBs *104*, *106* and *107* were replaced by new 55-foot boats from Thornycroft and the flotilla was shipped out to the Mediterranean. Three of the boats were sunk off Crete and two were lost off Tobruk. The 10th Flotilla was then re-formed with Elco boats from the USA.

It was a source of disappointment to Thornycroft that the Admiralty decided in favour of the hard-chine hull, on the grounds of its better sea-keeping qualities. They were also cheaper to construct, and there was a strong argument that the hard-chine hull afforded greater flexibility to alter the weight and position of the armament. However, Thornycroft was certain that its CMB-type hull would achieve better speeds than the designs of its competitors. This came out in discussion, following a post-war paper given to the Royal Institution of Naval Architects by W.J. Holt, the wartime Chief Constructor in the Admiralty's Naval Construction Department. J.W. Thornycroft claimed that the newcomer opposition boatbuilder (a thinly-veiled reference to British Power Boat) had applied high-pressure promotion and salesmanship to push the hard-chine design as something new and far superior to any traditional hull-shape. Although outweighed by the other arguments, Thornycroft's claim was proven because the fastest Coastal Force boats on the water between 1939 and 1945 were the CMB-type MTBs, which achieved around 48kt.

Thornycroft did build three of the Admiralty's 1938 programme for six hard-chine MTBs, powered with the Isotta-Fraschini engines. Eight more 73ft

9in hard-chine boats would be completed in 1941. Although designed and built by the company, its conclusion was that these boats were under-powered. They had four Thornycroft RY/12 on two shafts, amounting to 2,600bhp, but when fully armed with two 0.5in machine guns, two depth-charges and two 21in torpedoes, they had a maximum speed of only 29kt. They were eventually converted to target-towing launches.

The contribution of Thornycroft to the war effort should not be underestimated. Its Hampton works built many air/sea rescue craft, target-towing launches, and motor minesweepers. It undertook some assembly of prefabricated hulls, building five Fairmile B MLs and 19 HDMLs. It was also a valuable source of supply of marine engines and military shells.

Power Boats from British Power Boat Company

J.W. Thornycroft believed that the Admiralty and several influential serving naval officers had succumbed to the persuasive charms of the flamboyant Hubert Scott-Paine. This great opportunist had formed the British Power Boat Company in 1927 at Hythe, Southampton. He was not a naval architect in the mould of Peter Du Cane, his contemporary and, for many years, his arch-rival at Vosper, but he did have an outstanding vision which he passed on to a brilliant design team. Scott-Paine had accumulated considerable wealth by building flying boats during the First World War, having formed Supermarine Aviation when he was only 23. He had built two prototype flying boats for the Admiralty in 1916, which led to an order for twenty, keeping his firm in production for the rest of the war.

He was positive that there was a peacetime role for his flying boats, and, in 1920, introduced the first British commercial airline, flying from Southampton to the Isle of Wight and later to Le Havre and the Channel Islands. In the same year, he turned his attention to building *Sea Lion II*, a single-seater flying boat which would regain the Schneider trophy for Britain with a speed of 145.7mph. The lines of *Sea Lion II* were the inspiration of R.J. Mitchell, Supermarine's chief designer, who, years later, would achieve fame as the designer of the RAF Spitfire fighter.

"Our Coastal Forces engaged the enemy..."

THE BRITISH POWER BOAT COMPANY LTD.

Constructors of Scott-Paine Surface Craft

ENGLAND
CANADA
AMERICA
FRANCE
HOLLAND
NORWAY
SWEDEN

All chose
BRITISH **POWER** BOATS

THE BRITISH POWER BOAT COMPANY LTD.   *Constructors of Scott-Paine Surface Craft*

Advertisements in the nautical press extalled the designs of Scott-Paine.

An impression of the latest 70' 0" MOTOR TORPEDO BOATS now in active service with the Allied Naval Forces. These craft are designed by Mr. H. Scott-Paine and built by The British Power Boat Company, Ltd., Hythe, Southampton, England.

In 1923, Scott-Paine sold Supermarine Aviation to concentrate on building fast boats. There was a market in Britain for light, fast powerboats, which was being supplied almost exclusively by American boatbuilders. Scott-Paine recruited Fred Cooper, a young designer at the Saunders Yard in East Cowes on the Isle of Wight. They worked on Scott-Paine's ideas for a high-speed motorboat, which could be mass-produced for the leisure market. To achieve this ambition, he bought the Hythe Shipyard on Southampton Water, and the British Power Boat Company was formed.

Fred Cooper produced designs for a range of hard-chine planing hulls which would put the firm ahead of all the competition from America. They were also to gain considerable prestige with *Miss England*. This was a 26ft single-step hydroplane hull, designed by Fred Cooper for Lord Wakefield. *Miss England*, with Henry Segrave at the wheel, would win the world championships at Miami,

Boats of the 1st MTB Flotilla escort the Royal Family in a Scott-Paine admiral's barge for the opening of the National Maritime Museum at Greenwich on 27 April 1937. *Southampton City Heritage Services*

Florida. Then came *Miss Britain*, another record-breaker, which attracted a great deal of attention in the USA. Fred Cooper, however, never felt he was given sufficient recognition for designing *Miss England*, and left British Power Boat to work on *Miss England II*, another of Sir Henry Segrave's record-breakers. In 1930 he joined Vosper.

Scott-Paine passionately believed that the Royal Navy should be equipped with flotillas of fast motor boats carrying torpedoes. He also formed the opinion that the success of building such boats would be dependent on the development of suitable engines. One of the departments in the Admiralty had recommended that tenders should be invited to build a torpedo boat. Those with the purse strings in the Admiralty were not enthusiastic,

and were not impressed by this brash young businessman and his pursuit of orders for his revolutionary hard-chine hull designs.

Scott-Paine was having more success with the RAF, for which he had built a 37ft hard-chine seaplane tender. The prototype, *RAF 200*, was to attract considerable interest both at home and overseas. It was tested by Aircraftman 1st Class T.E. Shaw (the charismatic Lawrence of Arabia), who played an important role in developing *RAF 200* and in gaining wide acceptance of the new hull design.

Anticipating that the Admiralty would come round to his vision of a 'mile-a-minute' navy, Scott-Paine and British Power Boat, in great secrecy, started planning what would be *MTB 01*. The 60ft hull, based on an earlier Fred Cooper design, was single diagonal planking above the chine and double below. The deck and wheelhouse would be made of aluminium alloy sheeting that had been used successfully on craft built for the leisure market. The Admiralty had already taken delivery of a British Power Boat hard-chine 45ft admiral's barge, and with this Scott-Paine was able to demonstrate the performance of the hard-chine hull in all sea conditions. In September 1935 the authorities decided to order two experimental 60ft boats. Four weeks later, without the benefit of any trials on the prototype, the Admiralty ordered another four boats, to create a six-boat MTB flotilla to send out to Malta. Mussolini had invaded Abyssinia, and the C-in-C Mediterranean, concerned about the build-up of Italian torpedo boats, had requested similar craft to meet the emergency.

The money to purchase the six British Power Boat craft came out of the 1935 Emergency Naval Building Budget. Those responsible for administering the budget asked Scott-Paine for his detailed costings of the first boat, which would include time spent on development, research and building a full-scale replica on which to base the final drawings. These figures were supplied to the

British Power Boat 70ft prototype MTB (*PV 70*) designed by George Selman was a private venture, built by Scott-Paine to compete for Admiralty orders with Vosper's prototype MTB.

Admiralty, where the information was read as the cost per boat, and then multiplied by six. Several years later, Scott-Paine was virtually accused of sharp practice by his adversaries, in obtaining such a large sum from the Admiralty. When he appeared before a Parliamentary Standing Committee, he bitterly disputed the allegation, claiming that it was hardly his fault if the Admiralty insisted on throwing money in his direction.

The first two boats (now officially classified as MTBs) were handed over to the Navy early in 1936 and officially designated MTBs *01* and *02*. Scott-Paine would continue to be closely involved with development work on the boats. As yet, no design had been worked out for carrying and firing torpedoes. The solution, according to Scott-Paine, was to mount the torpedoes in recesses in the hull. Prior to firing, the torpedoes could be turned outwards. Scott-Paine felt his ideas were so far advanced that his firm should reap the commercial rewards from a patent. The Admiralty was upset, claiming that any patent should be Crown property, as it had funded all the development work. It was also felt that the launching gear was too vulnerable

Hubert Scott-Paine (far left) aboard one of the pre-war 60ft MTBs, supervising loading of a stern-launched 18in torpedo. *Southampton City Heritage Services*

when, for example, going alongside a stone jetty. Torpedo launching went back to the drawing board, and Scott-Paine and the torpedo school at HMS *Vernon* came up with the stern-launching principle through holes in the transom. This method was adopted for the first eighteen MTBs built by Scott-Paine, but the design was then dropped in favour of forward launching, developed by HMS *Vernon* on a 1937 Vosper prototype.

The doubters at the Admiralty would finally come round to accepting Scott-Paine's new hull-form after witnessing *01*'s rough weather trials off the Isle of Wight. Scott-Paine personally took the wheel, and his own experience of driving small fast boats in open waters paid dividends. More than anyone else, he had established the hard-chine hull as the future shape for so many of the boats built for wartime service with the Royal Navy and the RAF.

Two months before the 1st MTB Flotilla set sail for Malta, Scott-Paine pulled off a magnificent publicity coup for his small boats. The occasion was the opening of the National Maritime Museum at Greenwich. The four latest boats (MTBs *03–06*) would act as escort to the Royal Family as they processed down the Thames from Westminster. And the icing on the cake was that the King would be leading the procession in an admiral's barge built by British Power Boat at Hythe. There was more press coverage for Scott-Paine when the 1st MTB Flotilla, under its own power, reached Malta ahead of schedule. It had crossed the Bay of Biscay, stopping off at Brest, Corunna, Lisbon, and Gibraltar.

By now the ambitious Scott-Paine had grandiose plans for building on a vast scale for the Royal Navy and RAF. He had orders to build another twelve 60ft

MTBs, planned for Hong Kong and Singapore. The Admiralty was formulating its ideas of a wartime role for Coastal Force craft. It wanted a torpedo boat which could also be used as a submarine-hunter and a minesweeper. Scott-Paine, keen to establish another use for his 60ft hulls, came up with the motor anti-submarine boat (MA/SB). ASDIC trials were conducted in the prototype (*MA/SB 1*) and the Admiralty was sufficiently impressed to order five more of these boats. MA/SBs *1–5* would make up the 1st MA/SB Flotilla, which was based at Portland at the outbreak of war; *MA/SB 6* was built as a 70ft boat.

Vosper, anticipating the future requirements of the Admiralty, had embarked on its own private venture, a 68ft craft. Scott-Paine saw this early involvement of Vosper and Peter Du Cane as a threat to his success with the Admiralty, and was particularly put out when the Navy decided to buy Du Cane's prototype as an experimental hard-chine boat (*MTB 102*). To rub salt in the wound, the money spent to buy the Vosper boat had previously been earmarked for developing an experimental 66ft craft from British Power Boat.

Already worried about competition from Vosper, in March 1938 Scott-Paine had to face intense criticism from a certain Lt-Cdr Reginald Fletcher MP. During a debate on Navy Estimates in the House of Commons, Scott-Paine was the subject of an extraordinary attempt at character assassination. Fletcher's speech, published in Hansard for anyone to read, cast doubts on some of the payments made to British Power Boat by the Admiralty, and virtually accused Scott-Paine of industrial espionage. There was an extraordinary suggestion that Scott-Paine had purchased second-hand Napier Lion engines for a few pounds and then, having installed them, passed on costs to the Admiralty of several thousand pounds per engine. It was quite true that Scott-Paine had acquired some second-hand engines, but he was a great believer in first building an actual-size mock-up of a hull shape, with engines in position, from which his designers could take the lines; it was for this use that the engines had been purchased. Fletcher also demanded an explanation as to why the Admiralty had ordered more of the 'obsolete' Scott-Paine boats when there was a much better boat available from Vosper.

The Admiralty made it known that it was looking for an MTB longer than the 60ft boats, which could carry two 21in torpedoes. Although Scott-Paine already had an overflowing order book, he was convinced he could build a boat which would be superior to the Vosper prototype and meet the Navy's current thinking. Scott-Paine and his chief designer, George Selman, started work on a private venture MTB which they called *PV 70*. Scott-Paine was to make a huge personal investment in *PV 70* and in the development of her Rolls-Royce engines.

One can only speculate on the tension between Scott-Paine and Peter Du Cane of Vosper when, in March 1939, both were summoned by the Admiralty to demonstrate their prototype MTBs in rough weather off the Isle of Wight. *PV 70*, loaded with specialists from the Admiralty, went out in the morning. Vosper's shorter boat (*MTB 102*) would be demonstrated in the afternoon, accompanied by *PV 70* as a more than interested spectator.

Scott-Paine knew he had the better boat, and was extremely upset when the Admiralty decided to adopt a Vosper 70ft design as standard. He must have felt that there was something of a vendetta against him because, while the opposition had been searching for the right engine, he had negotiated with Rolls-Royce for a regular and exclusive supply of its Merlin engines, and spent a considerable time converting and testing the first three for marine use. These were the 1,000bhp engines that powered *PV 70* so successfully, attaining a top speed of 44.4kt.

There was undoubtedly bad feeling between several members of the Admiralty and Scott-Paine, partly fuelled by Lt-Cdr Fletcher's extraordinary outburst in the House of Commons and his subsequent demand for an enquiry. Years later, Scott-Paine discovered that the main reason for the Admiralty's decision was that he had undertaken his development of *PV 70* in secrecy, whereas Vosper had always worked closely with the Admiralty.

PV 70 had already attracted interest from overseas, including Henry R. Sutphen and his designer Irwin Chase of Elco, still based at Bayonne, New Jersey. It was a strange reversal of roles because, as we have seen, during the First World War it was Henry Sutphen who had been approached by the Admiralty to construct MLs in the USA and Canada for shipment back to the Royal Navy in Britain; at the beginning of the Second World War, Sutphen was looking for an MTB design suitable for the US

Navy. Apart from the 70ft Scott-Paine prototype (*PV 70*), Elco wanted to evaluate the latest from Vosper and Thornycroft.

Despite the Admiralty's lack of interest, Scott-Paine never had any doubts about *PV 70*; successful demonstrations to the Americans resulted in the sale to Elco of a 70ft boat based on *PV 70*. Elco in turn, sold it on to the US Navy as an experimental craft (*PT 9*). Scott-Paine left for America in September 1939 to negotiate a licensing agreement with Elco to build his boats at its yard in Bayonne. He wanted to set up a similar licensing arrangement in Canada with Canadian Vickers.

The order for Elco was constructed with some urgency and shipped out to the USA just days before the outbreak of war. Extensive trials were undertaken at Bayonne, during which the new boat, powered by Rolls-Royce Merlin engines, reached a top speed of 47.7kt. Scott-Paine was duly summoned to the White House to meet President Roosevelt, who confirmed that Elco had been awarded a contract to build another 23 boats. These would be made up of 12 PTCs (submarine-chasers) and 11 PTs (torpedo boats). The last of the batch of PT boats (*PT 20*) was 'stretched' by an additional seven feet towards the stern. This extended version of the original 70ft design would be adopted for the next four squadrons of PT boats. To meet these orders from the US Navy, Scott-Paine immediately entered into negotiations with Packard for an exclusive supply of a marine version of its M-2500 engine. Scott-Paine would spend the war years in America and Canada, anticipating that Elco would be building MTBs to be shipped back to Britain, as well as supplying the US Navy. He was to be disappointed.

Back home, eight British Power Boat MA/SBs were completed as MGBs to form the 6th MGB Flotilla. Working out of Fowey and then Felixstowe, the 6th Flotilla achieved some remarkable successes, despite the constraints of the modified boats. One of the COs in the flotilla was Lt Robert Hichens, RNVR, who would take over as Senior Officer and would become one of Coastal Forces' greatest tacticians. Hichens had already served with

Lt-Cdr Hichens' *MGB 77* was ordered as a motor anti-submarine boat but was subsequently re-designated a motor gunboat in January 1941.

great distinction at Dunkirk, for which he was decorated with his first DSC. Serving aboard the fleet minesweeper *Niger*, which was involved in evacuating troops from La Panne, to the north of Dunkirk, he had been put ashore to take charge of transferring the troops from the beach to small boats that would ferry them to the larger ships lying offshore. In his diary he recorded his dismay at the total lack of organisation he found on the beaches, and noted the reluctance of many of the small boats' civilian crews to return to the scene once they had embarked their first load of soldiers. He was nevertheless able to impose order amidst the chaos, and volunteered to continue ashore when *Niger* departed crammed with soldiers. It is reckoned that he was personally responsible for the successful evacuation of more than a thousand personnel who would have otherwise been killed or taken prisoner.

The hulls of the converted MA/SBs were really not suitable for taking heavier armament, and the Admiralty was looking for a more purpose-built MGB. In Scott-Paine's absence, the Navy approached his chief designer, George Selman. He worked closely with the office of the Director of Naval Construction at Bath, and produced a design for a highly successful 71ft 6in hull. Work on the prototype MGB started in December 1940, and by February 1941 the general arrangement of the boat had been approved by the Admiralty. The hull was laid down in April and she was launched at the end of 1941. Trials were completed in February 1942 and this first 71ft 6in MGB was commissioned the same month. Communication between Scott-Paine in America and George Selman was difficult; having to rely on surface mail Scott-Paine was not pleased when he learned of the plans for the Hythe yard to produce this new boat; he felt isolated from what was going on at Hythe, believing he should have been consulted.

MGB 87 was one of twelve Elco 70ft submarine chasers built for the US Navy and transferred to the Royal Navy as MGBs. IWM FL16301

The prototype MGB was a hard-chine hull, built of double diagonal mahogany planking and powered by three 1,250bhp supercharged Packard petrol engines. The strength of the hull would be sufficient to carry a 40mm gun on the foredeck. There was a certain irony that, of all the wartime production of 'short' boats for the Royal Navy, the Selman-designed 71ft 6in British Power Boat would prove to be the most successful, and Scott-Paine had no hand in it.

Robert Hichens first heard about this new boat at a Coastal Forces meeting with the C-in-C Nore in December 1941. He formed the 8th MGB flotilla, taking over the new boats as each one came off the production line. Until his death in April 1943, Lt-Cdr

35th MTB Flotilla was made up of 1942 British Power Boat production 71ft 6in Mk V boats.

Hichens worked closely with George Selman to improve the boats, suggesting modifications based on his experiences operating MGBs in the North Sea. Between them, they designed a new underwater exhaust system which considerably reduced the noise level.

Twenty-eight Hythe-built 71ft 6in British Power Boat craft were commissioned as MGBs. A later boat was selected for trials as a combined gunboat and torpedo boat, a development that had been enthusiastically promoted by Hichens. The trials were a success and British Power Boat then switched its production, building 67 more 71ft 6in hulls, which would enter RN service as MTBs. As more and more armament was added, George Selman was able to make modifications to maintain the performance, helped by the power increase of the later Packard engines from 1,200 to 1,500bhp.

British Power Boat had a full order book for the rest of the war, building various craft for all three branches of the services. Scott-Paine was having less success in America. He had failed to secure orders from the Admiralty for the construction of MTBs to be shipped back home. After 49 of the 77ft Elco boats had been built, the US Navy decided it wanted 80ft boats to carry four 21in torpedoes. There was then a parting of the ways between Hubert Scott-Paine and Henry Sutphen. The latter claimed the 80ft boats would be built to an exclusively Elco design in which Scott-Paine had no financial stake.

In Canada, Scott-Paine's fortunes were no better. Canadian Vickers, concentrating on larger craft, was no longer interested in a licensing arrangement to build Scott-Paine-designed boats. He then formed the Canadian Power Boat Company Ltd. With some interest from the Canadian government, arrangements were made for *PV 70* to be shipped out to New York. The Merlin engines, which belonged to Rolls-Royce, were removed before she was loaded on the first available freighter. To complete the last leg of the passage, she had to be towed along waterways from New York to Scott-Paine's boat-yard at Montreal.

PV 70, now powered with two Packards, was re-launched in Canada in November 1940. With a boat to demonstrate, Scott-Paine was able to secure orders from the Royal Canadian Navy and Royal Canadian Air Force and the Royal Netherlands Navy. This was sufficient work to keep the yard busy for about 18 months after which, with no more orders in the offing, most of the staff had to be laid off.

Scott-Paine could only watch Elco go from strength to strength, and by the end of the war it had built 326 PT boats. Thirty-two of the 71 early US-built, Scott-Paine-designed Elco boats did eventually get shipped across the Atlantic as Lend-Lease supplies. Amongst these were the original 70ft PT boats (PTs *10–19*), which would operate in the Mediterranean as MTBs *259–268*. The original

twelve 70ft submarine chasers (PTCs *1–12*) would operate in home waters as MGBs *82–93*, working out of Lowestoft as the 7th MGB Flotilla. Under Lend-Lease arrangements 29 boats constructed by the US builder Higgins Industries were also shipped across the Atlantic. These were a mixture of MA/SBs, MTBs, and MGBs, of varying lengths, some of which had been ordered for overseas navies. Of the thirteen boats that stayed in home

waters, ten were sent to Tough Brothers and Brook Marine for rebuilding, but these boats never operated satisfactorily in Coastal Forces and the majority were transferred to the Royal Army Service Corps to be used as target-towing launches. To the distress of Scott-Paine, the only direct Admiralty orders placed with American boatbuilders was for 64 Vosper 71ft MTBs.

At its peak the Hythe yard was building 71ft 6in

MGB 123 was the prototype Mk VI 71ft 6in from British Power Boats that was used for experiments with torpedo tubes. She was later re-designated MTB 446. Southampton City Heritage Services

MTBs at the rate of one a week. Towards the end of the war, some of the orders placed with British Power Boat began to be cancelled. By late 1946 the Hythe yard had closed, and the country had lost one

MTB 494 at speed. Note her 2pdr gun armament and torpedo tubes.

MTB 494 was one of the highly successful Mk VI 71ft 6in British Power Boats equipped for the dual role of MTB/MGB. These vessels had exceptionally strong hulls and suffered few structural failures. *Southampton City Heritage Services*

of the finest small-boat design teams and the most efficient mass-production boat-yard in Europe.

Two years later Hubert Scott-Paine became a citizen of the USA. He had contributed a great deal to the development of the wartime MTB and air/sea rescue boat and he had secured for the Allies a regular supply of Packard engines. Ill from overwork and disappointment, he felt his contribution to the war effort had never been properly recognised. He never appeared in the Honours List, unlike his rival

Peter Du Cane of Vosper, who was awarded the OBE in 1942 and the CBE in 1964.

MTBs from Vosper and Samuel White

Vosper, Scott-Paine's main competitor in the UK, has a long history of shipbuilding for the Admiralty. The company was started by Herbert Edward Vosper, who had established a small dock at Camber, on the east side of the entrance to Portsmouth harbour. His first production of small ships was in 1880, when he was still only in his twenties. Under his guidance the firm grew rapidly before the turn of the century. Originally 'general engineers and boiler makers', the business soon diversified. Ideally situated for the marine market, his firm turned to designing, developing,

Vosper's 70ft Private Venture.

manufacturing, and assembling marine engines, boilers, and pumps. In addition to the comprehensive engineering facilities, the yard specialised in maintenance (with a slipway for smaller ships and waterside frontage to receive larger vessels), and also undertook traditional boatbuilding and repairs in wood. H.E. Vosper retired in 1919 by which time he had built up a firm with a fine reputation, but, like so many shipbuilders, it had to scale down its operations in the aftermath of the First World War.

Two great names in the development of high-speed motor boats joined Vosper in the early 1930s, when there was a growing interest in building small, fast, hard-chine craft for the pleasure market. The first, as noted earlier, was Fred Cooper, previously employed by Hubert Scott-Paine, and the designer of both *Miss England* and *Miss England II*, in which Sir Henry Segrave had achieved 95kt – a world water-speed record in 1930. The other was the legendary Cdr Peter Du Cane, who joined Vosper in 1931 and after a few months became the firm's managing director and chief designer, and subsequently a principal shareholder. He managed the firm for 35 years, relinquishing the post in 1965 to become research director of what would be an amalgamation of Vosper and Thornycroft. He retired in 1973.

Peter Du Cane had joined the Royal Navy as a Dartmouth cadet in 1914. At the end of the First World War he specialised in engineering, and served as senior engineer in a Yangtze River gunboat. Frustrated with the peacetime navy, he resigned his commission and then qualified as a pilot, before joining Vosper.

Peter Du Cane made the name of Vosper synonymous with high-speed small craft. He was a brilliant designer with an enthusiasm for speed on the water. His skills had a worldwide influence on the design of small warships, pleasure cruisers, racing craft, and record-breakers (including Malcolm Campbell's *Bluebird II* and John Cobb's *Crusader*). He guided Vosper through the difficult interwar years, the war effort – in which the firm was to play such an important role – and the postwar years that so many shipbuilders failed to survive. During his time with Vosper he was responsible for the design and testing of numerous prototype high-speed craft, and in the process earned the company an international reputation.

At a time when Vosper design staff were gaining valuable experience with the production of Sir Malcolm Campbell's record-breaking hydroplane *Bluebird II*, plans were being developed for a high-speed motor torpedo boat. Impressed by the performance of the Thornycroft coastal motor boats (CMBs) in the First World War, Peter Du Cane was convinced that there was a market for a two-torpedo vessel, capable of tight manoeuvring, and powered to approach enemy shipping at high speed and make an equally speedy withdrawal after launching her torpedoes. In 1936, therefore, Vosper decided to build a private-venture MTB with no commercial partnership, either with the Admiralty or with overseas navies. She was completed in May 1937. The 68ft prototype (job number 1763), on which hundreds of wartime MTBs would be based, had a hard-chine hull, which was built in double-diagonal mahogany planking.

Pre-war MTB hulls under construction at Vosper's Flathouse yard in Portsmouth Harbour. *Vosper Thornycroft*

In any design of high-speed small coastal warships, the prime considerations are the water-resistance to the hull when travelling at speed, the choice and installation of marine engines, and the weight distribution of the armaments and the fuel tanks. Rolls-Royce, with its exclusive agreement with Scott-Paine's British Power Boat Co, was unable to supply the appropriate engines to Vosper. After considerable research, Vosper concluded that there was no available British-designed marine or aero engine suitable for powering its prototype MTB. Instead it ordered 1,050bhp Italian Isotta-Fraschini engines, which had been specifically developed for the Russian Navy for use in the high-speed MTBs that it had been building between the wars. Two Ford V8 auxiliary wing engines were added to the Vosper prototype, and installed as standard on many future boats, to enable them to

close on a target at about 8kt in almost complete silence.

Without armament, the prototype reached 47.8kt. Armed, she could still reach 43.7kt – a remarkable performance – carrying two 21in torpedoes (one firing through an aperture in the stemhead, the other being launched over the stern). Vosper's initial trials were encouraging, and the Admiralty was sufficiently impressed to buy the prototype in October 1937. Further evaluations of the performance were then undertaken, including the famous rough weather sea-trial in competition with

A 1938-class Vosper being used for torpedo trials at HMS *Vernon* in late 1939. *Vosper Thornycroft*

the British Power Boat prototype. This was carried out in gale-force winds in open waters to the south of the Isle of Wight. The boats were accompanied by a destroyer, to be on hand if one of them started to break up in the gale-swept seas. Du Cane personally took the wheel of the Vosper, using the enclosed wheelhouse in preference to the upper steering position. The hull, which had already been strengthened with additional frames, impressively

survived its pounding off the Isle of Wight.

After the rough weather trials, the Admiralty formally advised Vosper that it had been selected to build the new generation of MTBs for the Royal Navy. After extensive fitting out by Vosper, *MTB 102* (as she was now designated) was delivered to HMS *Vernon*, the torpedo school in Portsmouth harbour. For a trial period she was armed with a Swiss Oerlikon gun, mounted off-centre. The Oerllkon, previously unseen in home waters, proved extremely effective during these trials, and would be adopted by many of the wartime high-speed coastal craft.

102 paved the way for a long and fruitful association of Vosper with the Admiralty. She carried out many invaluable trials for the Navy, particularly in the firing of torpedoes. The experts at HMS *Vernon* perfected an arrangement using two 21in torpedo tubes mounted on *102*'s deck. This became accepted as standard for future MTBs and made the rear-launching system, as built into the early British Power Boat MTBs, look pretty antiquated. Trials also included the first power-operated twin Vickers 0.5in machine guns and chloro-sulphuric acid smoke-making equipment.

The wartime Vosper boats, built in the UK for the Royal Navy, were of two overall lengths (71ft and 73ft). There were also a few 60ft and 70ft boats, some of which had been built for overseas navies. All the wartime production was based on the highly-successful prototype *102* with its un-stepped hard-chine planing hull. Some still argued that a stepped hull should be adopted, believing that when the hull was planing there would be less resistance with more of the hull raised out of the water, and that therefore such a hull would be capable of greater speeds. Vosper, however, believed that its un-stepped hard-chine hull was a better sea boat, more manoeuvrable, and offered considerably less water resistance when not planing. These differing views prompted the Admiralty to commission Vosper to build an experimental 70ft stepped-hull MTB (*103*) which was begun in 1939, but progress was delayed when the planned Isotta-Fraschini engines became scarce, and she had to wait for imported Packard

T.3 was ordered for the Greek Navy, then taken over by the Royal Navy and renumbered *MTB 70*. *Vosper Thornycroft*

55

MTB 36: above, the engine room with 900bhp Hall-Scott engines; *left*, the wheelhouse. *Vosper Thornycroft*

engines. The test results were inconclusive, as she had been designed to be powered by the Italian engines. Vosper continued to supply un-stepped hulls throughout the war, and *MTB 103* became a target-towing launch (*CT 05*).

In 1939 Vosper was concentrating on completing its overseas orders and the first twenty 71ft MTBs for the Royal Navy. Excluding the boats built for foreign navies and those built under licence abroad, 118 standard short MTBs were delivered by Vosper. The wartime production programme was:

Year	Quantity	Numbered	Length
1939	10	*31–40*	71ft
1939 (extension)	10	*57–66*	71ft
1940	26	*73–98*	71ft
1941	24	*222–245*	71ft
1942	16	*347–362*	71ft
1943	16	*380–395*	73ft
1944	16	*523–538*	73ft

To meet the changing pattern of Coastal Forces warfare, towards the end of the war the 73ft boats had different combinations of armament. The 1943 production had four 18in torpedoes (taking advantage of a massive over-production of torpedoes for the RAF), while the last of the wartime production were armed to perform as dual-purpose MTBs/MGBs. These additional armaments were only possible at the sacrifice of some speed.

The production of Vosper boats ceased at the Camber yard after it was bombed in March 1941. Vosper had previously acquired Flathouse Yard on the north side of Portsmouth Dockyard, but when this was compulsorily bought by the Admiralty in 1938 Vosper had moved some of its production to a new site near Portchester, at the northern end of Portsmouth harbour. After the loss of Camber the Portchester yard was enlarged, and the company took over a small yard at Wivenhoe, Essex. Some of the construction work was contracted out to other well-established yards, including Camper & Nicholsons (Gosport), Berthon Boat Co (Lymington), Harland & Wolff (Belfast), Morgan Giles (Teignmouth), and two yards in Scotland, McGruer and Maclean.

There were other sources of supply for Vosper-designed boats, including sixty-four 71ft boats built under licence in the USA; of these eight were diverted to Russia, 24 supplied to the Royal Indian Navy, and 32 delivered to the Royal Navy in the Mediterranean.

J.S. White of Cowes, Isle of Wight, built 18 Vosper 71ft hulls as part of its 1940–1 programme. White had produced its own private-venture MTB, built on hydrofoils, but this design was never adopted. The company did, however, build 20 of its own design of MTB as part of the 1939 and 1942–3 programmes. The White boats were easily identifiable by their distinctive flared bows. Many MTBs built by J.S. White were powered by supercharged Stirling Admiral engines.

The Vosper building programme was largely determined by the availability of suitable engines. The Italian Isotta-Fraschini 1,050bhp engines installed on *102* had proved ideal for the Vosper design, and a modernised uprated 1,150bhp version was installed in the 1939 boats ordered by foreign navies, and in the first boats delivered to the Royal Navy in 1939–40. Italy, however, entered the war in June 1940, when an alternative to the Isotta-Fraschini had to be found as a matter of urgency. In order to maintain its building schedules, Vosper started installing American Hall Scott V-12 900bhp petrol engines, which proved to be a poor substitute for the Italian engines. Only 13 MTBs were built with the Hall Scott engine, which gave them a top speed of only 27kt. However, this had been only a stopgap measure until 1,250bhp Packard engines could be shipped over from the USA. These engines were adopted as standard in all Vosper boats built from 1941 to 1944, when the upgraded 1,350bhp Packards became available. The hull construction of the Vosper MTBs was along the lines of the original prototype, being hard-chine of double-skin mahogany side planking with triple-skin for the bottom planking. The deck was double diagonal mahogany. The 71ft boats were designed to be manned by two officers and eight ratings. With the introduction of the 73ft Vosper and more sophisticated armament and equipment, the complement was increased to ten and then eleven ratings plus two officers. The larger 73ft boats were also designed with three rudders, which made them considerably more manoeuvrable.

The basic equipment for the early 71ft boats consisted of W/T, echo-sounder, radar, and CSA smoke-maker. In addition to their two 21in

ABOVE: *MTB 83*'s wireless cabin. *IWM D12543*

torpedoes they were armed with a twin 0.5in Mk 5 (power-operated turret) Vickers machine gun. The later Vosper boats had W/T, three radar sets, echo-sounder, QH (electronic navigational aid), inter-ship radio sets, hydrophone, CSA smoke-maker, Aldis lamp, and loud hailer. Armament included a 6pdr cannon forward, two twin Vickers 0.303in machine guns midships, a twin 20mm Oerlikon aft, and two 18in torpedoes. The steering position on the later boats was on the upper bridge, which was built in 15lb bullet-proof steel; there was an emergency aft steering position, and the navigator had the luxury of a chart table beneath the upper bridge. This was a big improvement on the 71ft Vospers, which had a steering position in the armoured wheelhouse and a second position on the upper bridge.

RIGHT: The 73ft flush-decked Vosper *MTB 380* was launched in 1944 and carried four 18in torpedo tubes. *Vosper Thornycroft*

Fairmile series A, B, C and D

Apart from Hubert Scott-Paine and Peter Du Cane, there is another famous name associated with the development of Coastal Forces craft in the Second World War. This is Capt Noel Macklin, who was knighted in 1944 in recognition of his services in warship production. Eton-educated, in his younger days he raced cars at Brooklands, was a keen amateur jockey, and represented England at hockey. He had served in the Royal Artillery during the First World War, until, invalided out, he became an RNVR officer, serving in the Dover Patrol, an experience which gave him an enthusiasm for small craft and a valuable insight into the wartime role of motor launches.

As we have seen, in the First World War the Admiralty had sent one of its representatives over to the USA with a top-priority mission to purchase or

place orders for motor launches. Although at the outbreak of the Second World War there was once again an urgent requirement for MLs, the solution this time was to be found at home. Positive that there would be a demand for an anti-submarine patrol boat, the remarkable Noel Macklin had already approached the Admiralty not only with a design for a motor launch, but also a unique method of mass-producing hulls, using what is now known as marine-ply (a pre-fabricated waterproof plywood). The concept was brilliantly simple – furniture factories would produce standard cut sections of marine-ply, which could then be assembled by boatbuilders with even the most modest facilities.

In July 1939 the Admiralty, having been convinced that Macklin's construction plans were practical, placed an order for one motor launch, detailing the armament. What would become *ML 100* was laid down in October at Woodnutt's Yard in Bembridge, on the Isle of Wight.

Noel Macklin's Fairmile Marine Company started

MTB 523's engine room. The 73ft Vosper MTBs were powered by three supercharged Packard engines. *Vosper Thornycroft*

Building 73ft Vosper MTBs at Wivenhoe in 1943.
Vosper Thornycroft

modestly, with a handful of specialists working from his home in a Surrey village which had a pub called 'The Fairmile', after which his company was named. It was not an entirely new name in industry, Macklin having previously formed Fairmile Engineering, which successfully manufactured custom-built cars. This was the stable of the famous Invicta racing car, and the Railton Special, which was marketed as the Fairmile version of the American Hudson automobile.

Macklin had personal qualities which inspired those who worked around him, and in a matter of months an extraordinarily ambitious boatbuilding programme had developed, with Macklin seeking out many firms – ranging from sawmills to furniture manufacturers and foundries – which pre-war had no connection with boatbuilding. By 1944 the Fairmile Company was employing 550 staff. However, it never

attempted to establish itself as a wartime boatbuilder. The organisation was a brilliant example of what today would be labelled production control, covering the design work, technical specifications, ordering up of prefabricated parts, and allocation of the kits to boatyards around the British Isles for assembly; Fairmile would also schedule the supply of engines and armament, standardise and contract the manufacture of a whole range of fittings, and establish a huge spares department at Brentford in Essex.

Even before the prototype had been started at Woodnutt's Yard, the Admiralty increased its order to 24. The Norman Hart-designed Fairmile A would be 110ft long, with a hard-chine double diagonal mahogany on plywood frame, and eight

61

71ft MTBs designed and built by J.S. White at Cowes. *R.G.R. Haggard*

The bridge layout of *MTB 523* was complex . . .

prefabricated bulkheads. The three 600bhp Hall Scott engines would give the boats a top speed of 25kt, and a cruising speed of 22kt. The accommodation, which did not prove entirely satisfactory, was planned for two officers, two petty officers, and twelve ratings. Production of the first twelve boats had been spread among ten boatbuilding firms. This initial Admiralty order allowed Fairmile Marine to gain valuable experience in the management of mass-production boatbuilding. The A-Class, however, fell between a long MGB and an all-purpose ML. The hard-chine hull-form made them uncomfortable in head seas. The fuel tanks held 1,200 gallons, which gave them a range of only 600 miles at 12kt. These early A-Class Fairmiles would soon be converted to minelayers.

Independent of Fairmile, W.J. Holt's Naval Construction Department at the Admiralty had been experimenting on various ideas for a new ML, using the test tank at Haslar. The department was looking for something about the same length as the Fairmile A, but more robust, to perform a wider range of duties. Several models were tank-tested. At the end of 1939, the lines of a hull and bridge, and the armament, had been established. Fairmile was considered eminently suitable for managing the construction of a large number of the new design. In the end only the first 12 of the A-Class boats were built and, by the end of 1939, all the resources of the Fairmile organisation would be concentrated instead on the 200-boat order from the Admiralty for what would be designated the B-Class ML. Macklin went into partnership with the Admiralty, working as an arm of the Naval Construction Department, to provide the MLs that would operate in various roles all round the British Isles, in the Adriatic, and the Mediterranean. The success story says much for the healthy working relationship

. . . compared with earlier Vospers such as
MTB 83. Vosper Thornycroft

between Noel Macklin and W.J. Holt. 'Deafy' Holt
was himself a considerable character, perhaps a
little dogmatic, but a dedicated hard-working zealot
in the cause of small warships. He controlled
discussions by switching off his hearing aid.

It is perhaps a hackneyed phrase, but 'maid-of-all-work' is one that immediately comes to mind when
considering the B-Class ML. It was used in anti-submarine and anti-E-boat roles, as a minelayer, an
enemy-mine spotter (looking out for those dropped
from aircraft), a minesweeper, a convoy escort, and
a troop carrier. A remarkable innovation included in
the design was the provision of deck fittings which
would enable an ML to be converted at short notice
from one role to another, so that one week she
might be laying mines off the Dutch coast, and the
next week hunting submarines with depth-charges.

The B-Class ML was fractionally longer than the
A, with more beam and considerably less draught.
The main difference, however, was the round-bilge
hull-shape. The fuel capacity was doubled and, with
additional deck fuel tanks, the B-Class MLs could
carry 5,000 gallons of fuel, giving them a range of
1,500 miles at 12kt. Accommodation, improved
compared with the A, was for two officers, two
petty officers and twelve ratings. The original boats
were armed with two Lewis machine guns, a 3pdr
cannon and twelve depth-charges, but this
configuration was constantly being changed to
meet the differing roles of the ML. Typical
armament might be a 3pdr forward, an Oerlikon aft,
twin 0.303in gas-operated Vickers aft of the bridge,
two 21in torpedo tubes and two depth-charges.

Once the Admiralty had decided on the lines and
armament of the new B-type ML, the whole
production was handed over to Fairmile, to design
the framing and prepare the plans for prefabrication

and assembly. Fairmile would also appoint builders all round the coast, who would be visited regularly to ensure quality control. The one problem area was the engines. The Admiralty had originally specified three Hall Scott Defender engines, which had to be imported from the US and were consequently in short supply. This would influence the final specification, with only two of these 600bhp engines being fitted, reducing the top speed to 20kt. Speed was sacrificed in order to increase the building programme by 50 per cent.

Forty-five boatyards all around the country, some experienced only in the maintenance and winter storage of wooden yachts, would take delivery of keel, stemhead, and transom, to which eleven bulkheads and frames would be secured. The pre-cut bulkheads had notches in them to take the fore and aft stringers. To these were secured the double diagonal mahogany planking. The construction was closely supervised by Fairmile Marine at every stage. Engines and electrics were installed by Fairmile specialists, who also undertook sea trials before handing the boats over to the Admiralty. Each ML took about six months to construct, although several of the better-equipped yards, working a seven-day week, were able to knock several weeks off the average.

Production of the B-Class MLs for the Royal Navy continued both at home and overseas until December 1944. Between 1941 and 1944 the MLs would be upgraded from time to time with additional or improved equipment. Radar, ASDIC, and hydrophone became standard.

The C-Class ML was ordered as a temporary measure, to provide 110ft gunboats. The hulls were prefabricated, using the original A-Class Fairmile jigs. It was felt that, although the B-Class was proving to be an excellent sea boat easily equipped to undertake a whole range of duties, a faster boat was urgently required for use in an offensive role against the German E-boats. Only 24 of these C-Class MGBs were built, each powered by three supercharged Hall Scott 900bhp engines, giving them a top speed of 26.6kt. After some

The last series of the wartime Vosper 73ft MTBs carried two 18in torpedo tubes but was more heavily armed, with a 6pdr gun in a power-operated mounting forward. *Vosper Thornycroft* experimenting with armament, each boat was equipped with 2pdr pom-poms forward and aft, two twin 0.5in Vickers machine guns, two twin 0.303in Vickers machine guns on the bridge wings, and a single Oerlikon amidships. These 110ft boats, underpowered for their role, were no match for the German E-boats, and would soon be superseded by the famous D-Class MGBs and MTBs.

In the build up of Coastal Forces craft in the early part of the war, Vosper and British Power Boat were producing the short MTBs and MGBs, and Fairmile the all-purpose ML. Month-by-month, Germany was building up the numbers of its own well-tried round-bilge E-boat. The Royal Navy was still looking for a suitable craft which, heavily armed, could take on the E-boats in all weathers.

One of the models being tank-tested by W.J. Holt in late 1939 was a hard-chine hull design which would be 110ft in waterline length, with 3ft more beam than the B-Class to accommodate the installation of four marine engines. This was the origin of the D-Class MGBs and MTBs, which have been described as having the bows of a destroyer attached to the stern of a fast motor boat. They were affectionately known as 'Dog-boats', and served extensively at home and overseas. Many flotillas were despatched to the Mediterranean in 1943, making the passage entirely under their own power.

The prototype D-Class MGB (*601*), built in four months by Tough Brothers at their Thames-side yard at Teddington, was launched in October 1941. With increasing pressure on the Admiralty to put in service a powerful craft over 100ft long, the first batch of D-Class boats were commissioned without torpedo tubes; thereafter, however, these craft would be armed as they were originally conceived, so that they could function as MTB/MGBs.

Although the waterline length of the Dog-boats was only about 4ft more than that of the B-Class MLs, the projected displacement was substantially greater. In design terms, these D-Class boats represented a considerable challenge. To achieve a reasonable speed, the hull would have to house four 12-cylinder, 1,250bhp supercharged Packard petrol engines. The first MGBs would be armed with a 2pdr forward, a twin Oerlikon aft, and twin 0.5in Vickers machine guns either side of the bridge, with

twin 0.303in gas-operated Vickers machine guns on the wings of the bridge.

There were various re-armaments of the D-Class boats. The heaviest configuration consisted of four 18in torpedo tubes, depth-charges, a 6pdr forward and aft, twin 0.5in Vickers machine guns either side of the bridge, with a twin Oerlikon midships. The large fuel tanks to hold 5,200 gallons would give the boats a range of about 1,200 miles at 10kt, which could be significantly extended with deck tanks providing an additional 3,000 gallons. It was hardly surprising that the projected hull displacement of 85 tons soon climbed to 105 tons. The projected top speed of 35kt dropped to 30kt with the addition of direct drive. Over 200 D-type MGBs/MTBs were built by the many boatyards which, in peacetime, would have been working on large, expensive cruisers for sale or for hire (several were located on the Norfolk Broads).

More so than any of the other classes of Coastal Force craft, the Dog-boats would be expected to maintain high speeds irrespective of sea conditions. Inevitably, these prefabricated hulls could not take endless crashing into head seas at relatively high speeds without weakening the frames. Those boats whose operational requirements dictated making long passages in all weathers required heavy maintenance. The hulls often had to be strengthened, and the over-worked Packards needed frequent overhauls. A typical D-Class complement was three officers, coxswain, chief petty officer, engineer, five stokers, and 23 seamen ratings.

Camper & Nicholsons MGBs/MTBs

Another outline design to come out of the Admiralty's Naval Construction Department was for a combined MTB and anti-submarine boat. W.J. Holt's staff produced this outline at about the same time (late 1939) as they were working on the D-Class lines. In waterline-length, both boats were very similar (about 110ft), but unlike the 'Dog-boat', this addition to the range of Coastal Forces craft would be round-bilge, and constructed using traditional methods of shipbuilding. Web-type steel frames with intermediate elm frames would be

Twin 0.5in machine guns in a power-operated turret. *R.G.R. Haggard*

incorporated which, with steel bulkheads, would make them much stronger than the same-sized prefabricated Fairmiles.

Once financial approval had been given to the Naval Construction Department, Holt approached Charles Nicholson of shipbuilders Camper & Nicholsons. For over two centuries this firm had built, at its Gosport shipyard in Portsmouth harbour, some of the most prestigious yachts available. It was this yard which launched several of the famous J-Class contenders for the America's Cup, including *Endeavour I* and *II* raced by Tommy Sopwith, as well as large steel motor yachts, and a number of small commercial vessels. Now Charles Nicholson, grandson of the firm's founder and a naval architect with a considerable reputation, was provided with plans of the general layout and proposed armament of the required MTB, and produced the detailed construction plans, basing his design on a popular range of Camper &

Nicholsons day-cruisers.

The Admiralty entered into a commitment to provide similar boats to the Turkish Navy, based on the original design, but with more armament and a correspondingly greater displacement. The Turkish government would never receive them, as the order would be re-allocated to the Royal Navy. Eight boats (*502–509*) would simply be treated as an extension to the original order for *MTB 501*.

It was to be an ill-fated order. Camper & Nicholsons would finish up building an additional four boats, to replace hulls destroyed on their stocks during the blitz of Gosport on 10 March 1941, when over 80 per cent of the yard was razed. A fifth hull was blown off its keel blocks and badly damaged aft, but it proved possible to lift her back on, line her up, and eventually make a new stern. It would be six months before the yard would be fully operational again and work could be started on new boats to replace those lost.

The first of the 500-Class was eventually commissioned in April 1942. During construction, it was decided to complete her as an MGB. Her armament would be a Mk VIII 2pdr with manual

A-Class Fairmile. The first of the Fairmile range of Motor Launches (ML) was launched in time to take part in the Dunkirk evacuation. *IWM HU2082*

mount forward, two 0.5in twin machine guns abreast the bridge/wheelhouse, a 20mm Oerlikon aft, and two 21in torpedo tubes. She had excellent accommodation for three officers and 18 men. With 5,000 gallons of fuel, *MGB 501* had a displacement of 95 tons. The original specification had been for diesel engines, but because of a shortage at that time *507* was fitted instead with three petrol-driven 1,250bhp Packards. Speed on trials was 30kt plus. With the exception of *509*, which reverted to petrol engines, the rest of this batch of boats would be powered by three 1,000bhp Paxman Ricardo 16V RBM diesel engines.

Several months prior to the completion of *501*, a top-secret department had been formed by Capt Frank Slocum at the Admiralty. He had been looking

The launch of the first of the successful B-Class MLs at Tough Brothers yard on the Thames at Teddington. *Tough Brothers*

round for boats to form the 15th MGB Flotilla, which would be involved in undercover operations along the coasts of Brittany, Normandy, and Norway (*see Chapter 10*). He made a successful bid for the first three of the Camper & Nicholsons boats (*501, 502,* and *503*) to join a C-Class MGB (*318*) and *MA/SB 36*.

On 27 July 1942, just weeks after being commissioned, *501* was at sea, resplendent in her Plymouth Pink colour scheme. Her CO was Lt Dunstan Curtis, DSC (who commanded *MGB 314*, leader in the famous St Nazaire raid, *for which see*

Chapter 8). Captain Slocum was also on board to view his new acquisition. When they were between Lands End and the Scillies there was a serious explosion below deck, which blew out the side of the boat. The cause was thought to be the spread of fire from the galley – which was fitted with a Taylor paraffin stove – to the adjacent 2pdr magazine. Mercifully, there were no serious casualties. *501* had been in company with *MA/SB 36* and *MGB 318*, which picked up her crew before she sank and landed them at Falmouth and Penzance.

Captain Slocum was eventually able to take delivery of MGBs *502* and *503*. These were more heavily armed than *501*, with a 2pdr in a power-mounting forward, twin 0.5in P/O machine guns abreast the bridge/wheelhouse, two twin 0.303s on pedestal mountings alongside the after edge of the bridge, a twin 20mm power mounting amidships, and a 6pdr aft. The displacement went up to 109 tons, and speed on trials was 28kt.

By late summer 1943 *MGB 504* had also been completed, and was lying afloat moored between two buoys; fully armed, she was ready for handing over to the Royal Navy. Ronald Merritt, the then assistant manager at Camper & Nicholsons' Gosport yard, recalls summoning the foremen aboard *504* and telling the assembled company that as a matter of great urgency *504* and four other boats nearing completion had to be torn apart, gutting all the midship and aft accommodation. A deckhouse was to be built aft to make up for the accommodation lost below decks, and the existing bridge had to be re-sited on top of the deckhouse. Any explanation to the foremen for these radical changes would have been a serious breach of security. Plans were drawn up in great secrecy by Merritt, working behind locked doors with the naval architect of the Ellerman Wilson shipping line. The five converted boats would achieve considerable fame as the Kattegat blockade runners.

A serious shortage of ball-bearings had arisen following the heavy bombing of the UK's main supplier, Ransom & Marles. War production, particularly of tanks, would be severely held up unless an alternative supply could be found quickly,

B-Class Fairmiles at Vosper's Wivenhoe yard for refit. Over 650 of these 'maids of all work' were built at home and overseas. *Vosper Thornycroft* and orders were placed with SKF in neutral Sweden. It had been decided that five of the 117ft Camper & Nicholsons boats, with their wooden construction and drawing only 4ft 3in as MGBs, even when fully loaded, would stand the best chance of getting through the German blockade of Swedish waters to collect the order. *504, 505,* and *506* were converted at Gosport, while *507* and *508,* finished at Northam, would be taken by RN crews to Smith's Dock, Hull, where Camper & Nicholsons' shipwrights assisted with their conversion.

The five boats would sail with Ellerman Wilson crews, and their Admiralty numbers were replaced by names. They became *Gay Viking, Gay Corsair, Master Standfast, Hopewell,* and *Nonsuch.* Being now classified as merchant ships, their statutory requirements came under the jurisdiction of the Ministry of War Transport (MOWT). Still working in secrecy and unable to explain their vital role, Ronald Merritt recalls his brush with the local

MOWT surveyor, who was reluctant to accept the height of the coamings around the cargo hatches and the arrangement of the ventilators. Being cargo boats, each had to have an official loadline. In steel ships, this would normally be cut into the hull, but the surveyor reluctantly had to accept an easily removable steel plate, secured to the double diagonal mahogany planking.

The boats were redesigned to provide cargo holds to take 25 tons of ball bearings forward, 15 tons aft, and six tons on the deck. Even when fully loaded at about 150 tons, the ships could still make 20kt. Armed with Oerlikons forward and aft, and with machine guns either side of the bridge, these small ships would make nine trips between Immingham and Lysekil, near Gothenburg. There were casualties – the Germans captured *Master Standfast* when her engines failed just inside

B-Class Fairmile *ML 159* of the 7th Flotilla in the Channel on convoy escort duty.

The view of the armament looking aft on a Fairmile C-Class MGB.

Swedish territorial waters, and *Gay Viking* was in a collision with a coaster, but was successfully repaired by Smith's Dock in Hull.

MGB 509, completed at Gosport, was fitted with Packard 1,250bhp petrol engines. She was later renumbered *2009*, and after the war was used as a floating test-bed for the Metropolitan Vickers 'Gatric' gas turbine, which replaced the central Packard engine. Eight more boats (*511-518*) were completed in 1944-5.

A 6ft wooden model had been built of both the early series and of what would become the new series. These were run together on Haslar Creek from a tow-beam fitted on one of the yard boats. From these tests evolved the shape of the new boats, which would be more heavily armed but with no loss of speed. Similar in profile to the first Camper & Nicholsons, they were 3ft longer on the waterline and had a larger displacement (115 tons); with a greater beam (22ft 2½in) they could carry four 18in torpedo tubes with 6pdrs forward

and aft and Oerlikons either side of the bridge and amidships. They were powered by three Packard W14 1,500bhp engines, achieving a top speed of 31.25kt on trials. With a full fuel-load of 5,000 gallons they had a range of 2,000 miles at 11kt. They had to accommodate a crew of three officers and 27 men.

Because of the additional weight the first class of boats (*502-509*) had to carry, they had settled lower in the water than originally planned, and proved to be uncomfortably wet up front in certain sea conditions. To overcome this, an effective spray strake was added to these earlier boats. The improved hull-form of the second series included a knuckle forward to keep the foredeck clear of water. Fitted out to an exceptionally high standard and bone dry below deck, the Camper & Nicholsons boats were considered the *crème de la*

MGB 664, a D-Class Fairmile. Known as 'Dog-boats', these were operated with great success at home and in the Mediterranean. The hard-chine hull provided an excellent gun platform. *IWM A25317*

crème of Coastal Force craft in terms of construction and accommodation. They were lovingly built by craftsmen who had learned their trade building the many famous pre-war cruising and racing yachts.

As well as the 117ft Camper & Nicholsons boats, the Gosport yard built six Vosper-designed MTBs. Two were ordered by the Admiralty before the war, and were equipped with Isotta-Fraschini engines. Charles Nicholson always insisted that the yard would only build the boats if the order was placed direct with the yard, and there was no suggestion that the firm would be used as a subcontractor to Vosper. The shipyard also turned out many landing craft in both wood and steel, minesweepers, and numerous motor fishing vessels (MFVs). They also built the surfboats carried on deck by the

clandestine 15th MGB Flotilla based on the River Dart (*see Chapter 10*).

Harbour Defence Motor Launches

In addition to firms like Camper & Nicholsons, there were many smaller, traditional boatbuilders making their own contribution to building yet another class of boat for Coastal Forces.

The design of the 72ft harbour defence motor launch (HDML) originated in the Admiralty's Naval Construction Department, which supervised the building at every stage. The first HDML was completed in September 1940, and by the end of the war 293 had been built by 23 firms around the British Isles.

Unlike the Fairmiles, the HDMLs were constructed using basic wooden-boatbuilding

LEFT, RIGHT & BELOW: Different stages in the construction of the prototype D-Class Fairmile (*601*) at Tough Brothers' yard, Teddington. The Fairmile principle of using prefabricated parts is well illustrated here. *Bottom right* shows the completed structure of *601* prior to being 'planked up'. *Fairmile Marine Consultants*

Camper & Nicholsons' MTBs (this is *MTB 2018*, ex-*518*) were considered to be the very finest Coastal Forces craft. *Camper & Nicholsons*

principles. No prefabricated parts were supplied, so all the firms engaged in building HDMLs had to be equipped to construct the entire hull from the keel upwards, and have suitable launching facilities. The round-bilge hull was of double diagonal mahogany or larch planking. With a specified top speed of only 11 or 12kt, there was a choice of suitable British-manufactured engines. These were diesel, generating between 130 and 160bhp. The suppliers were Thornycroft, Gleniffer, and Henty & Gardner.

The HDMLs could carry over 1,500 gallons of fuel, which would give them a range of 2,000 miles at 10kt. When loaded with full fuel tanks and armed (with a 3pdr gun forward, an Oerlikon aft, two twin 0.303in Lewis machine guns, and eight depth-charges) the boats displaced 54 tons. Later boats had in addition an armoured bridge.

These smaller versions of the ML were originally conceived for inshore use, patrolling the entrances and approaches to harbours, where they carried out ASDIC sweeps to detect enemy submarines. They were also of a length that made them suitable for being shipped overseas as deck cargo, although many reached distant operational areas on their own keels. Some even made long passages overseas equipped with a suit of sails, to conserve fuel.

The HDMLs were to play a much more varied role in Coastal Forces. They proved to be excellent seaboats, highly manoeuvrable, with two large rudders, and able to stay out at sea for extended periods. Their diesels were exceptionally reliable, and did not carry the fire risk of their faster sisters, with their high-octane petrol. The crews consisted of two officers, two petty officers and eight ratings. Some of those who commanded the HDMLs were trawler skippers. With their intimate knowledge of coastal waters, the Navy employed them as 'skipper-lieutenants', with no formal training in the disciplines of the Royal Navy.

HDMLs were often stationed in remote parts of the British Isles, where they would be the sole representatives of the Royal Navy, and on hand to carry out at short notice such diverse duties as air/sea rescue, or the investigation of reports of sighted mines. Some of the boats were equipped with minesweeping gear, while later in the war a few were fitted with sophisticated equipment and radar, and used as navigational leaders for assault landings. Even

with their limited armament, some HDMLs scored remarkable successes in an offensive role.

Rescue Motor Launches

Another variation of the ML was the rescue motor launch (RML). Towards the end of the war there were eight RML flotillas in home waters, mostly with eight boats in each flotilla. They were used for air/sea rescue, and operated from bases all around the British Isles. There were also some MA/SBs designated for air/sea rescue.

The popular Fairmile Bs made up most of the boats in RML flotillas. They carried the armament of a B-Class ML except for the depth-charges and the midships Oerlikon, which made deck space for a tiny box-shaped sick-bay. Like the RAF boats which performed similar duties, the decks of early RMLs were painted yellow, to signify their specialist non-combatant role, but after some successful skirmishes with the enemy, both on the water and from above, the RMLs' decks were painted Admiralty grey. Some of them would be called on to

King George VI aboard Rescue Motor Launch (RML) *529* inspects the invasion fleet assembled in the Solent. RMLs were built with a small sickbay abaft the funnel. *IWM A23619*

make up numbers in an ML flotilla going out at night on E-boat patrol. It was not until late summer 1941 that a close working relationship would be formed between the rescue services of the Royal Navy and the RAF. This stemmed from a high-level conference on all aspects of air/sea rescue, chaired

Harbour Defence Motor Launch (HDML) *ML 1031.*
IWM A28339

by the Deputy Chief of Air Staff, with the Royal
Navy's Assistant Chief of Naval Staff also in
attendance. Rear Admiral Power committed 14
MA/SBs to the overall strength of air/sea rescue,
with a promise of 50 converted Fairmile Bs
operational from March 1942.

The RAF air/sea rescue boats were called high-
speed launches (HSLs) or 'crash boats'. They used
the same radio wavelength as the Navy's rescue
service, and between them would patrol areas
beneath the air lanes of bombers and fighters. On
many occasions, when the weather was unsuitable
for the RAF to make a high-speed mercy dash in
their 63ft hard-chine hulls, the RMLs would be
called out instead.

Steam Gunboats

At the other end of the scale of Coastal Force craft
were the 156ft steam gunboats (SGBs). The Naval
Staff in the Admiralty had been looking for a
substantial, fast gunboat that could match the
reliability and comparative safety of the E-boats'

diesel engines. At the outbreak of war Germany was
years ahead in development of the powerful lightweight diesel, thanks to research and development
at the Daimler-Benz works at Stuttgart. Steam
turbines were then considered for Coastal Forces.
They were in service in most of the larger ships in
the Royal Navy, where the weight of the engines
and excessive use of fuel were not so critical.

The skills of the Admiralty and two ship builders
(Yarrow and Denny) were pooled, to try to achieve
a design which could accommodate the weight of
the steam turbines, carry 50 tons of diesel fuel, and
still be able to achieve a speed of over 30kt.
Building began in October 1940, and the first of the
steam gunboats commenced trials in November
1941. A total of nine had been planned, but only
seven would be launched, as two SGBs were never
started because of bomb damage to one of the
shipyards during an air raid. The hulls were round-
bilge and strongly built in steel, so that the vessels
could operate in all weathers. They were initially
armed with a 2pdr power-operated gun forward, a
2pdr hand-operated gun aft, twin 0.5in machine
guns in power-operated turrets either side of the
bridge, and two 21in torpedo tubes. The crew

envisaged for these craft was three officers and 24 ratings. By the end of the war, with their additional equipment and armament, crew strength had risen to over 50, including the officers, eight engineers, and a cook (SGBs were the only craft in Coastal Forces to have this luxury).

Orders for steam gunboats were farmed out to Yarrow, Denny, Hawthorn Leslie, and J.S. White. In the middle of June 1942 the 1st SGB Flotilla was formed at Portsmouth under the command of Lt G. Pennel, RN. Within days, three of the boats, accompanied by a Hunt-Class destroyer, were in their first action in the Baie de la Seine; their targets were two merchant ships and their R-boat escorts. *SGB 7*, under the command of a Free French officer, Lt René Barnet, torpedoed one of the merchant ships, but was herself stopped by an R-boat, with most of the crew being taken prisoner after scuttling their boat. In the debriefing following the action it was established that, after her successful torpedo attack, *SGB 7* did not have the speed to make a rapid withdrawal. It was thought that she might have been stopped by a single shot in the boiler room. In view of this experience, the Admiralty reconsidered both the design of these boats and the future building programme, which was originally planned to total 50.

On the trials of the first steam gunboat, the maximum speed, even with only 30 tons of fuel aboard, was disappointing. Redesigned propellers and a new specification for the boiler increased the top speed by 5kt, to 35kt, with a displacement of 170 tons. With only one boiler, one feed pump, and one extractor pump, it had been graphically demonstrated that the lack of protection around the main steam piping meant that just one shell or machine-gun bullet could put both 8,000bhp steam turbines out of action, often at a time when maximum speed was required, either to disengage or to pursue the enemy. The Admiralty decided that the crews of the SGBs should be highly trained to take in tow any boat in the flotilla stopped by gunfire.

The value of the many towing practices was appreciated in an action off Cherbourg in July 1943. Two SGBs were in collision when taking avoiding action after encountering a group of E- and R-boats and armed trawlers. *SGB 8* was severely damaged and down by the bows. It took less than three minutes for *SGB 3* to pass a tow-line to the stricken vessel and get under way, making about 6 to 8kt. By this time it was nearly dawn, and enemy aircraft were expected. Strong destroyer support was sent out from Portsmouth, but the air attack did not materialise, and the SGBs made it safely back to port.

The last of the 'steamers', as they were called, was *SGB 9*, which was laid down in January 1941 at J.S. White's yard at Cowes, Isle of Wight. She was completed in July 1942 and underwent trials with her newly-appointed commanding officer, Lt Peter Scott, RNVR, the ornithologist and painter. She was worked-up at HMS *Bee*, Weymouth. Scott was appointed Senior Officer of the SGB Flotilla towards the end of 1942 and promoted to the rank of lieutenant-commander. Under his guidance, the SGBs were cleverly camouflaged with a mixture of light blues, whites and greens, which was particularly effective at night.

Another contribution Peter Scott made to the SGBs was to obtain Admiralty authority to give the boats names instead of numbers. He believed this would engender more pride for the boats amongst their crews. After making extensive enquiries he had discovered that any craft under 130ft could only carry numbers. With glee, he pointed out to the secretary of the Ships' Names Committee that his flotilla was made up of 156ft boats. After several weeks, he was advised that the Committee would be pleased to consider his proposals. He wanted a series of six names linked together in some way. Scott liked the idea of 'geese', and wanted to call *SGB 9* 'Grey Goose', which was the name of the first boat he owned – a custom-built duck punt he designed himself. The choice of names was democratically decided, and his other COs did not want a flotilla of 'geese'. They considered ducks, finches, and waders, but none had unanimous support. There were more rejections – butterflies, moths, and goblins. Then came the suggestion that if the SO wanted to call his boat 'Grey Goose', why not link the names with 'grey', with each CO adding a name of his own choice? Eventually the following list was submitted to, and approved by, the Ships' Names Committee: *Grey Seal* (SGB 3), *Grey Fox* (SGB 4), *Grey Owl* (SGB 5), *Grey Shark* (SGB 6), *Grey Wolf* (SGB 8) and *Grey Goose* (SGB 9). It nevertheless remained obligatory to prefix the names with 'SGB'.

Peter Scott's *Grey Goose, SGB 9.*

Lt-Cdr Peter Scott aboard SGB *Grey Goose*.
IWM A15866

In addition to their names, several of the boats could be identified by a signature tune, played loudly over their speakers as they left Newhaven or Dover, and again on their dawn return. Dennis Pratt, who was one of the two radar operators in *SGB 4 Grey Fox*, can still recall the exhilaration experienced when the 'Post Horn Gallop' reached its climax as *Grey Fox* gathered speed on her way out for offensive action.

Scott felt that the element of surprise in Coastal Forces warfare was more important than the ability to approach the enemy and disengage at high speed. Once having engaged the enemy, the SGBs should have sufficient fire-power to make their presence felt. He campaigned successfully for heavier armament. A 3in gun, fitted to *SGB 9* for trial purposes, proved highly effective. By D-Day, the steam gunboats bristled with armament – a 6pdr power-mounted forward, 3in hand-operated

HA/LA gun aft, four sets of 20mm twin Oerlikon hand-operated mountings either side of the bridge and aft, and six sets of twin Vickers 0.303in machine guns (two on the bridge, two below the bridge, and two on the ends of the torpedo tubes). They also carried two 21in torpedo tubes and four depth-charges.

The Admiralty had reluctantly decided that both the boiler-room and the engine room were too vulnerable, and should be protected with ⅝in thick armour plating. The torpedo-men and below bridge Vickers 0.303 gunners would also be better protected. This, together with the additional armament, increased the displacement of the SGBs from 170 tons to 260 tons, reducing top speed to 27kt. One of the firms involved in the major refits required to make these changes was the Southern Railway Marine Department at Southampton. There, the marine superintendent showed great interest in the SGBs, and was particularly concerned about the loss of speed. He was convinced that extending the hulls by six feet would restore the lost speed. He produced plans for this modification to the hull, but the Admiralty naval architects at Bath turned it down.

No more steam gunboats were ordered. This was mainly because construction of a steam gunboat, in terms of man-hours and cost, amounted to much the same as building a destroyer. The original concept of a fast gunboat had not been realised. They were not always able to achieve the same element of surprise as their Coastal Force cousins, as they had a comparatively large silhouette. Their operational use was also limited by their range of only about 400 miles with a full load of fuel. With their considerable fire-power, however, they were treated as a formidable adversary by the German Navy.

Schnellboote and Raumboote

At the outbreak of the Second Word War, the Germans were well ahead in the race to build up the strength of their fleet of light motor torpedo boats, or 'E-boats' as they were to be subsequently known by the Allies ('E-boat' being an abbreviation of 'Enemy War Motor Boat', a term adopted by the Royal Navy during the 1930s to describe the MTBs of hostile powers). They had a head start, having concentrated on building this type of boat between the wars, and on development of the 1,320bhp Mercedes-Benz lightweight diesel required to power it.

After the First World War, the terms of the peace treaty restricted the number of large ships in the German Navy. Germany was quick to spot a loophole in the treaty, however, which made no reference to 'speed-boats'. Unobtrusively, development work was carried out on the design of a high-speed torpedo boat for use in coastal waters. Some restrictions on building German warships were lifted in 1926, by which time the Bremen shipyard of Lurssen Werft had designed several successful racing boats, some features of which would be incorporated in a new generation of motor torpedo boat.

In 1930 Lurssen was developing the first prototype *Schnellboote* (*S1*). Powered by three 950bhp Daimler-Benz 12-cylinder, four-stroke petrol engines, *S1* had a top speed of 35kt. To disguise the project, *S1* was initially referred to as a submarine chaser, and had detachable torpedo tubes to maintain the secrecy of her ultimate use. The 81ft round-bilge hull was based on a privately owned large motor-cruiser. She would be armed with two 530mm (approximately 21in) torpedoes, two reloads, a 20mm AA gun, and a machine gun.

S1 proved to be a good, albeit wet, seaboat, but the German Navy was reluctant to accept the inherent risks of carrying high-octane petrol. It approached two firms – Daimler-Benz and MAN (Maschinenfabrik Augsburg-Nürnberg) – to carry out development work to produce a lightweight marine diesel.

The next four German motor torpedo boats (*S2–S5*) were completed in 1932. They still had the same engines, but performance was increased by supplementing them with compressors. Even at this early stage, the German Navy realised the importance of providing the boats with a means of running without excessive noise and with a

An early German *Schnellboot* or S-boat.
Lürssen Werft Bremen

LÜRSSEN WERFT

BREMEN—VEGESACK

GERMANY

Sole suppliers of M.T.B. to the GERMAN NAVY

MOTOR TORPEDO BOAT

ARMAMENT : 2 Torpedo Tubes as Chosen
1 A.A. Automatic Gun as Chosen
Depth Charges
Smoke Developing Equipment

ABOVE: Lürssen of Bremen developed and built most of the S-series of Second World War E-boats.

minimum of wake, in order to achieve the element of surprise. A 100bhp engine, coupled to the centre shaft, enabled the boats to make headway almost silently at 6kt.

These early boats were constructed with skins of mahogany mounted on metal frames. *S1–S5*, with crews of one officer and thirteen ratings, were formed into the 1st S-boat half-flotilla. *S6–S13* were launched in 1934–5. *S6–S9* were powered with 1,320bhp MAN diesel engines, which were upgraded to 2,000bhp in *S14–17*, but these MAN engines were considered unreliable and too heavy, and all subsequent boats would be powered with Daimler-Benz diesel engines. The hull-form of the 1934–5 production included a knuckle forward, to improve the seaworthiness of the boats by reducing

LEFT: *Räumboote* or R-Boats were small minesweepers designed to operate in shallow waters. Many were fitted with horizontally mounted Voith-Schneider propellers that made the craft very manoeuvrable.
Bundesarchiv MW 1916/25A

Schnellboot S100 showing her low profile. *Lürssen Werft Bremen*

the tendency for the bows to plunge into head seas in foul weather. The first five boats, which had proved invaluable in the ultimate development of Germany's wartime E-boat, were decommissioned in 1936 and taken over by Spain. (The numbers were re-allocated at the beginning of the Second World War to one boat building for Bulgaria, and to four boats originally built for Yugoslavia, taken over by Italy in 1941, and then by Germany in 1943.)

By the outbreak of war, Germany was operating 18 E-boats. More significantly, a high standard of construction, engineering, and armament had been established. The Lurssen Shipyard had developed a composite sheet metal to form the outer hull, which was inner-lined with plywood. By this means the same dimensions could be maintained as in the earlier boats but, with a reduced displacement, the 1939 E-boats were able to achieve speeds in excess of 40kt. The standard engine was now the 2,000bhp

20-cylinder Daimler-Benz diesel. The boats were about 115ft long with a range of about 700 miles at 30kt. Armament comprised two 20mm AA guns and two 21in torpedoes with two reloads. The torpedo tubes were built-in beneath a raised foredeck, while the forward AA gun was positioned in a well between the tubes. This arrangement was adopted for all the wartime production of E-boats, giving them better seagoing qualities, with less wind resistance on the bows, and, with a low bridge, the E-boats had a lower profile compared with the British Coastal Forces craft. Another innovation was in their rudder arrangement, which consisted of a central rudder and two side rudders. By angling the side rudders outwards, the boats could add an additional 2kt to their speed. The additional rudders controlled the trim of the boat's stern, so that the hull remained almost horizontal. This reduced their stern wave which, with their silent-running engine and their grey-white low-profile hull, allowed them to move around at night almost undetected. They had a crew of 23. Over 100 of these boats were

built, some by the Schlichting shipyard at Travemünde, but mostly by Lurssen.

There was a projected figure of around 450 for the second and last series of E-boats. By the end of the war, however, only a hundred had been built, the balance being uncompleted, broken up, or scuttled. The second series had supercharged light-weight Mercedes-Benz diesels rated at 2,500bhp, which enabled them to carry more armament with no loss of speed. There were various permutations of the armament of the later E-boats, although this remained primarily defensive. The spare torpedoes were sometimes removed and replaced with several mines. The aft 20mm AA gun was replaced with a 37mm AA, and an additional twin 20mm AA was mounted midships.

Apart from the E-boat, the Germans did try one or two alternative designs of motor torpedo boat. Some small craft were built to be carried aboard larger ships, but this use was never adopted. Sixteen boats built in 1940–1 were slower and more economical than the E-boat, with a greater range (800 miles at

Besides their main task, R-boats were also used for convoy escorts, search and rescue missions, and escorting U-boats in and out of their bases. *Bundesarchiv MW 1877/1*

30kt), while in 1943 eight 57-ton, 92ft boats were built in the Dutch yard of Werf Gusto, Schiedam.

The other significant class of coastal craft, again built extensively before the Second World War, was the *Raumboot* or R-boat. These were similar in some respects to the Fairmile MLs. Between 85ft and 135ft long, they were used as escorts for coastal convoys, as minelayers and minesweepers, for air/sea rescue, and for general patrol duties. The larger boats had a crew of 38. Diesel-powered, their top speed was about 20kt with a range of 1,000 miles at 15kt. They were typically armed with six 20mm AA guns. Forty R-boats were in service at the outbreak of war. Lurssen built *R1* and *R8*, but the rest of the production was spread amongst three boatbuilders and four shipyards. Of the 368 *Raumboote* ordered by the German Navy, 325 were completed.

Chapter Four

And Train the Crews

A young naval officer serving aboard HMS *Sussex* in the Mediterranean in 1937 witnessed the arrival of the 1st MTB Flotilla; the boats were to take part in Fleet exercises, during which *Sussex* acted as their target. He decided there and then that his future should include service in these fast, small craft. They presented the opportunity of a command at an early age in what he believed would be a powerful and formidable type of warship. The officer was Christopher Dreyer, who would later have a distinguished wartime record in Coastal Forces, and, after the war, maintained his connections with this branch of the Royal Navy, firstly as sales and commercial manager of Vosper, then as a director of Vosper Thornycroft, and, in later years, as president of the Coastal Forces Veterans' Association.

It was while Sub-Lt Dreyer was carrying out his six-months' sea-training for his watch-keeping certificate that he applied to the commanding officers of *Nelson* and of *Revenge* for an appointment to motor torpedo boats. He took every opportunity to persuade his peers, including visiting the captain of HMS *Hornet*, who was operating the handful of MTBs then in commission under the overall control of the torpedo school at HMS *Vernon*.

Along with two RNVR officers, he joined the MTB service at HMS *Vernon* at the beginning of 1940. For the next few weeks they would go out, for the experience, in any boats that happened to be available. In March, at the age of 21, he was appointed commanding officer of the Vosper-built prototype *MTB 102*, which was to be used for

Coastal Forces Wrens became expert in engine maintenance.

training. Christopher Dreyer remembered the joy of driving *MTB 102* in those early months of the war. Being a prototype, she had been lovingly constructed by Vosper, with remarkably spacious accommodation for a boat of her size.

In April, *102* was joined by *MTB 100* which had been originally built by British Power Boat as *MMS 51* – a 60ft high-speed motor minesweeper. After an extensive refit, *MMS 51* was converted to an MTB at HMS *Vernon*. At a time when 'Coastal Forces' had not yet been formally established, MTBs *100* and *102* would provide the basic sea training for RNVR officers appointed to the 'Little Ships'.

Lt Courtney Anderson, CO of *MTB 100*, had been sent over from *Vernon* in late 1939 to the RAF air/sea rescue centre in Haslar Creek, Gosport, to assess its suitability for an MTB base instead of continuing to use the torpedo school across the water in Portsmouth harbour at HMS *Vernon*. Named HMS *Hornet*, this first designated base exclusively for Coastal Forces opened at Gosport in December 1939 (but was not commissioned until April 1940). Coastal Forces' own training centre, HMS *St Christopher* at Fort William, with a large expanse of water nearby on Loch Linnhe, was commissioned in October 1940.

The modest recruitment of personnel for Coastal Forces at the beginning of the war had to increase rapidly to keep up with the boatbuilding programmes. There was, however, an important nucleus of RNVR officers already in existence prior to 1939. Before the war, these volunteers in civilian employment had joined one of the reservist training establishments where they would spend one or two evenings each week on naval training. Each year they would spend two weeks at sea with the Royal Navy gaining practical experience. The London branch of the RNVR in HMS *President*, moored alongside the Thames embankment, would provide training for many of those who, by day, worked in finance in the City. Those who attended their branches regularly would have the opportunity of sitting before a selection board for a commission in the RNVR. This pool of enthusiastic RNVR officers provided the sub-lieutenants drafted by the Admiralty to the 1st MTB Flotilla at Malta in 1939 before the outbreak of war.

Another, less formal, bunch of volunteers had, during their peacetime occupations, gained commissions in the Royal Naval Volunteer (Supplementary) Reserve (RNV(S)R). Four years before the outbreak of the Second World War, the Admiralty had invited experienced yachtsmen and other seamen to enlist in the RNV(S)R, the idea being that the supplementary reservists could, at short notice, transfer from their civilian jobs to the Royal Navy in times of national emergency. This was the origin of what was later referred to as the 'yachtsmen's navy'. Advertising in yachting magazines and trade journals, the Admiralty had underestimated the huge response to its call for volunteers, and almost immediately the maximum age had to be reduced from 39 to 25.

These enthusiastic amateurs received no pay or allowances as members of the RNV(S)R; they organised their own training; if they had contacts with serving seagoing RN officers, the Admiralty had no objections to the volunteers gaining sea experience, providing this was at the invitation of the ship's commanding officer. Such was the enthusiasm of these RNV(S)Rs that they would pay their own fares, organise their own lectures, and enlist for any courses for which the Admiralty had spare places; one of the RNV(S)R divisions actually purchased and ran its own ex-naval steam pinnace. However, not all supplementary reservists were successful in retaining their commissions at the start of the war, many of them being ruled out on medical grounds. Colour blindness, for example, automatically precluded a commissioned supplementary reservist from wartime service as a seaman officer.

On 11 September 1939, eight days after the outbreak of war, Hove Marina was requisitioned by the Admiralty and renamed HMS *King Alfred*. The buildings available at that time might nowadays be

MTBs *100* and *102* photographed before the
outbreak of war. They later formed the 3rd MTB
(Training) Flotilla. *Vosper Thornycroft*

Lancing College, Sussex, where many RNVRs undertook some of their officer training. *Lancing College*

referred to as a part-completed leisure centre. A large bathing pool was under construction, but other facilities, like the smaller pool and indoor bowling greens, had already been completed, together with a large underground car park.

Commissioning Hove Marina as a naval training camp had to be completed in a matter of days. Buildings had to be converted, catering organised, arrangements for local billeting made, and a comprehensive training syllabus and timetable worked out. The first trainees to arrive at *King Alfred*, some with uniforms and some without, were those already holding RNV(S)R commissions. They were a mixed bunch from different backgrounds and occupations, but they had two things in common – their love of the sea, and their enthusiasm to serve in the Royal Navy. Those with seagoing experience could be something of an embarrassment for their RNVR instructors, whose schooling in seamanship was sometimes not as

good as their own. Their length of stay would be no more than ten days.

By the time all the pre-war volunteers had been accepted or rejected, a new system of officer recruitment and training had to be introduced, as a matter of some urgency, to meet the demands of the rapidly expanding Navy. After the supplementary reservists, those next considered for an RNVR commission would have begun their naval service on the 'lower deck'. Bankers, Old Etonians, titled gentlemen, stockbrokers – all would be just part of an ordinary batch of new recruits, reporting to their nearest barracks to be issued with bellbottoms and to learn the disciplines of the parade ground. For those 'hostilities only' enlisted personnel used to a more flamboyant lifestyle, there had to be a rapid adjustment to the basic duties of cleaning, ironing, working in the kitchens, and taking a certain amount of abuse from the divisional petty officer.

After basic training, new recruits would be drafted to a ship. For many, this too came as something of a shock. Now they had to adjust to living in a crowded mess deck, which had to be kept spotlessly clean. Here they would sleep in hammocks, each of which had to be lashed up the 'Navy way', so that it could be neatly stowed along with all the other trussed-up bundles. Some of these new recruits would already be under observation for officer training, and after serving a minimum of three months at sea, and on the recommendation of their CO, those with 'officer-like qualities' (OLQ) would be put forward as CW ('commission and warrant') candidates, to attend an officer selection board.

Officer selection and training, becoming increasingly more sophisticated, took place in various centres around Brighton. The importance of the vital task they performed is reflected in the situation at the end of the war, by when 90 per cent of the Navy's commissioned officers were reservists, and around 22,500 personnel had undertaken their initial officer training at what, throughout the wartime Navy, was called 'KA' (*King Alfred*). All the RNVR officers, who played such an important part in Coastal Forces, had worked their way through *King Alfred* before completing their training at HMS *St Christopher* at Fort William. By the end of the 'KA' course, those who were left had been taught something about gunnery, torpedoes, knots, chartwork, boat drill, general administration, codebooks, and rule of the road. The last two weeks of the course, with everyone now under considerable pressure, would be spent revising for comprehensive examinations and attending interviews with their divisional officer and instructors.

The incentive was not just to pass the examinations and the final selection, but also to achieve really good results. Those who did well stood the best chance of getting a posting of their own choosing. In effect this meant that those with the top marks were generally destined for Coastal Forces, submarines, or destroyers, which were the most sought-after appointments. One successful CW candidate who went on to serve in MLs remembers the pressures of *King Alfred*. Ronald Woods' intake numbered about 40, of whom only about 30 succeeded in passing through the selection board. Throughout his course the numbers dwindled as, in ones and twos, candidates were dropped and returned to their ships.

The staff at *King Alfred* exerted considerable pressure on their pupils. Although the teaching was

of a high standard, and their instructors were pleasant and encouraging, none of the candidates really knew how they were progressing. The pressure was applied from day one, and the opportunities to relax were few and far between. The final hurdle, being confirmed as an officer, was mainly up to the individual's divisional officer.

Ronald Woods felt that the course was excellent, but that 'KA' exhibited a certain heartlessness in the final selection. At the end of four months, the course survivors were lined up on the parade ground. The names of the successful candidates were called out, and they formed themselves into another group. Those that remained had failed the course, and these included Woods, who went through feelings of acute disappointment and despair until they checked the number of the successful candidates and discovered one was missing – they had forgotten to turn over the page. Woods was then called forward, while those less fortunate were doubled off the parade ground to pick up their kit and climb into a waiting lorry; by midday, they would be back in barracks. Tailors around 'KA' who specialised in making uniforms cut these for trainee officers on the understanding that if the candidate failed to obtain a commission, there would be no charge.

The newly appointed acting-temporary midshipmen and sub-lieutenants would collect their uniforms, hand back the rest of their kit, and, after a passing out parade, would be sent away for a few days' leave. Those destined for Coastal Forces would then make their way up to the Scottish Highlands.

Fort William, in the shadow of Ben Nevis and at the head of Loch Linnhe, is a popular holiday resort; it is about 30 miles from Fort William's pier to the sea at Oban. It was to these picturesque surroundings that naval personnel in their thousands came, between October 1940 and December 1944, for training for Coastal Forces. To cope with this influx, four hotels were taken over by the Royal Navy. The administrative base, HMS *St Christopher*, was established in the resort's main hotel, the Highland. Senior naval officers were in the Grand, and the Wrens (members of the Women's Royal Naval Service – WRNS) occupied the Waverley, the Station Hotel, and an annexe to the Palace Hotel. However, many of those who arrived for Coastal Forces training were billeted

with families in the town. There was also the inevitable sprawl of Nissen huts, which provided additional sleeping accommodation and classrooms.

Before the formation of HMS *St Christopher* and the Commando training centres around Lochaber, the local population was by no means unaffected by the war. Like most of those living in towns across Britain, they had formed an ARP section, built shelters, prepared to take evacuees from densely populated areas, observed blackout restrictions and rationing, and would soon be issued with identity cards, which were required to cross from one side of Loch Linnhe to the other, and were used by certain individuals to gain access to normally prohibited military areas.

Light and heavy anti-aircraft batteries were set up to protect possible targets within the vicinity. The British Aluminium plant at Fort William, for instance, was one of the main producers of aluminium for military use, with many employees classified as being in 'reserved occupations'. In September 1940, a solitary Dornier, carrying additional fuel to give it the range, dropped bombs on the factory, but these failed to explode. The local history society has recorded that during this air raid, the CO of the AA battery defending the works was away at lunch in the town and the NCO left in charge had no authority to fire the guns. The other targets in the vicinity were six ammunition ships moored at the head of Loch Eil.

The social life of Fort William was certainly enlivened by the arrival of the Navy and the Army. The Playhouse Cinema reopened. There were frequent dances at the town hall and the Braxy at Inverlochy. The Garrison Theatre, which was a large Nissen hut put up by the Army, was primarily used by both services for concerts and tombola evenings, but they also held occasional dances, to which the young locals would be invited. Inevitably, on Saturday nights there had to be a naval shore patrol and a military police presence to deal with clashes between the Army and the Navy, but there were never any serious disturbances recorded. Various nationalities were trained for Coastal Forces

ABOVE LEFT & LEFT: Coastal Forces Wrens' duties included moving gunboats and MTBs ashore and loading torpedoes.

at Fort William. At one time, there were both Russians and Poles under training, and it was considered prudent to make certain that they were not on leave in the town at the same time.

One estimate puts the number of those passing through HMS *St Christopher* at around 50,000, some of whom would be drafted direct to Coastal Forces bases overseas. There were over 30 full-time officers employed on the naval base, either in an instructional or administrative capacity. Many of these had come out of retirement, including *St Christopher*'s first CO, Cdr A.E.P. Welman, DSO, DSC, who was a First World War CMB veteran. He was destined to be posted to Coastal Forces in the Adriatic, and was replaced by Capt D. Hammersley-Johnson, who employed the Laird of Muck (Lt-Cdr W. McEwen) as his First Lieutenant. Over 100 Wrens were on the accountancy staff, which gives an indication of the size of this shore establishment.

It was about five minutes' walk from the centre of town to the small pier, where those undergoing training would jump into small open launches to be ferried across Loch Linnhe to the boat moorings at Camusnagaul. Those clutching kitbags would be joining boats which would leave the placid waters of the loch for a few days, perhaps making for the Western Isles to give those under training some real sea-going experience.

At one time, there were nineteen MLs, eight MTBs, and nine MGBs at Fort William. All the boats were manned by permanent, albeit scaled-down, crews. PO Hopkins, the coxswain of one of these, *ML 133*, was killed in a tragic accident in 1943 when, on the morning of 11 May, there was an explosion which blew out the side of the boat, wrecking a forward bulkhead, the galley, and the coxswain's cabin, killing Hopkins. The cause of the explosion was thought to be petrol in the bilges, which was ignited when a stoker started up one of the auxiliary Stuart-Turner engines used for charging the batteries. The stoker was blown through the hole in the side of the boat but managed to reach the shore. With the fire gaining, the rest of the crew were unable to reach the coxswain; they escaped by means of the forward hatch.

Archie Maclean, who ran the ferry between Fort William and Trislaig, saw the fire on *ML 133*, and was able to bring his boat close enough to the bows of the burning ML for her crew to scramble on board. There was a second explosion when the flames reached the fuel tanks, ammunition store, and depth-charges. The ML's stern was blown off, and the wrecked hull settled on the bed of the loch where it can still be seen today. The sound of the explosion was heard 30 miles away in Oban. Members of the Coastal Forces Veterans' Association used to visit Fort William every year, and attend the cemetery at Glen Nevis to lay a wreath on the grave of PO Hopkins. On the Sunday afternoon, the CFVA would hire a boat to take them to the spot where *ML 133* sank, where another wreath was thrown onto the water.

The scaled-down crews of these boats were there to oversee those under training. COs had to stand to one side as their boats were brought alongside, sometimes too aggressively, by young sub-lieutenants whose only experience of boat-handling may well have been the few hours spent in the confines of Shoreham Harbour, while undergoing training at *King Alfred*. Motor mechanics would get their first 'hands on' experience, and seamen would take the wheel under the watchful eyes of an experienced coxswain. The silence of the loch would regularly be broken at night by the noise of engines as the boats went out on night exercises, which would often involve realistically staged torpedo attacks.

Most of the acting-temporary midshipmen and sub-lieutenants, wearing their new uniforms and self-consciously acknowledging the salutes of other ranks, came direct from *King Alfred*, or within a few weeks of gaining their commissions. The other ranks, often with no sea training, were drafted to Coastal Forces and arrived at *St Christopher* by a less circuitous route, after a few weeks' basic training. Those with even the remotest connection with a trade would be drafted for initial training to become motor mechanics, stokers, telegraphists, gunners, torpedo-men, writers, or chefs. Those without a trade invariably started as ordinary seamen.

Having left school at 14, Bob Lawrence worked in a garage at Dover. Within two weeks of the outbreak of war, he became chauffeur to Vice-Admiral Ramsay, Flag Officer Dover, who was to take charge of the planning and execution of the evacuation of Dunkirk. Lawrence was in this job for 18 months, in which time he drove many famous naval and military commanders. However, to Lawrence there was a certain glamour attached to the MTBs and MGBs he regularly saw in the harbour. It was not unusual for a message to be flashed on the screen of a cinema, requesting the crew of a certain boat to return to their craft immediately. To those who lived within earshot of the harbour, the roar of engines as darkness fell, as the boats headed through the harbour entrance into the open sea, became a familiar sound. Anyone down at the harbour at first light would invariably see the boats return, berthing alongside to refuel for their next night operation.

The local papers at this time were carrying advertisements for young men with a trade to volunteer for the Navy and join Coastal Forces, and Lawrence enlisted. One of an intake of about 20, he arrived at Chatham Barracks (HMS *Pembroke*) on 31 March 1941. The joining routine, completed during the first day, included visits to the medical officer, dentist, clothing store, victualling store, and gas school (for instruction and provision of a gas mask). One of the first issues was kitbag and hammock; few slept well that first night. With the joining routine completed, the group were marched to a workshop in the Dockyard to undergo individual trade tests. Expecting to be examined on the internal combustion engine and fault-finding, he was asked instead to carry out an endurance test on the use of worn-out files and hacksaw blades.

Having successfully passed the trade test, the new recruits returned to RN Barracks, Chatham, after a few days' leave to await their next posting. This was to the intimidating surroundings of the borstal, or young offenders' establishment, near Rochester. Here the group of trainee motor mechanics learned drill movements, rifle-handling, route-marching, and how to give orders. Proper mechanical training started when Leading Motor Mechanic Lawrence arrived in the Fairmile Marine yard in rural Esher, Surrey, for a course on Hall Scott engines and the general mechanics of the Fairmile B ML. The clue to ownership of the premises was the two Railton cars on display, easily recognised by the dome-shaped chrome rivets which secured the centre hinge of the bonnet.

A hectic four weeks was divided between the classroom and practical mechanics. Bob Lawrence recalls not being over-impressed on his introduction to the Hall Scott V12 engine. Besides the main

MTB 23 test-fires torpedoes in Weymouth Bay.

engines, they familiarised themselves with the 3bhp and 1bhp Stuart Turner auxiliaries. The larger of the two charged the boat's main batteries and pumped out the bilges. The smaller Stuart Turner charged the ASDIC batteries, and another would be installed in later MLs to provide the power for the radar.

The training on the Lockheed hydraulic steering gear failed to prepare the course for the troubles experienced by most of those drafted to B-Class MLs. Bob Lawrence had taken the advice of his father, and strove to become thoroughly familiar with the engine's ignition system and, when he had finished the Fairmile course, he was feeling reasonably confident. His one criticism was that the course did not specifically relate to running engines in heavy weather, when the revs would race up as the boat rolled one way and drop as she started to roll the other way, not to mention the frequent attention needed to revs whenever the props came out of the water.

When he returned once more to RN Barracks, Chatham, it was not long before a party of motor mechanics, stokers, ABs, and telegraphists had been mustered and fully kitted out: their destination – HMS *St Christopher*, Fort William. To Lawrence's dismay, he was put in charge of the draft, and had to contend with the Londoners in his party disappearing for a few hours while those left behind dealt with transferring bags, hammocks and suitcases across London. The same thing happened when they arrived in Edinburgh, but as the train chugged its way through the Highlands a count established that there were no absentees.

Most days, Leading Motor Mechanic Lawrence was out on Loch Linnhe, undergoing rudimentary training aboard one of the *St Christopher* MLs. This amounted to driving the main engines as instructed on the telegraph, which would invariably be worked by some trainee coxswain or newly commissioned sub-lieutenant on the bridge or in the wheelhouse. He also familiarised himself with the auxiliary engines, starting and stopping them, adjusting the charging rate or pumping out the bilges. This was invaluable experience, but Lawrence felt that motoring across the mirror-like surface of Loch Linnhe hardly prepared him for working in the engine room of an ML plunging into a sick-making head sea.

Some, like John Bone, attended HMS *St Christopher* on two separate occasions. Between leaving school and being called up, Bone worked for a merchant bank in the City of London, commuting with some difficulty, because of the Blitz, between Chislehurst and the capital. He joined a machine gun battalion in the Home Guard, and remembers his section's 0.303in Vickers being transported around Kent in a two-wheel trailer behind the major's Riley. Called up on 13 August 1941, he was drafted to HMS *Raleigh*, Plymouth, for his initial training, which lasted about three months. With his Home Guard experience, he volunteered as an AA3 LC (Anti-Aircraft Gunner 3rd Class – Light Coastal Forces) and attended a gunnery course on the 0.5in Vickers and 20mm Oerlikon at Whale Island.

Having completed his course, AA3 LC Bone was sent up to Fort William to complete his training in an ML and an MTB on Loch Linnhe. Gunnery ratings also boarded *St Christopher*'s armed training ship, *Aberdonian*, which was moored alongside the British Aluminium pier. Two or three days a week, a Westland Lysander or Blackburn Skua would fly overhead to provide a gunnery target. At the end of his training, John Bone departed for the Coastal Forces base at HMS *Hornet*, Gosport, to await a drafting to his first boat. Two days before Christmas 1941, he joined HMS *Beehive*, Felixstowe, as spare gunner on *MGB 6*. Early in the New Year, he was appointed to *MGB 60* as the after Oerlikon gunner.

MGB 60 was part of the 6th MGB Flotilla, led by Robert Hichens. Bone spent nine months in the flotilla, and saw some action off the Dutch coast. At the end of nine months, AA3 LC Bone was summoned by his CO and told that he had recommended him for a commission. Having passed his medical, Bone then reported to HMS *King Alfred*, where he passed the selection board to train as an officer. He distinguished himself by passing out of 'KA' with the top marks in Effingham Division, and was able to choose to remain in Coastal Forces, but this time as an officer. Before renewing his acquaintance with HMS *St Christopher*, the newly commissioned Sub-Lt Bone attended more courses. The first of these was known as the 'knife and fork' newly commissioned RNVR officers' course, in the impressive surroundings of the Naval College at Greenwich. In addition to being told which way the port was passed round at formal naval dinners, he was taught about King's Regulations, naval protocol, discipline, and cyphering. He then attended a Coastal Forces gunnery course at Whale Island and a torpedo course at the famous girls' public school at Roedean, on the outskirts of Brighton. Taken over by HMS *Vernon* in May 1941, Roedean seems mostly to be remembered for the printed notice in the showers: 'If you require a mistress in the night, please ring the bell.'

At the end of the officers' course at *St Christopher*, there would be an assessment of each individual's progress and skills, which could influence those responsible for appointments to Coastal Forces. Newly-commissioned officers eagerly awaited the CW list, with their first appointment to Coastal Forces. Sub-Lt Bone's appointees advised him that, because he had previously served at Felixstowe in Coastal Forces as a rating, it was not their policy to appoint such individuals to the same base in an officer capacity. He was, therefore, posted to HMS *Wasp* at Dover, where he served as spare officer on an MA/SB and an MGB before joining the 3rd MGB Flotilla as First Lieutenant on *MGB 42*.

There were two more establishments which played an important part in training many of those who served in Coastal Forces. One was the anti-submarine school commissioned at Ardrishaig in January 1941. Little more than a village before the war, Ardrishaig is on Loch Gilp, an offshoot of the larger Loch Fyne, at the entrance to the Crinan Canal, about 60 miles south of Fort William. At one stage the establishment at Ardrishaig, called HMS *Seahawk*, had an attachment of three MLs, two MA/SBs, and an HDML. These boats would work in Loch Fyne, carrying out sweeps with ASDIC equipment to locate one of two midget submarines allocated to the base for training purposes. Later in the war, HMS *Seahawk* assumed greater importance as a working-up base for HDMLs.

Another training base involved in the development of Coastal Forces was HMS *Bee*. Established firstly at Weymouth in July 1942, HMS *Bee* would put the crews of newly commissioned or re-commissioned boats through their paces. It was established at a time when Coastal Forces' warfare was becoming more sophisticated. Operational tactics developed by the likes of Lt-Cdr Hichens and Lt Dickens had to be passed on to new crews, working a new generation of improved boats. HMS *Bee*'s first CO was Cdr R.F.B. Swinley, RN, and his much-revered organisation was known as 'Swinley's Circus'. The base at Weymouth consisted of an hotel, the Pier Theatre, requisitioned boarding houses, and several workshops. Cdr Swinley's staff was made up of officers and ratings who already had considerable experience in Coastal Forces. He had a training commander and a tactical commander, together with experienced specialists in gunnery, torpedoes, and anti-submarine warfare. Crews spent between four and eight weeks here, being prepared to join an operational flotilla.

The syllabus for new crews was comprehensive and the training intense, with equal emphasis on classroom studies and exercises at sea which closely resembled actual warfare conditions. One of the strengths of the working-up programme at HMS *Bee* was that progress of the crews was continuously under review, so that problems (both human and material) could be put right at an early stage. The working-up base was also able to undertake useful trials of new equipment or tactics. Towards the end of 1943, when South Coast ports were being included in the master-plan for the invasion of France, HMS *Bee* was moved to Holyhead, and stayed there until paid off in July 1945.

When considering the recruitment and training of those who served in Coastal Forces, it is important to establish that, for every operational crew, there was a similar number of shore-based staff. There were the specialists in radar, gunnery, torpedoes, and engineering, each Coastal Forces' base having a senior officer in charge of each specialist branch. Many flotillas had their own radar, torpedo, and gunnery officers who, although shore-based, would sometimes put to sea in one of the boats for the operational experience. The CO of a Coastal Forces base would have his First Lieutenant and also his 'Staff Officer Operations'. The latter would usually be a highly-experienced Coastal Forces officer, whose number of operations as senior officer of one or two flotillas had earned him a period ashore. Whenever the boats were deployed in an offensive or defensive role, it was the SOO who would brief the COs. The SOO would have the latest intelligence reports on the movement of enemy shipping; he would also have been advised whenever possible of the German identification signal operating until midnight and have details of any British shipping within the vicinity, as well as the latest weather report.

In addition to the shore-based officers, there were those who provided the essential back-up services to the boats themselves when they returned to harbour after each operation. They would need refuelling, rearming, and revictualling, as well as routine engine maintenance. If a boat had been in action, the First Lieutenant's defects list might be extensive, and the boat might be urgently required to be fully operational again within a matter of hours. In this capacity the WRNS played a particularly vital role, perhaps more so than in any other branch of the Royal Navy. A team of Wrens would board the boats as they returned to base, to service the armament, engines, radio, and radar, while ashore there would be Wrens in the torpedo and shipwright workshops and operating the tractors which moved the boats in and out of the boat-sheds.

It is perhaps too easy to concentrate on the crews of the MGBs, MTBs, and MLs, identifiable by their white polo neck jerseys and caps worn at a jaunty angle, the RNVR officers making a point of having the top button of their uniform jacket undone (a practice wholly unacceptable on any Royal Navy ship larger than a 'Dog-boat'). They enjoyed a certain glamour not always associated with the crews of bigger vessels. By contrast, there was not much glamour in being a Wren in oil-stained overalls, stripping-down an Oerlikon or loading depth-charges. Nevertheless, no one who served in the 'Little Ships' ever underestimated the vital contribution of the shore-based personnel, who worked so hard to keep their boats operational.

Chapter Five

End of the Phoney War

For those back home in Britain, the first months of 1940 were called the 'Phoney War'. It was a time of uncertainty, while Germany and Britain each waited for the other's next move. The only 'bombing' raids that took place over Germany involved the release of millions of propaganda pamphlets – a vain attempt to persuade the German public to overthrow their wicked military regime. There were those who felt that Britain's declaration of war against Germany should have been more aggressively implemented, and that the failure to help embattled Poland was a disgrace. But, on both sides, the lull provided an opportunity to build up arms and train personnel.

After Chamberlain's declaration of war, the public believed the skies above them would immediately fill with German bombers. The blackout was imposed. Everyone was issued with a gas mask; sandbags appeared around public buildings; shopkeepers boarded up their windows; children were evacuated to the country; the Women's Land Army was formed; and food rationing was introduced. Nevertheless, there seemed still to be hope of a peace settlement, and thoughts of a direct confrontation with Germany began to recede. Churchill called it the 'twilight war'.

It was during this period that the 1st MTB Flotilla arrived back in Britain after its remarkable trip from Malta. For the crews of the MTBs, the next few months would be something of an anti-climax. They rejoined their depot ship *Vulcan* in Portsmouth harbour and the boats were thoroughly surveyed to decide which were in good enough condition to resume their duties as MTBs, operating in the North

Loading a torpedo aboard one of the 1st MTB Flotilla boats at Felixstowe.

Sea. Most of the older boats – MTBs *01, 02, 05* and *19* (the original prototype) were disarmed, to serve as air/sea rescue craft, or relegated to finishing their days being driven at high speed into booms to test the defences of Portsmouth harbour. The serviceable boats went round to Felixstowe in two groups, except for *MTB 14*, which was the last to be repaired.

Delayed from setting off from Portsmouth for several days because of the weather, *14* finally left on 27 January. With a reasonable forecast, the crew had hoped to make Dover on the first day. When they reached the Owers Light Vessel, off Selsey Bill, the weather had already started to deteriorate, and by the time they were off Brighton their CO, Lt Mason, was becoming concerned that they would damage the boat in the mounting seas. Cold, wet, and miserable, they put into Newhaven. No one really wanted to know them here, and the duty officer found it difficult to believe that any ship in the Royal Navy could not stay at sea in any weather. They were stuck in Newhaven for three days, until the weather improved enough to make Dover. They reached Felixstowe the following day, joining MTBs *03, 04, 15, 16, 17,* and *18* berthed in the southern half of the dock. On the way *MTB 14* had passed through the sea area called the Downs, off Ramsgate. There were many ships about and a number of wrecks, serving as a stark reminder of the effectiveness of Germany's magnetic mine. The crew of *14* spotted a couple of floating mines, and expended a great number of rounds sinking them with their machine guns.

Felixstowe was destined to become HMS *Beehive*, one of three main bases for Coastal Forces on the East Coast. Over a thousand naval personnel would eventually be based there. In peacetime the main users of the port of Felixstowe were barges supplying a large flour mill. There had also been an RAF flying boat station here, which was used at the beginning of the war to train RAF personnel and accommodate those responsible for the barrage-balloon defences. The crews of the 1st MTB Flotilla were housed in the RAF base, where the officers used the somewhat cosmopolitan RAF mess.

The first four months of 1940 were a frustrating period of inactivity for the 1st MTB Flotilla. Before the fall of France, the German Navy was usually well out of the range of the MTBs. Much time was spent on navigation exercises or going out to investigate reported sightings of periscopes which were never to be found by the time the MTBs arrived on the scene. In one respect, however, the war off the East Coast and in the Channel was already deadly serious. There was nothing phoney about the casualties caused by German magnetic mines. These losses were not widely reported to the public. It took some time before the extent of German infiltration of convoy routes off the East Coast and Thames estuary was realised, enabling such raiders, undetected, to drop sizeable quantities of deadly explosives on the seabed or to leave them floating on the surface. The Germans used light cruisers, destroyers, submarines, and E-boats in these operations, all of which were able to slip in and out of the East Coast convoy routes without detection. They even employed low-flying seaplanes. By contrast, at this stage no Royal Navy vessels were available for general patrolling offshore, and there was no effective radar cover. Consequently, in the first weeks of the war, there were many unexplained sinkings. Particularly hazardous were the waters north of Margate, around the Tongue Light Vessel, which was a crossroads where shipping coming out of the Thames estuary met up with the East Coast convoys. The month before the 1st MTB Flotilla had come round to the East Coast, enemy mines around the Tongue Light Vessel had sunk 14 ships, including two warships.

The only way to devise an effective means of sweeping for magnetic mines involved first getting hold of and dismantling one. In November, a mine dropping by parachute was spotted coming down over the mudflats at Shoeburyness. Later that night Lt-Cdr J. Ouvry, from the Naval Torpedoes and Mines Branch at HMS *Vernon*, crossed the mud with a party of volunteers to inspect the mine. They had been patiently waiting in London to get their hands on one, and within the next few hours they would learn everything they needed to know about such devices.

One of the jobs of the Felixstowe MTBs was to take off at high speed in response to the sighting of a mine by one of the many local lightships. With no means of manoeuvring, the crews of the lightships sometimes had no alternative but to push mines clear with a boat hook. In the early part of the war, the lightships were also subjected to German air attacks, which the British government angrily claimed was a flagrant disregard of international law, as they were positioned purely for the safety of shipping from all nations. The lightship crews must have felt very isolated and always welcomed the visit of an MTB crew, who might bring newspapers and reports of what was happening on the mainland. Because they continued to be targets for air attacks, however, the lightships were gradually replaced by unmanned light floats, or removed altogether. The Oaze lightship was sunk with no survivors, and two more were so badly damaged they had to be abandoned.

The MTBs were routinely employed on DWI (directional wireless installation). For these light, fast craft, DWI duties must have seemed particularly tedious. The boats were employed as markers while an RAF Wellington aircraft, with a 51ft diameter magnetic coil fitted beneath the fuselage, flew low over the sea to try to activate magnetic mines. The only excitement was when a Wellington crew forgot to switch off the magnet as they were supposed to do when approaching the marker boats – one mine was touched off within a hundred yards of *MTB 03*.

Another job dreamt up for the MTBs was to deploy them astern of ships with equipment specially designed to detect E-boats. It was an ingenious plan, which required much more than the standard ASDIC equipment being developed for the Royal Navy. Before the war, there had been two telegraph cables laid on the seabed to connect the UK with Germany. At some stage during the early part of the war, the Germans had cut the cables near the East Coast, but were able to re-energise them; with listening-in gear, the German E-Boats could use the cables to identify passing convoys

and, with an accurate fix along the cables, make their attack.

If the Germans could do it, there seemed no reason why British craft could not position themselves at the end of the telegraph cables, pick up the HE (hydrophone effect) noise of an approaching E-boat and despatch a waiting MTB. After four nights at sea without any contacts, *MTB 14* resumed other duties. On two occasions, their escort failed to turn up because of fog. Another experiment tried in the 1st Flotilla during this period was for the duty crew to man whatever boat was nominated, depending on availability. The reason for this was that at any time there would invariably be one or two boats out of commission, usually requiring urgent maintenance. The arrangement of putting to sea in someone else's boat was not popular, and was dropped after a few weeks.

Gradually, new MTBs were being handed over to the Royal Navy. In January, the first three newly-commissioned boats, forming the 4th MTB Flotilla,

Craft of the 1st MTB Flotilla at Felixstowe in February 1940. Note the outriggers, raised in the photograph but normally stowed inboard. They were hinged to the transom and lowered astern when firing a torpedo.

were sent up to Blyth, Northumberland, where they were fitted with deck fuel-tanks to give them a greater range. Intelligence reports and aerial photographs had indicated that major German warships were lying off Wilhelmshaven, without the protection of booms. The MTBs were on stand-by to launch an attack, but early 1940 was exceptionally cold and the entrances to all the German rivers became iced up. By the time the ice had cleared, protective booms had been positioned. The 4th MTB Flotilla moved round to Felixstowe.

By May, the 'Phoney War' was over. Norway had fallen to the Germans, to be followed on 10 May by the invasion of France, Holland and Belgium. Four boats from the 1st MTB Flotilla were then despatched to Sheerness for a secret mission. After

MTB 18's quadruple 0.303in Lewis guns in a practice shoot off Felixstowe in February 1940.

the COs studied charts of the Dutch coast, the boats returned to Felixstowe to load up all the armour-piercing ammunition they could carry. Later, they learned that their objective was the Netherlands Zuyder Zee (now called the Ijsselmeer), where they were to prevent German troops from crossing the water from east to west in barges. Next day, the operation was called off; later three boats of the 4th Flotilla (MTBs *22*, *24*, and *25)* did cross to Holland, and for a few days worked out of Ijmuiden. Their brief was to act as reconnaissance for the destroyers deployed to evacuate both Army and civilian personnel. When the flotilla was leaving on 14 May, they were strafed by two German seaplanes, one of which – a Heinkel He 115 – was shot down by the gunner on *MTB 24*, the first reported success against enemy aircraft by Coastal Forces.

On the same day, MTBs *15* and *16* set out from Felixstowe for Holland. *MTB 15* had engine problems and had to return to base. Lt P.F.S. Gould's boat, *MTB 16*, would be the last of the Royal Navy to leave Holland. She entered at the Hook to take off British nationals. Lt Gould waited for two hours with no signs of the evacuees. The German front was within a few miles. Nearby Rotterdam, which had been subjected to continuous bombardment, was on fire. The Dutch soldiers in the vicinity of *16*, resigned to defeat, had no wish to leave. *MTB 16* finally departed in the evening with a Dutch naval officer, five British soldiers, and three Dutch civilians. A few hours later, Holland formally surrendered to Germany. Lt Gould was one of the first officers in Coastal Forces to be mentioned in despatches, for this final trip to Holland.

Towards the end of May, MTBs *15* and *16* were sent down from Felixstowe to Sheerness to prepare for a top-secret mission with the destroyer HMS

Vega. Boulogne and Calais had fallen to the rapidly advancing German Army, and the Allied army had been cut off, with only Dunkirk and the Belgian ports remaining open. A plan had been evolved to block Ostend and Zeebrugge by sinking cement-filled blockships in their entrances. This had been devised several months earlier, and was to have been organised by the French; with the advancing German Army now within 12 miles of Zeebrugge, the next two or three days would be the last opportunity to carry out the operation. Unfortunately, the Belgians were unwilling to co-operate with the French. The responsibility for the entire operation was then handed over to the British.

Similar raids had taken place on these two ports in the First World War. The St George's Day raid of 1918, however, was on a totally different scale. To block German-occupied Zeebrugge and Ostend, a fleet of 166 ships had participated, including dozens of MLs and CMBs, all under the command of Vice-Admiral Sir Roger Keyes. MLs were provided to rescue the crews of the blockships and any other ships in trouble, and also to provide smoke-screens; the CMBs were towed across the North Sea and used for launching torpedoes to sink shipping in the harbours and to destroy the lock gates and basins. The CMBs also laid the inshore smoke-screens. At Zeebrugge, the offensive had also involved landing raiding parties on the giant mole. Zeebrugge had been heavily defended by the enemy, who illuminated the battleground with searchlights and star shells. There were many casualties and a considerable loss of ships, but the operation was considered a great success and a much-needed boost to morale. At Ostend, however, the blocking did not go according to plan. The Royal Navy bombardment started around midnight, followed by the arrival of the two blockships. Then the wind had changed, blowing a laid-down smoke-screen back out to sea and making the precise positioning of the blockships, already under heavy fire, extremely difficult. Both blockships were driven aground too far off position to make an effective barrier. A second attempt was made two weeks later, but again the elements and the strength of the German defences had proved too much.

Twenty-two years later, on the afternoon of 24 May 1940, the destroyer *Vega* sailed from Sheerness with two blockships, surrounded by fleet minesweepers, anti-submarine vessels, and two minesweeping trawlers to be used for clearing and marking the channel into Zeebrugge. The blockships had their holds filled with cement, and demolition charges had been placed around the hulls. Small concrete shelters were constructed on the blockship bridges where the captain would be housed, just before activating the time-delay fuses and abandoning ship.

The blockships had been moored-up in the River Medway for several months, and a first attempt to put them to use had been made a week earlier, when the plan had been to tow them across to Zeebrugge and Ostend, where they would be anchored ready for later deployment, thereby keeping the ports open so that evacuation of personnel and equipment could continue until the last possible moment. However, after a night out in the North Sea, the whole convoy had been recalled to Sheerness. In a rapidly changing military situation, four more such postponements occurred. When the convoy finally set out on 24 May, the objective was to concentrate on Zeebrugge; it had been decided that Ostend should remain open for a little longer.

Charles Coles was aboard *MTB 16* as the spare officer. He remembers leaving Sheerness in warm, sunny weather. In company with *MTB 15*, they joined up with the convoy off the North Goodwin Light Vessel. Some of the convoy escorts were busily engaged carrying out anti-submarine patrols while the minesweepers were clearing a channel for the destroyer and the blockships *Florentino* and *Transeas*. Overhead, three Wellington bombers were circling round and round, providing air cover in the broad daylight.

MTBs *15* and *16* patrolled some distance off the convoy and encountered two more boats from their flotilla, MTBs *14* and *18*, sent down from Felixstowe to Sheerness to take the Vice-Chief of the General Staff, General Sir John Dill, and his party to Ostend for an on-the-spot assessment of the desperate situation of the British Expeditionary Force. A distraction on board *MTB 16* was the discovery of a carpet of floating watertight boxes, some of which were gleefully seized and opened, to reveal highly superior ships' biscuits in some and dry boxes of matches in others.

Progress was frustratingly slow, with the convoy only able to make 6½kt. Navigation at this speed was difficult because of a 3kt tide on the beam, which meant a huge variation in the course steered to achieve the desired course-made-good. By now there was full moon lighting up the calm sea. In the distance they could hear the rumble of guns and bombs as the enemy advanced through Flanders. There was no mistaking Ostend in the distance, alight with fires.

One of the leading boats reported sighting two torpedoes tracking through the water close by; the escorts immediately carried out a submarine search and one of them dropped depth-charges. Around midnight, the convoy was spotted by enemy aircraft. One approached with the moon behind and dropped a bomb about 50yd from *Transeas*, the leading blockship. The plane, thought to be a Junkers, then turned to make a second run, again approaching from the direction of the moon. This time the gun crews on the destroyer opened fire, but, looking directly into the full moon, were unable to line up on the target with any accuracy. The senior officer on *Vega* considered trying to take evasive action, but his priority had to be to maintain speed and course so that the blockships arrived as planned. *Vega* endured four more attacks, and then the aircraft disappeared into the night.

Aboard *MTB 16*, they had donned tin hats, kicked off seaboots, and inflated lifebelts. As she approached Zeebrugge, the crew made ready for battle. The confidential books were placed in a weighted bag ready to be thrown overboard at a moment's notice, a rifle and ammunition were placed in every hatch, blankets were spread out below decks for any wounded, and the medical chest was opened. Mills bombs were handed out. It was then about two o'clock in the morning.

A naval trawler was the first into the harbour, laying dan buoys and sweeping for mines. Then came *MTB 15* with the demolition officer aboard. *Vega* dropped a dan buoy to provide an outer mark for the blockships, and then told them to proceed into harbour and wished them luck by megaphone. The destroyer and other escorts then lay off the seaward side of the mole to provide anti-aircraft cover.

The blockships had to proceed with great caution, closing the shore under their own power at a speed so slow that they only just had steerage way. They had hoped that there would be lit buoys and shore lights to assist them in their approach. There were none, and to make navigation that much more difficult, they had to allow for a strong cross-current and evade extensive shoals off the entrance. *Florentino* was the first to attempt the difficult entry. Aboard *MTB 15*, the crew realised she was being swept off course. They overtook the blockship, secured temporarily to the inner breakwater with a grappling hook, and attempted to provide a guide by using a torch. It was to no avail, for *Florentino* was already on the mud with no prospect of being refloated. Her CO decided he had no option but to scuttle her where she was, some way off the planned position.

As *Florentino* settled in the mud, a flare illuminated two paratroopers descending from the skies. Tracer bullets were flying everywhere. A paratrooper appeared from behind a shed on the mole and started blazing away at *MTB 16*, which had been lying low on the sea side of the mole. The port gunner, a leading torpedoman, requested permission to return the fire. 'Let the buggers have it,' was the immediate reply from the CO. There was gunfire from almost every direction. At first it was thought that Zeebrugge had already fallen to the enemy. The probable explanation was that the convoy had arrived at the same time as the first drop of German airborne troops. The gunfire was a mix of German and Royal Navy, along with that of Belgian troops uncertain who the enemy was. *Florentino*'s crew leaped into boats and rapidly withdrew under oar, and there was a terrific explosion as the captain and coxswain detonated the charges. *Florentino* settled firmly on the bottom.

Aboard *MTB 16*, the Lewis machine guns were blazing away in all directions. Those who were not on the machine guns were using rifles. Her charge, the blockship *Transeas*, was manoeuvring with difficulty and, like *Florentino*, finished up on the mud. Her crew scrambled into their boat, which was then towed beyond the mole by *MTB 16*, where they transferred to *Vega*. During this operation, those aboard *MTB 16* could clearly see the mud-banks either side of the channel and too close for comfort; they knew if they grounded, there would be no escape.

It was already light as *MTB 16* joined up with *15*. Although their crews had carried out their duties faultlessly and courageously, it was doubtful that the raid on Zeebrugge had achieved its objectives. There was a feeling that the port and entrance to the Bruges–Zeebrugge canal still remained open. (An aerial photograph soon confirmed that the two blockships had been scuttled well outside the fairway, providing no obstruction to shipping using the harbour and the Bruges canal.) Miraculously there had been no casualties.

Meanwhile, 13 miles to the south-west, MTBs *14* and *18* had endured a miserable night off Ostend, which was suffering appalling damage from German air raids. General Dill and his party had been safely landed, saying that they hoped to be back some time the following day. Lt Mason, *14*'s CO, was told that if the German tanks expected from the west should reach the outskirts of the town, he was to leave Ostend and rendezvous with Dill's party at Zeebrugge. *MTB 14* spent the night directly beneath the path of enemy bombers. In the morning they moved out to the seaward end of the harbour breakwater so that they could make a rapid departure. After what seemed like an interminable wait, Dill arrived in the afternoon, and *MTB 14* then made her way back to Sheerness. In the evening, *14* and *18* returned to Felixstowe as did *15* and *16* after their unsuccessful attempt to block Zeebrugge.

It was decided to have another shot at blocking Zeebrugge 36 hours later. This time MTBs *14* and *15* were selected to accompany *Borodino* and *Atlantic Guide*, two of the blockships originally planned for sinking in Ostend. The same destroyer would take part, along with the anti-submarine vessels, but the minesweepers were not involved. Lt Gamble in *MTB 15* was briefed to enter Zeebrugge at dawn with a prominent display of her White Ensign to clarify her identity to the Belgian troops. *15* would then act as a guide for both blockships, to help them reach the entrance to the lock gates. If *15* was shot up from the shore, then Lt Mason in *MTB 14* would take her place.

The North Sea was again calm, with the slow-moving convoy clearly visible in the moonlight. Torpedo tracks were seen from *Atlantic Guide*, which had fallen behind the convoy. Her escort immediately encircled the blockship with a smoke-screen. Half an hour later came the ominous sound of German aircraft. MTBs *14* and *15* had been sent on ahead, and were closing the shore at speed to establish that all was clear for the convoy to maintain its course and speed towards Zeebrugge. One of the approaching Heinkels, spotting the wakes of the MTBs, swept down on them, flying low over the water and releasing its bombs close enough to shake up their hulls. It then disappeared.

At dawn off Zeebrugge, all seemed quiet and going according to plan. Once again *Vega* dropped a dan buoy to show the blockships the start of the approach channel. When *Borodino* reached the dan buoy she stopped, took the way off with her engines and then let go her anchor. The rest of the convoy stared across the water in disbelief. A message was relayed to the senior officer aboard *Vega* that her steering gear had broken down.

It was now broad daylight, and *Borodino* had to be positioned and sunk without delay. One of the escorts secured alongside her and together they made painfully slow progress towards the harbour entrance. When they had reached the end of the mole, *Borodino*'s CO signalled that his engine room staff had managed to repair the steering gear. The lines of the escort were slipped, and *Borodino* proceeded towards the inner harbour under her own steam. By this time *Atlantic Guide* was in position and ready to follow *Borodino* up the harbour. *MTB 15* took up position to guide *Borodino* to the exact spot, close to the lock gates, where she was to be sunk to provide the best possible blockage. There was no sign of anyone, friend or foe, ashore.

The senior officer in *Vega* was so confident that he waved to *MTB 14* to come alongside to take him up into the harbour and possibly land for a grandstand view of the proceedings. This was not to be. Suddenly a dozen Heinkels swooped down on the convoy, singling out the two blockships and *MTB 14* as their main targets. The tide had set *Borodino* onto a shoal so the Heinkels had a stationary target, and it was amazing that she was not hit. She managed to struggle free from the shoal and manoeuvre towards the lock gates only to find that her passage was blocked by a sunken dredger. The CO still managed to slew his craft half across the lock entrance, and the crew then hurried into the ship's lifeboat. The first attempt to detonate *Borodino* failed. There was an anxious delay, with eyes looking upwards, waiting for the German aircraft to return and resume their attack. The captain and a torpedoman scrambled back aboard *Borodino* and disappeared below to check the wiring. They found the propeller shaft had fouled a lead, which had become disconnected. This was quickly put right and they jumped back into the boat. Once at a safe distance they had the satisfaction of witnessing the explosion and seeing *Borodino*, with her hold full of cement, settling on the bottom.

Atlantic Guide was enthusiastically waved on to close up alongside *Borodino* to make the blockage doubly effective. This she did with great skill, and her crew jumped into their boat. The elated crews of the blockships, some of whom had already celebrated their success with several days' rum ration, had a light-hearted rowing race to reach the waiting MTBs. At 0715hrs, flushed with success, the convoy set off at high speed for the return passage. Above them came the sound of aircraft, which this time turned out to be friendly Spitfires providing air cover, albeit 45 minutes late. They disappeared once they saw the convoy was heading for home. (A plan to sink blockships in Ostend about three weeks later was abandoned by the Admiralty when the RAF said it was unable to provide appropriate air cover.)

The larger ships, and particularly the destroyer, were attacked four times by bombers on the way back, but there was no damage and no casualties, as, unhampered by the blockships, they could now manoeuvre at speed to keep out of trouble. Once the convoy arrived safely off the North Goodwin Light Vessel, the MTBs were released to return to Felixstowe.

Just 20 miles down the coast from Zeebrugge another MTB was involved in locating Nieuport and motoring up the canal. The previous day, the 10th MTB Flotilla had put into Dover en route between Portsmouth and Felixstowe. The SO, Lt Courtney Anderson, was ordered to leave Dover in *MTB 67* with three Belgian cabinet ministers to return them to their homeland and bring back to England their sovereign King Leopold. Anderson recalls a dreadful passage, all being soaked to the skin in the little open cockpit of his 55ft Thornycroft MTB. The ministers had complete faith in their mode of transport, believing that, just like on a train or a ferry, they would be delivered safely to their

destination. They did not know the peculiarities of *MTB 67*. She had no navigational aids apart from an unswung compass veering 20 degrees either side, and they arrived off Belgium to find only a dark, low, unlit coast. Lt Anderson had no idea where they were so he nudged the boat into the shallows and asked the ministers if they would paddle ashore, find out where they were and come back and tell him so that they could locate the entrance to the canal at Nieuport. His passengers were wonderfully co-operative, disappearing into the night and, after a long anxious wait, returning with the Belgian equivalent of 'It's that way!' Anderson

then found the canal and identified the boat to a voice challenging them at the entrance. Back came an urgent response 'Allez, allez! Boches ici. Boches partout!' ('Hurry, hurry! Germans here. Germans everywhere!') They crept up the canal feeling rather like rats entering a trap. Then, suddenly, they saw lights ahead and a huge car (probably belonging to the British Embassy) being tipped unceremoniously over the side into the canal. There was no sign of the King, but they were able to embark Admiral Keyes who was Churchill's special envoy to King Leopold and the same Admiral Keyes who had led the 1918 raid on Zeebrugge. To their

Boats of the 1st MTB Flotilla operating off Felixstowe.

surprise, at the entrance to the canal, they met up with an MA/SB sent by someone on the same mission. The admiral was transferred to the MA/SB to give him a slightly more comfortable run home. Both boats then returned to Felixstowe.

Soon, all the boats based at Felixstowe would be back at sea, off the French coast. The fortunes of the war had reached their lowest point: 29 May was the start of the evacuation of the British Expeditionary Force from Dunkirk.

Chapter Six

Dunkirk and the Navy's 'Little Ships'

Winston Churchill called it 'a miracle of deliverance'. On 24 May 1940, 400,000 British and French troops were trapped along a short stretch of flat, featureless coastline on the Franco-Belgian border, between Dunkirk and Nieuport. On the other side of the water, from his HQ in Dover Castle, Flag Officer Dover, Vice-Admiral Bertram H. Ramsay, was directing Operation *Dynamo*. By 4 June, the operation was over. In twelve days, 338,000 men had been evacuated. Over 800 ships of all shapes and sizes had taken part in one of the greatest rescues of all time.

There were only about a dozen craft of the type soon to have the collective title of 'Light Coastal Forces' available at that time to take part in Operation *Dynamo*. They were a mixed bunch of MTBs, CMBs, MA/SBs, the first ML to be launched (*ML 100*), and an experimental DCMB (Direction Control Motor Boat). During this period they would work out of Dover, Harwich and Felixstowe.

MTBs *14*, *15*, *16*, *17*, and *18* were sent out nightly from Felixstowe, to form a protective screen on the northern flank of Dunkirk during the hours of darkness. Their brief was to lie stopped between two and five miles offshore, and intercept any E-boats coming down from the north. The crews of these boats from the 1st MTB Flotilla slipped into a punishing routine, finishing up with an average of two hours' sleep a day for six successive days. The boats would leave at 1800hrs, be in position to the north of Dunkirk by dusk, and patrol the area for six hours until first light. They were back in port for refuelling at around 0630hrs. After a bath and breakfast, the COs would attend a briefing for their next patrol. Then a couple of hours' sleep was grabbed in the afternoon, before putting out to sea again the next night.

Sub-Lt Peter Williams was sent to pick up the almost completed *MA/SB 10* from British Power Boat at Hythe, Southampton Water. She was in the water, but much of her painting had to be abandoned unfinished. He was joined by an inexperienced crew and Lt Richard Eyre, who admitted he knew nothing about navigation. *MA/SB 10*'s trials consisted of a short run up Southampton Water and back, which was insufficient for those in the engine room to master how to put the engines into astern mode. In her brief life, *MA/SB 10* was always manoeuvred with the knowledge that her way could not be stopped with the engines. Thus ill-prepared, she sailed for Dover to take part in Operation *Dynamo*.

On the afternoon of 26 May, Lt Dreyer in *MTB 102* was summoned urgently by the captain of *Hornet*. He was told to prepare his boat for a passage round to Dover, where the Flag Officer would have further orders. Leaving his First Lieutenant, John Wilford, to top up the fuel tanks and take on stores, Dreyer then sought out the Staff Officer Operations in the C-in-C Portsmouth's office for his formal sailing orders. *MTB 102*, in her training capacity, had been unarmed, but Lt Dreyer returned to his boat to discover that his First Lieutenant had miraculously acquired a four-barrelled Vickers 'K' 0.303in machine gun from HMS *Vernon*. This was being mounted on the deck by *Hornet* base staff as securely as time permitted, positioned aft of the bridge between the torpedo tubes.

Having sailed through the night, *MTB 102* entered Dover harbour at about seven in the morning, berthing in the old submarine basin with several other MTBs and MA/SBs assembled to take part in Operation *Dynamo*. Lt Dreyer made his way up to Dover Castle, perched high up on the cliffs. The Staff Officer Operations outlined briefly the grim situation of the British Expeditionary Force, and then introduced Dreyer to Vice-Admiral Ramsay. *102*'s orders were to leave immediately for Dunkirk and once there report to the Naval Officer in Charge, Capt William Tennant.

Just along the coast, Ramsgate was already filling up with the yachts, motor boats, sailing barges, fishing boats, paddle-steamers, and ferries that would form the famous 'Small Ships' armada, crucial to the success of the evacuation. Among them was a 35ft motor yacht, which had been commandeered by the RAF as an air/sea rescue boat. She had an all-civilian crew, and was skippered by R.C.M.V. Wynn. He was to become an RNVR officer in Coastal Forces, gaining his commission in unusual circumstances.

Encouraged by his father, the late Lord Newborough, Wynn had joined the regular army in 1938. Invalided out just before Dunkirk, he went to Southampton, as a civilian, to take over the RAF motor yacht. They sailed firstly to HMS *Hornet*, and then on to Ramsgate. The boat made five trips to and from Dunkirk, taking 50 soldiers off the beach on each occasion. On the last crossing, returning to Ramsgate, a shell just above the waterline put paid to any more trips in this boat.

Some of the first wave of the armada from Ramsgate was already under way, these being quickly overtaken by *MTB 102* as she made the first of several trips across the Channel. Even with the most basic navigation aids (including a compass with unknown deviation), there was no difficulty in finding Dunkirk, which was identifieded by flames and dense black smoke above the bombed oil-storage terminal to the west of the port. *MTB 102* arrived around noon, and was soon berthed alongside. Christopher Dreyer vividly remembers the tragic surroundings. The locals were awaiting the inevitable occupation by the German Army, which was by then only 10 miles from the town. There were fires everywhere, and crowds of bemused troops, drained of all energy, some literally on their knees, others wandering about appearing to be totally lost. Tennant told Dreyer to take his boat along the coast as far as La Panne, which is seven miles north-east of Dunkirk and just inside Belgium. There were many destroyers lying

offshore, and he should offer the services of *MTB 102*, and then report back for further orders.

As they motored eastwards, *102*'s crew gazed at the grim scene. The sand dunes, a popular holiday attraction in peacetime, were black with men joining the long, straggling, vulnerable queues, four or five deep. Some waited instructions to board the small boats that would ferry them out to the larger ships. The magnitude of the evacuation was harrowing in the extreme – Christopher Dreyer likened it to attempting to empty a swimming pool with a fountain pen.

He had been warned not to go beyond La Panne, where the enemy were well established, and even as they approached the eastern end of the beaches he and his crew had their first taste of enemy fire. On their way back from La Panne, they were able to close the beach, using the echo-sounder to get as near inshore as possible, to take in tow boats packed with soldiers, and deliver them to the destroyers and other ships lying offshore. It was depressingly slow work, but by the end of the day *MTB 102* had managed to transfer several hundred soldiers from the beach.

Returning to the jetty at Dunkirk, Dreyer found Capt Tennant, who produced a hand-written note to be delivered to Admiral Ramsay. *102* then left for Dover, taking about 30 soldiers from the end of the jetty. Lt-Cdr Stratford Dennis, CO of the new MTB base at Dover, was waiting for *102*, and offered to take the communication up to the Castle. *102* was then refuelled, and her crew were turned in by midnight.

Vice Admiral Ramsay had decided that his Naval Officer in Charge at Dunkirk needed more help; on 29 May, Rear Admiral William Wake-Walker, with two commanders, embarked from Dover in the destroyer *Esk*. He would take over responsibility for everything afloat off Dunkirk. His flag was destined to fly from six different ships as he moved amongst his fleet and patrolled the shoreline. One of his flagships was *MTB 102*, and over the next few days the Admiral would become a familiar figure on her bridge.

Having first established himself aboard the destroyer HMS *Keith*, one of Rear Admiral Wake-Walker's initial meetings the next day, 30 May, was with Lord Gort, the Commander-in-Chief of the British Expeditionary Force. The Admiral and the

Under the command of Lt Christopher Dreyer
MTB 102 made several passages between Dover
and Dunkirk in May/June 1940.

Lt C.A. James and his First Lieutenant, Midshipman John Wilford, with the crew of *MTB 102*.

General dined together at La Panne, in the seaside villa which served as the temporary headquarters of the BEF. It must have been an extraordinary occasion, with Lord Gort coming to terms with what some have described as the greatest disaster in British military history. The following day Churchill ordered Gort to nominate another commander to take over the remnants of the BEF. The General let it be known that he wished to remain until the end of the evacuation, but Churchill was adamant; he wanted Lord Gort home immediately, anxious not to risk such a senior officer being taken prisoner by the enemy. General Alexander was then nominated to assume command.

Wake-Walker formed a plan whereby Lord Gort and his staff would be at a pick-up point on the beach, two miles west of La Panne, at 1800hrs. He laid on launches to take the party out to HMS *Keith*, which would then set sail for Dover. Unbeknown to Rear Admiral Wake-Walker, who never received the signal, naval liaison at GHQ had laid on four MTBs of the 10th Flotilla to race over from Dover to pick up the C-in-C and his staff from the beach and bring them back. Inadequately briefed, the Senior Officer of the 10th MTB Flotilla, Lt Anderson, reported to the flagship *Keith* only to be told by a slightly mystified flag officer that Lord Gort had no intention of leaving and the 10th Flotilla should make themselves useful off the beaches. This they did, transferring soldiers from the shallows off La Panne to the bigger vessels offshore until they were running short of fuel and experiencing the inevitable engine problems. They returned to Dover and found a large staff car and a bowler hatted individual with an umbrella, who was very put out when he found the boats had no C-in-C. Back over on the other side, the drivers of the cars carrying Lord Gort and his staff had misunderstood the rendezvous and found no launches to take the C-in-C's party out to Wake-Walker's flagship. Those waiting on the beach became separated and eventually Gort's staff were picked up and taken out to HMS *Keith*, while the General boarded the minesweeper *Hebe*, and his batman, driver and luggage finished up on the motor yacht *Thele*.

The government was becoming extremely worried that none of the MTBs had returned and there was no information on the whereabouts of the C-in-C and his staff. A message was sent to Rear Admiral Wake-Walker, asking for an explanation as to what had happened to the MTBs, and why they had not been used to bring home the General. By this time, Wake-Walker had discovered that the C-in-C had boarded HMS *Hebe*. He had, however, misjudged the situation. Believing that two or three hours' delay in returning the General would not be crucial, he had ordered the minesweeper to pick up as many troops as possible before returning to Dover. When he realised the anxieties of the government, he despatched an MA/SB to take the C-in-C off the minesweeper, only to find the General had already left this ship.

By nightfall, Lord Gort had become restless aboard *Hebe*, and, anxious to rejoin his staff aboard HMS *Keith*, so a white yacht was hailed to come alongside. The yacht, with her VIP aboard, disappeared into the gloom to find HMS *Keith*. While under way, she was involved in a near collision with *MA/SB 10*, under the command of Lt Richard Eyre. A shouting match ensued, during which Lord Gort made it very clear who he was.

The white yacht eventually found HMS *Keith*. Wake-Walker immediately called up Lt Everett in *MA/SB 06*, who came over to collect Lord Gort. On meeting Lt Everett, Lord Gort, referring to his earlier encounter with Lt Eyre in *MA/SB 10*, is reputed to have said imperiously: 'I did not know that there were two commanders-in-chief on the water today'. Much to the relief of Churchill and the government, Lord Gort and his party were finally landed at Dover at around six the following morning, 1 June.

Two hours later, *102* was under way again on another trip to Dunkirk, with instructions to report to Rear Admiral Wake-Walker. The 40-mile crossing

took about 90 minutes. *MTB 102* arrived when the many ships assembled off Dunkirk were being dive-bombed by dozens of Junkers 87 Stukas. The scene was one of turmoil. Large ships, with limited sea room, were under way and taking whatever evasive and defensive action they could. Lt Dreyer weaved *MTB 102* at 30kt between the many smouldering wrecks and large merchant marine vessels, patiently waiting to embark troops being ferried off the beach.

Someone spotted HMS *Keith*, but as *102* approached, the destroyer was under heavy attack from Stuka dive-bombers, and her steering had been severely damaged. The next wave dropped a bomb down the second funnel, which exploded in the number two boiler-room. *Keith* now signalled for *102* to come alongside – a tricky operation because, as *102* closed, it could be seen that, the destroyer was starting to list, and, with her rudder jammed, she was out of control, describing a circle. Nevertheless, *102* managed to get alongside and took off Rear Admiral Wake-Walker, his staff officers, and two wounded members of *Keith*'s crew.

The Admiral wanted to be landed quickly, to confer with Capt Tennant. As *MTB 102* shaped a course towards the harbour, three Stukas peeled off to concentrate their bombs on her. Lt Dreyer immediately rang down 'full ahead' to the engine room three times, which meant to his chief engineer 'give her everything you've got'. Some of the bombs were so close that they disappeared from view behind the transom, exploding near enough to be felt when they hit the seabed.

The Admiral told Dreyer to wait alongside the harbour jetty, while his party went ashore to get a first-hand impression of the situation. Moored close by was a drifter mine-recovery vessel, whose crew seemed oblivious to the noise and drama of the war being fought around them. One of the crew was fully occupied peeling potatoes on the foredeck while his skipper was working away on a loaf of bread and a tin of marmalade. The skipper managed to produce some morphine for the wounded, and then offered Dreyer a morning paper and a replacement tin hat for the one that he had at some point lost overboard.

While the admiral was away, *102*'s torpedoman, Leading Seaman Peter Dawkins, had made a rear admiral's flag out of a red-striped dishcloth, now bearing a St George's cross along with two blobs of red paint to denote his rank. When the Admiral returned to *MTB 102*, he was asked if the flag, denoting his presence on board, could be flown from the signal halyard. He was delighted to agree, and *102* sailed back to Dover as his flagship, the first of several occasions that she was to undertake this role over the next few days. On the last such trip with the Admiral, Christopher Dreyer presented him with the dish-cloth as a souvenir. Many years later this same dish-cloth was returned to *102*, this occurring in 1973, when the Norwich Sea Scouts acquired the old MTB as a working training ship. The Admiral's son, Capt Christopher Wake-Walker, presented the 'flag' to the boat, where it is framed and proudly on display.

MTB 102 made several more trips between Dover and Dunkirk. Christopher Dreyer recalls the remarkable collection of ships and boats manned by civilians. Some were pathetically inadequate for their mission, but their crews still demonstrated a remarkable bravery and single-minded determination; the term 'Dunkirk spirit' is still used today, by a certain generation, to describe a peculiarly British way of dealing with a crisis.

Before *MTB 102* set out on one of her trips back to Dunkirk, the CO of the MTB base, Lt-Cdr Dennis, reached an amicable agreement that he should come along as a spare officer. He was a charming Irishman who had fought in CMBs in the First World War. Senior to Lt Dreyer both in rank and many years, there was never any occasion when this influenced his status on board. As an observer aboard *102*, Lt-Cdr Dennis was subsequently able to file a report with the Admiralty on the operational effectiveness of these small boats. He drew attention to their ability to avoid heavy attack from the air; he had also been impressed by *102*'s success in entering Dunkirk virtually undetected at night, using her auxiliary engine. He recommended that spare crews should be considered, having witnessed first-hand the strain of operating these small boats with only a few hours' sleep between operations. He particularly singled out those in the engine room.

Manoeuvring *MTB 102* on main engines was particularly hard work for those below. She had large propellers, with a corresponding surge of power to accelerate or rapidly take the way off. The gear-boxes, operated by a handwheel, took eight full turns each way to engage; if there were many orders over a short period, those in the engine room could quickly get exhausted. There was also the fatigue caused by the noise level, and the constant worry of reliability. Between 26 May and 4 June, *102* remained in port for just one 24-hour period for long-overdue engine maintenance, when the Isotta-Fraschinis were showing a reluctance to start.

The concept of 'spare crews' was never really adopted in Coastal Forces, although there would nearly always be a spare officer in a flotilla. Experience would show that MTBs and MGBs rarely put to sea on successive days as complete flotillas; invariably there would be one or two boats out of the water, on the slips for maintenance and repairs. Operational sorties night after night in MTBs and MGBs would hardly ever be to quite the same intensity as experienced by the handful of crews that took part in Operation *Dynamo*.

Apart from the MTBs operating nightly from Felixstowe, patrolling the northern approaches to Dunkirk, there were those, like *102*, which were used primarily as despatch boats, carrying reports between the commanders, or ferrying senior officers in and out of the war zone. When not engaged in these duties, they would help with the transfer of soldiers between the beach and the big ships waiting offshore.

Wake-Walker and his staff transferred to the destroyer *Venomous*, anchored off Dunkirk, but continued to use *MTB 102* to patrol off the beaches. By 2 June much of the army had been taken off, but there remained a large number of wounded. There was a stiff wind blowing, and *MA/SB 10*, under Lt Richard Eyre, was despatched to the harbour to help berth some of the larger ships, by acting as a tug. This involved pushing ships alongside the mole, which was hardly appropriate work for a fragile wooden MA/SB. Her bows were pushed in to such an extent that when she returned to British Power Boat, the yard declared her uneconomical to re-build.

When most of the wounded had been transferred, *MA/SB 10*'s tiny wardroom was used for a meeting between General Alexander and Rear Admiral Wake-Walker. Meanwhile, the indefatigable Capt Tennant and his shore-party were embarked on *MTB 102*.

Lt Hamilton Hill and the crew of *MTB 14*.

Admiral Ramsay, meanwhile, had been advised that, although the majority of the remnants of the British Expeditionary Force had been rescued, there yet remained a large force of French soldiers, who had fought an heroic rearguard action which had taken some of the pressure off the evacuation of the British Army. The French requested assistance in embarking their troops, who were estimated at around 30,000. Admiral Ramsay agreed, immediately reassembling much of the fleet that had returned from Dunkirk.

HMS *Malcolm* sailed for Dunkirk at 0200hrs on 4 June. Admiral Wake-Walker resumed his flag officer duties, directing the last of the evacuation from the bridge of *MTB 102*. The French troops were taken off with some difficulty, for the wind and tide were pushing the rescue ships away from the mole. The Luftwaffe had mercifully withdrawn, to concentrate on their next offensive. Nevertheless,

this final evacuation was only a partial success, as many Frenchmen who had not been involved in the rearguard action swarmed on to the boats, taking up so much space that 15,000 French soldiers ended up being left behind to be captured by the Germans.

On the final night of the evacuation, a new motor gunboat was on the scene. With a young RN sub-lieutenant in command, R.C.M.V. Wynn had been roped in to help crew her. Admiral Ramsay had come from Dover in her, and Wynn was taken out from Ramsgate to join her on her way to Dunkirk. The Admiral was going out to have a final look around and see the last ship out before blockships were drawn across the entrance. The late Lord Newborough remembered his amazement that the Admiral carried out his rounds without protective

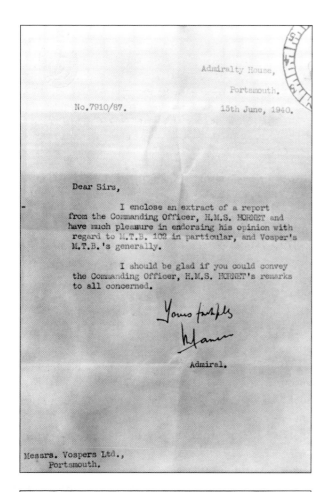

Admiralty House,
Portsmouth.

No.7910/87.   15th June, 1940.

Dear Sirs,

I enclose an extract of a report from the Commanding Officer, H.M.S. HORNET and have much pleasure in endorsing his opinion with regard to M.T.B. 102 in particular, and Vosper's M.T.B.'s generally.

I should be glad if you could convey the Commanding Officer, H.M.S. HORNET's remarks to all concerned.

Yours faithfully

Admiral.

Messrs. Vospers Ltd.,
Portsmouth.

Enclosure to Portsmouth No.7910/87 of 15.6.40.

EXTRACT FROM H.M.S. HORNET'S REPORT.

x x x x x x x x x x x x x x x x x x x

It may be of interest to the designers and builders of M.T.B. No.102 to know that she took an important part in the evacuation of the B.E.F. from Dunkirk. By Builders, I mean all the Vosper craftsmen and workmen who helped to build her, and are building British M.T.B.'s.

The fact that this boat, over three years old, attacked by German aircraft, by bombs and machine guns, going alongside piers already damaged by shellfire and bombs, and constantly being bombed and shelled, came out at the end of it unscathed, with hull and engines in perfect condition, is a tremendous tribute to the Firm and the workmanship. M.T.B. 102 had many bombs dropped close to her, several within 10 yards, and one within two yards of her transom, and in spite of this, no defect developed.

Knowing this, one can imagine that confidence the M.T.B. Officers and Men have in Vosper M.T.B.'s.

x x x x x x x x x x x x x

LEFT & BELOW LEFT: Extracts from HMS *Hornet's* report of 15 June 1940. *Vosper Thornycroft*

headgear, and merely brandishing a walking stick. The Admiral ordered Wynn to carry out the gruesome task of recovering identity cards from the bodies of British servicemen, while a civilian colleague managed to lay his hands on a motorbike, which he used to take a final look round for any soldiers who might still need to be embarked.

The blockship convoy consisted of three old freighters, escorted by the destroyer *Shikari*, along with *MTB 107* and *MA/SB 10*. This was to be a second attempt to sink blockships in the entrance to Dunkirk harbour. Perhaps the Germans had anticipated it, for mines had been dropped in the vicinity, and *Gourko*, the leading blockship, exploded and sank. The remaining two blockships attempted to position themselves in the harbour entrance, but the strong cross-wind and current pushed them away, and they were scuttled well clear of the entrance channel. As *MA/SB 10* picked up the crews of the blockships, Lt Cameron in *MTB 107* motored into the harbour to have a last look round.

Jock Cameron, an eminent KC in Scotland, had assumed command of *MTB 107* at the relatively ripe old age of 40 (he had served as a midshipman in the First World War). Because of his seniority in years his naval colleagues, who were mostly half his age, affectionately called him 'Grandpa'. *MTB 107* was equally remarkable. She was a 40ft experimental CMB-type Thornycroft boat, designed to be lowered from the deck of a cruiser, and carried a single torpedo. Ordered in April 1939 as a Distance Control Target Boat, she had a single 650bhp Thornycroft petrol engine, which gave her a top speed of 33kt.

MTB 107 was the last warship to leave Dunkirk. Lacking any form of astern gear, she was still able to motor round in circles, scooping up soldiers out of the water by the light of the burning town, all the while under attack from the shore by enemy machine guns. Many years later, an account of *MTB 107*'s exploits appeared in the Coastal Forces Veterans' Association newsletter. Rear Admiral Courtney Anderson, referring to Lt Cameron, wrote: 'Grandpa and his dreadful little *107* upheld the finest traditions of Coastal Forces.'

Chapter Seven

Kekewich's Navy

Following the evacuation of the remnants of the British Expeditionary Force from Dunkirk, the mood of the nation quickly changed from a sense of relief to despair for the future. The retreating British and French armies had lacked the training and the equipment to take on the might of the advancing German Army, and those soldiers who had been rescued had returned dispirited and resentful of the military leadership that had led them to humiliating defeat. The defence of the country was now in the hands of the Royal Navy and the Royal Air Force. There was no disguising the threat of a German invasion, and air reconnaissance photographs would soon start showing that hundreds of landing craft were being assembled in the French and Belgian Channel ports.

MTBs and MLs became involved in a desperate attempt to disrupt Hitler's plans by trying to destroy at least some of his invasion fleet. Reputedly emanating from Churchill, Operation *Lucid*, as it was code-named, involved sending in fireships to block Calais and Boulogne. As at Zeebrugge and Dunkirk, the role of Coastal Forces would be to take off the crews of the blockships. The initial plan concentrated on Calais, making use of an old tanker which had been prepared at Sheerness as a fireship, loaded with petrol and strategically placed explosives. The idea was to position her in the harbour entrance, and then, with an onshore wind, allow her to drift in amongst the assembled invasion fleet, causing maximum damage and at the same time blocking the harbour. On the first attempt, the tanker fouled the boom off Sheerness and was forced to return to port. On the next attempt, a diversionary air raid failed in its objective, and the Calais shore defences were ready and waiting, illuminating the small fleet of ships by searchlight.

Rear Admiral Anderson recalls a final attempt in October 1940 to carry out Operation *Lucid*. His boat, *MTB 67*, was in Sheerness, and at the last minute he was told to remove his torpedoes and sail with the fireships to take off their crews. The dockyard crane driver refused to operate the crane until he had had his tea break so, in view of the urgency, *67*'s crew removed the torpedoes themselves. All hell then broke lose, and the dockyard staff threatened a general strike unless Anderson was severely reprimanded.

MTB 67 was being towed out to sea by a destroyer but, just before heading south off Ramsgate, the destroyer displayed a blue signal lamp, indicating that the operation had yet again been cancelled. Courtney Anderson was told that it was not a conventional fireship being used on that night but that instead she was carrying some new and secret chemical, which would spread fire across the surface of the sea when ignited. The idea was to release the chemical in a position where the flood tide would carry the flames into the invasion ports. On this final attempt, one of the destroyer escorts, which had been degaussed, was mysteriously mined. Since a fireship might suffer the same fate off the English coastline and the tide might then carry the flaming sea into Dover and Ramsgate, Operation *Lucid* was abandoned.

Hitler had decided that, before launching his planned invasion along the South Coast of England, the Germans had first to win control of the skies, and, simultaneously, to attack the all-important convoy routes that carried essential supplies along the East and South Coasts. To this end, wave after wave of German fighters and bombers were directed towards towns and ports in the south of England, while sometimes two or three convoys a day were subjected to similar harassment by the Luftwaffe. The merchant ships, with a sparsity of escorts, were also easy targets for German submarines and surface raiders (particularly E-boats). German mines posed an even greater threat, claiming an alarming tonnage of both Merchant and Royal Navy shipping.

Between 8 and 18 August 1940 the fight in the skies grew to an intensity which would never again be matched. This was the Battle of Britain. The Luftwaffe was throwing in every available fighter and bomber, putting up over a hundred aircraft to attack single convoys. On one occasion as many as 168 planes targeted a convoy off the Isle of Wight, sinking two ships; on the same day, another wave of 139 planes attacked a convoy off Bournemouth. Three days later, Germany launched a bombing raid on Portland and Weymouth and attacked more convoys off Harwich and in the Thames estuary. This pattern of air raids was to be repeated with ever-increasing frequency, some towns, like Dover, being attacked two or three times a day. On one occasion Dover underwent ten hours of air raids in a single 12-hour period, during which the harbour suffered considerable damage, and the electricity supply was cut off. In the MTB office, work continued by the light of oil lamps.

What would be designated 'Coastal Forces' was still in its infancy in the summer of 1940. With the war at sea having advanced into the Channel, the shore establishment, HMS *Hornet*, at Gosport in Portsmouth harbour, became an operational base (having previously been the MTB administrative and training centre). The base at Dover was meanwhile being developed, and a new base was opened up at Fowey. The British Power Boat motor anti-submarine boats (MA/SBs) were forming at Portland, but were proving to be unsuitable for their role (some would soon be converted to the Navy's first Second World War motor gunboats).

On 21 June 1940, the 11th MTB Flotilla, comprising MTBs *69*, *70*, *71*, and *72*, arrived in Dover. Ten days later, the destroyer flotilla there was built up to seven ships, and the strength of 11th MTB Flotilla was increased with the arrival of the Norwegian-manned MTBs *N5* and *N6*. These new 60ft Vospers had two Isotta-Fraschini engines, two Ford V8 auxiliaries for silent running at 8kt, two upper deck 18in torpedo tubes with cordite

discharge, four depth-charges, but only twin Lewis machine guns for defence, which were totally inadequate for any close combat with German E-boats.

Sub-Lts Coles and Rickards, both RNVRs who had been First Lieutenants with the 1st MTB Flotilla in Malta, were appointed liaison officers to the Norwegian boats. Their first priority was to familiarise the Norwegians with the disciplines of the Royal Navy and RN codes and signals. The boats' crews were made up of the commanding officer and nine ratings plus the seagoing British liaison officer and telegraphist. Sub-Lt Coles' CO on *MTB N6* was the deceptively reserved Per Danielsen who, later in the war, would lead daring raids by the all-Norwegian flotilla on their enemy-occupied homeland.

Charles Coles vividly recalls the war as it was fought in the Straits of Dover during the height of the Battle of Britain. His diary entry on one day was twice interrupted by Dorniers bombing the harbour and the convoy outside. On these occasions, he would usually grab his tin hat and go up top to witness the Spitfires chasing off the Dorniers as the port's ineffective AA guns opened up. All the crews of the 11th MTB Flotilla lived on board, using the submarine depot ship *Sandhurst* as their base. Here they would usually eat breakfast and supper, which was invariably interrupted by an air raid, when half-finished meals were abandoned as the crews sprinted the half-mile back to the MTBs. Without the comforts of an established shore base, meals had to be grabbed whenever there was the opportunity. Sub-Lt Coles and the CO shared *MTB N6*'s tiny wardroom, in which there were two bunks, each with minimal headroom, and precious little else. The duty officer for the flotilla would usually set up a camp-bed beside the telephone, in the quayside hut that served as the MTB office.

The 11th Flotilla was invariably out at night, responding to the frequent reports of E-boats operating in the Straits. Apart from these night patrols, it was used extensively for crash-boat duties, picking up ditched fighter pilots from the sea and survivors from merchant ships which had been damaged by the Luftwaffe or torpedoed by submarines or E-boats. These sea rescue duties were grim. Frequently officers and crews alike would strip to the waist and jump into the water to put a

Lt Denis Jermain and the crew of *MTB 31.*

bowline around survivors trying to keep afloat in the oily seas. Some would be desperately wounded and only with the greatest difficulty could these be brought alongside and hauled inboard. The MTB would then motor at high speed back into Dover, where cars or ambulances would be waiting to take the casualties to hospital

Aerial dogfights were intently watched by the MTB crews. If a plane was sighted coming down from 25,000ft, an MTB could be under way and circling around within 50yd of the pilot splashing down. Charles Coles tells of one remarkable rescue by *MTB N6* when a Spitfire pilot was picked out of the water just off the harbour and raced back to shore, where he was met by car, and within 30 minutes of taking off was back reporting for duty at his aerodrome. When he returned the dry clothes he had borrowed he also sent a letter of appreciation to Coles, claiming that, thanks to the MTB, he must have established a record for a pilot

taking off, ditching in the sea, and returning to his squadron.

Along the coast to the east, the 10th MTB Flotilla took over air/sea rescue duties in the Thames estuary. Courtney Anderson, at that time SO of the flotilla, recalls competition amongst the crews to be the first boat to catch a parachuting pilot on the deck. Nobody made it, but some got pretty close.

The boats would also pick German airmen out of the sea. These were usually terrified, having been told they would be shot if captured. On one occasion *MTB 70* stopped for a young German pilot in the water who was desperately yelling that he was unable to swim. One of the MTB's crew jumped into the water with a knife to cut free the pilot's parachute. As he did this, a Dornier screamed down on them, strafing the boat at close quarters and wounding three of her crew. The CO

Lt-Cdr Robert Hichens displays the German flag beneath his White Ensign aboard *MGB 64* after sinking *Schnellboot 41* on 20 November 1941. *IWM 7631*

opened up the throttles and, with the seaman in tow, *MTB 70* sped off, having no choice but to leave the German to his fate.

All through July and August, the Luftwaffe kept coming, wave after wave of aircraft targeting convoys, Navy ships in or off Dover, and RAF airfields. Spitfire and Hurricane crews were scrambled from airfields all over the south and south-east, including Biggin Hill, Lympne, Hawkinge, Kenley, Detling, Martlesham, Manston, Croydon, Dover, and Deal. Numerically the odds favoured the Luftwaffe, each bomber being usually accompanied by three fighters, but, as history has recorded, Germany had underestimated the skill and bravery of the young RAF pilots who would eventually scupper Operation *Sea Lion*, Hitler's

planned invasion of Britain. At the height of the battle the number of enemy aircraft destroyed on a single day was estimated at 180.

How close Germany came to achieving its invasion plans is left to the historians to debate, but the relentless destruction of Allied convoys and their escorts continued. At this stage of the war off Dover, the MTBs were out for every air battle, racing to the assistance of bombed freighters or tankers as soon as they were seen to be in difficulties. On one occasion the crews of the 11th MTB Flotilla were alerted to the fact that a 21-ship convoy was shortly expected through the Straits of Dover. By the time the flotilla was on the scene the first ship in the convoy had already been hit, the second was on fire and the third was listing badly. On board Sub-Lt Coles' boat, the Norwegian gunner had his sights on a dive-bomber, raking it from tail to nose until smoke appeared, and, to the cheering of the MTB's crew, it hit the sea and burst into fragments. Another dive-bomber came dangerously close, and again the

Norwegian gunner opened up, but this time succeeded only in firing off short bursts. Coles yelled at him to keep his finger on the trigger, but then noticed the gunner's crumpled-up binoculars and a dark red patch on his blue overalls; he had been hit in the stomach and wrist by shrapnel.

The next day, picking up yet more convoy casualties off Dover, *MTB N6* came across an old Scots fireman in the water, who raised a mangled arm to show that he could not reach the boat unaided. The CO stripped off and plunged in to help. Once on board, Sub-Lt Coles applied a tourniquet to the remains of the arm and then provided blankets, brandy, and a cigarette. The following day, he was visiting the wounded Norwegian gunner in hospital when someone in the next bed tugged at his coat. It was the Scots fireman who shook him warmly with his left hand, expressing his gratitude. Coles had never expected him to live.

In between the rescue work by day and the E-boat patrols at night, the 11th Flotilla was used on operations on the other side of the Channel. It never ceased to amaze Charles Coles just how close they were to enemy-occupied France. On a clear day, it was possible to make out the high cliffs of Cap Gris-Nez, flanked by Calais on one side and Boulogne on the other. On one of their operations, five boats of the 11th MTB Flotilla roared out of Dover at dusk. As they approached the enemy coastline a searchlight beam started sweeping around, looking for them. Then, just as the telegraphist on *MTB N6* was decoding a signal, passed to friendly aircraft in the vicinity, that E-boats had been sighted on a course suspiciously similar to their own, the flotilla was suddenly illuminated by a parachute flare, presenting an easy target both for the shore batteries and any aircraft overhead. Then two bombs dropped quite close by. The MTBs had been mistaken for E-boats and were under attack by the RAF!

The first time the MTBs were picked out by searchlights on the enemy coast was an alarming experience. They subsequently developed a technique for dealing with searchlights, which had a range of about three miles. The boats would cross the Channel at full speed; once detected, they would continue directly into the beam, still at full speed, until close inshore, when the high cliffs would protect them from the probing lights. Here they would switch off engines and wait, seeing the occasional small ship slipping by to seaward of them. Sometimes *MTB N6* would launch the small tender to ferry an agent ashore and, on one occasion, Lt-Cdr Dennis joined the boat for a night passage and decided to go ashore to have a look round.

Another patrol incident involved MTBs *69* and *70*. These had already been out twice in the day to rescue convoy survivors, but this time the destroyers *Boreas* and *Brilliant* accompanied them. The port war signal station at Dover had previously alerted the C-in-C Nore that a dozen E-boats were putting to sea at around 1400 hours. These were duly sighted from the air off Cap Gris-Nez, and appeared to be making for the slow-moving remnants of a convoy which would soon be rounding Dungeness. Fighter aircraft had failed to stop any of the E-boats. Dover Command decided to despatch, with all haste, *Boreas*, *Brilliant*, and the two MTBs. At around 1700hrs the E-boats were in range of the destroyers' heavy guns and soon dispersed, turning back towards the French coast. Half an hour later *Brilliant* reported that she had again sighted E-boats, which she intended to engage. The E-boats made smoke to screen their rapid departure, but by now the destroyers were in range of German shore batteries, which opened fire. The vice admiral at Dover, whose flotilla of destroyers was already critically depleted by war damage, signalled *Boreas* and *Brilliant* to withdraw. This they did, helped by a smoke-screen provided by MTBs *69* and *70*. By this time, the Luftwaffe had also been alerted. The destroyers escaped unscathed by the first air attack, but the Stukas returned, hitting the bridge of *Boreas*, penetrating to her galley and engine room, killing fifteen of her crew, and seriously wounding many more. Although only three miles from harbour, *Boreas* was unable to raise steam to get home. *Brilliant* had also had been hit, two bombs through the quarterdeck having destroyed her steering gear, fortunately without causing any casualties. MTBs *5* and *6* had witnessed the battle and raced out of Dover to assist. *MTB 6* was signalled to call up tugs to take both the destroyers in tow. The MTBs then rushed over supplies of morphia and medical aid for treatment of the injured.

The 1st Destroyer Flotilla at Dover sustained considerable damage within a matter of weeks of the Battle of Britain beginning. *Boreas* and *Brilliant* would be out of commission for some time; *Brazen* had been sunk; *Griffin* and *Greyhound* had been badly damaged; enemy bombers had sunk their leader HMS *Codrington* when she was lying alongside the depot ship, *Sandhurst*, undergoing boiler cleaning. A few days later *Sandhurst* herself was badly damaged by bombing and was towed out of Dover for repairs. The MTB crews then took over the Lord Warden Hotel, which became HMS *Wasp*, the Dover base for Coastal Forces. Some of the 11th MTB flotilla would now, at last, have the comfort of cabins and hot baths ashore.

Because of the constant bombing the decision was taken that, except under special circumstances, the local destroyers should not enter Dover harbour. The MTBs would be disguised with fishing nets. Though this proved impractical, the resourceful crew of *MTB 6* dragged their net from one end of the dock to the other and caught 23 mackerel. Barrage balloons, which proved to be an effective obstacle for the Luftwaffe, now floated above the convoys and around Dover harbour.

Although the population of Dover had suffered appallingly from the bombing, they had stoically grown to accept air raids as a routine part of their daily lives. Towards the end of August, however, there was a different sort of menace. Charles Coles remembers the first time Germany's Big Berthas were pointed towards Dover. Alerted that an east-bound convoy was approaching the Dover Straits, he was awaiting the air raid warning announcing the inevitable arrival of the Luftwaffa's dive-bombers. Instead, there came the unfamiliar sound of what was thought to be heavy calibre bombs exploding. Mysteriously, there was still no sign of enemy planes and so no air-raid warning. He listened carefully to the initial crack, then there was a long pause followed by a deep explosion. He could hardly believe it, but the only explanation was that huge German guns, 25 miles away on the other side of the Channel, were shelling the convoy nearly off Dover. The flash from the French coast could be seen, followed by the bang of a gun firing and eventually, after an eerily long pause, the shell-burst. On this first occasion, the barrage from the Big Berthas lasted for about an hour, as the shelling

uncannily followed the convoy through the Dover Straits and the two escorting destroyers raced backwards and forwards making smoke. The huge guns were being trained by an enemy plane, flying above the convoy until eventually driven off by Hurricane fighters.

There was a markedly different war at sea being fought off the East Coast. The greatest menace here was the magnetic mine, which, as we have seen, during the first few months of the war the German Navy and Luftwaffe had been devastatingly successful in laying all along the convoy routes between Hull and the Thames estuary. Then came a number of mysterious sinkings. Denis Jermain (another of those who had served at Malta in the 1st MTB Flotilla) was to provide the explanation. He was CO of *MTB 31*, which was one of the new Vosper boats operating out of Felixstowe. On passage alone, in swept, narrow channels along the East Coast, his boat was blowing up mines which had dried out on nearby sandbanks. Returning to port he reported this manifestation, and a party of mine experts from HMS *Vernon* was soon at sea, hunting out more of these mysterious objects. It had always been assumed that the mines were activated by magnetic contact, but here was something else – the Germans had now perfected the acoustic mine, which was activated by the mere sound of a ship's propellers. This was the explanation for some of the recent losses of shipping off the East Coast.

One of the worst mining disasters was at the end of August 1940. There was a report of enemy shipping off the Dutch coast, under way in a westerly direction. The minelaying destroyers *Express*, *Esk*, and *Ivanhoe*, all of the 20th Destroyer Flotilla, were on passage to intercept them off the Frisian Islands when they were all mined in an uncharted minefield off Texel, the southernmost of the islands. *Esk* sank with only one survivor and *Express* had most of her bows blown off, with the loss of many of the crew; *Ivanhoe* was only slightly damaged, but in the process of taking the wounded off *Express*, she hit another mine which broke her back and resulted in the loss of another 50 lives.

An armada of boats went to the scene to give assistance, including tugs, minesweepers, Capt Mountbatten's destroyer *Jupiter*, and MTBs 29, 30, and 31 from Felixstowe. Denis Jermain in *MTB 31*

The Lord Warden Hotel became HMS *Wasp*, the Dover base for Coastal Forces. *Dover Express*

recalled one of the strange incidents of war, when a German seaplane flew low overhead, directing the MTBs towards the survivors from the destroyers. Having accomplished his task, he dipped his wings in salute and disappeared. *Express* was towed back to the Humber, through the same uncharted minefield. *Ivanhoe* was signalled that more MTBs were on their way, again from Felixstowe, to embark the seriously wounded. The boats involved, all from the 1st MTB Flotilla, were MTBs *14* (Lt E. Hamilton-Hill), *15* (Lt J.A. Eardley-Wilmot), *16* (Lt P.F.S. Gould), and *17* (Lt R.I.T. Faulkner). Three of the MTBs took off the wounded and returned to base; Lt Eardley-Wilmot in *15* stayed on the scene to give further assistance. The unfortunate captain of *Ivanhoe*, Cdr P.H. Hadow, had reluctantly given the order to abandon ship. Several attempts were made to scuttle her, but without success, so *MTB 15* was ordered to sink her with a torpedo. The whole operation had turned out to be a tragic disaster. From the three destroyers, over 400 personnel had been killed, severely wounded, or taken prisoner (some of the survivors of *Ivanhoe*, having taken to the boats, finished up on Dutch beaches). Apart

from Dunkirk, this turned out to be the Nore Command's greatest loss over a 24-hour period.

In the early part of the war, with so much depending on the constant flow of British and Allied convoys, the toll of shipping sunk by German mines tells its own story. In a single command, Nore, of 249 Allied ships sunk between September 1939 and December 1940, 179 were mined. These statistics represented an appalling loss of life, particularly in the Merchant Navy. Nevertheless, it would be wrong to give the impression that mine warfare was all one-sided. British forces were equally active in minelaying off the French Channel ports, in the Elbe and the Schelde, and on the German convoy routes from Scandinavia. Mines destroyed more shipping than the total losses attributed to torpedoes, gunnery, and bombing. Coastal Forces would make a significant contribution to laying minefields off the enemy coastline. This work was frequently carried out right under the noses of the enemy. The exact positions, accurate to within 40–50yd, had to be carefully recorded to warn other shipping of their presence.

However, until the RAF was in a position to disrupt the railway network across Europe, Germany was not reliant on a constant stream of convoys. Those that were necessary, generally preferred to be under way during daylight, surrounded by escorting vessels, at risk only to the RAF. It followed that there were correspondingly fewer targets for the Felixstowe MTBs over this period, so that along with newly-launched MLs employed as minelayers, the early MTBs were also used for this purpose. Denis Jermain recalled minelaying with the 4th MTB Flotilla. With a dearth of targets in the North Sea, the boats put to sea with four mines, two either side on chocks. Thus armed, the boats would make for the shallow, narrow, known channels off Boulogne, Calais, and Dunkirk, or the entrances to their ports. On other occasions their destinations might be the Dutch coastline and the Schelde Estuary.

Laying mines was not popular with the crews of the 4th MTB Flotilla, as this took them away from

the role for which the boats were originally designed. But they did feel that they achieved considerable success so close inshore, off harbour entrances, or in the shipping lanes off the enemy coastline. With the basic navigational equipment they possessed at this early stage of the war (a steering compass), it required considerable skill to minelay to within the required degree of accuracy, particularly in some of the remoter spots. Hand-bearing compasses were not yet available, and to take a bearing it was necessary to swing the bows round until pointing in the required direction, and then read off the ship's head from the steering compass. Dennis Jermain particularly remembered the Schelde Estuary, where an effective lead and line for taking depth soundings would have been especially useful. His First Lieutenant, however, came up against the bureaucracy of Naval Stores, which decreed that small vessel leads should be no more than seven pounds. This might have been fine

Recognition signals displayed in the wheelhouse of a 70ft Elco MGB for quick reference.

in some areas, but in the Schelde fresh water comes down over salt water, and when a lead is handed down through the top layer it then meets the salt water and will sink off the perpendicular, to give a totally false reading.

On one of their minelaying operations, a quarter of a mile from the entrance to Dunkirk, *MTB 31* and two other boats were illuminated by what is known as St Elmo's Fire. This is caused by certain thundery weather conditions, in which a boat receives a static charge which causes all its aerials to be ringed with bright light. On this occasion it outlined the boats like Christmas trees as they floated across the entrance to Dunkirk. The crews could never understand how the enemy managed to miss this dramatic display.

The Felixstowe MTBs did not have the opportunity to mount a torpedo attack against enemy shipping until 13 August 1940. Three boats from the 1st MTB Flotilla, led by Lt Mannooch, with Lt Gould and Lt Hamilton-Hill in the other boats, were patrolling with destroyers off the Dutch coast when what was thought to be a group of E-boats was sighted. Lt Mannooch attempted to ram the nearest ship, only realising at the last moment that his boat was taking on a motor minesweeper. His MTB was damaged in the bows seriously enough to require being taken in tow. Lt Gould's boat then took over the attack on the minesweeper, sustaining some damage in turn. As Lt Hamilton-Hill took in his stern torpedo-firing outriggers, preparatory to taking Mannooch's boat in tow, six armed trawlers steamed by. With one MTB with her bows stove in, the second with no launching gear at the ready, and the third unable to increase speed sufficiently to launch with safety, a glorious opportunity was lost.

It would be over 12 months from the outbreak of war before Coastal Forces would launch a successful torpedo attack. Three MTBs from the original 1st Flotilla left Felixstowe on 8 September 1940, when aerial reconnaissance sighted a large convoy approaching Ostend. *MTB 14* had to be left behind with engine trouble, but MTBs *15* and *17* (commanded by Lt Eardley-Wilmot and Lt Faulkner, who had been together in Malta before the outbreak of war) went on in search of the enemy. The MTBs were not the only force to have been alerted, because when *15* and *17* arrived off Ostend the battle had already started, as Harwich

destroyers opened fire on the port; RAF bombers were also in action. MTBs *15* and *17* separated, selected their targets, and each made two torpedo runs. In the general confusion of attacks from all sides it was difficult to say for certain who scored direct hits, but an ammunition ship, which blew up spectacularly, was credited to the MTBs, with one or two other possibles.

In October there was another success. Felixstowe-based MTBs *22*, *31*, and *32* had set out from Dover, led by Lt-Cdr Cole, SO of the 4th MTB Flotilla. To the north of Calais, they unexpectedly encountered two trawlers. The SO decided to check by radio whether they were friendly. Back came the reply 'negative', and the MTBs then launched a torpedo attack on what were then assumed to be armed German trawlers. Both enemy vessels were sunk and their crews taken prisoner, but only after Lt Jermain had dropped a depth-charge under the bows of one of them. He had perfected this daring form of attack by practising the manoeuvre many times in the estuaries along the East Coast. He would drive his boat at speed within a few feet of the bows of the practice ship, let go a dummy depth-charge, and then have to turn sharply to avoid going aground.

In December, Jermain had another opportunity to use depth-charges at close quarters. With his SO (Lt-Cdr Cole) and Lt P.M. Corsar, the three boats from the 4th MTB Flotilla were on patrol off Flushing and the estuary to the River Schelde. Lt-Cdr Cole's boat had to return to Felixstowe with engine problems. Still under power on their main engines, the other two boats suddenly came on a large convoy at anchor, further out than was expected. The convoy escorts, alerted by the noise of the MTBs' engines, immediately opened fire. Lt Jermain lost contact with the other MTB, which was hit several times, sustaining damage to her steering and torpedo firing equipment. *MTB 31* was now on her own. Twice she attempted to torpedo one of the armed escorts, but on both occasions Jermain had trouble with the firing mechanism and the torpedoes failed to reach the target. With no torpedoes, he selected the largest ship at anchor, and made two runs with his depth-charges. On the second of these, *MTB 31* actually scraped the bows of the German ship. Both depth-charges exploded beneath the target, and although Jermain did not

A 21in torpedo is lowered onto the deck of *MTB 232* in Felixstowe Harbour. *MTB 232* was part of the 21st MTB Flotilla, commanded by Lieutenant Peter Dickens. Amongst those on board are Leading Seaman John Valentine, Lt N.S. 'Norrie' Gardner (CO, *MTB 32*), Sub-Lt Douglas 'Gertie' Gill (CO, *MTB 232*), and Lt Bob Morgan (CO, *MTB 69*). Three other MTBs can be seen to the left (*L to R: MTB 69, MTB 70,* and *MTB 72*).

stay to see the results of his attack, she was believed to have been a vessel of over 6,000 tons.

Along with these early successes, came the casualties. Only one of four boats in the 1st Flotilla (MTBs *14*, *15*, *16*, and *17*, which had frequently operated together) would survive a six-week period in September and October 1940. *MTB 15* was mined on a return passage to Felixstowe, *MTB 16* suffered the same fate in Barrow Deep, and *MTB 17* was sunk by a mine off Ostend.

Although Coastal Forces had marked up some notable victories in the first two years of the war, the exact role of these 'Little Ships' was still something of a mystery to the commands in which they were operating. The lack of targets contributed to this and, numerically, the build-up of Coastal Forces craft had been slow. Operation of the early boats was frequently frustrated by engine failure, or by damage to the hulls sustained in rough seas, or by poor design. Most of the motor gunboats (MGBs)

Inspection of boats' crews by Rear Admiral Piers Kekewich.

operating in the first two years of the war, for instance, had been originally conceived as motor anti-submarine boats (MA/SBs), but, being found unsuitable for this role, some had been converted, and others had been completed as MGBs. They hunted targets on their own, but, with their modest speed and armament, were ill-equipped to take on the German E-boats. Against the odds, however, these early MGBs did achieve some remarkable successes, and produced one of the great names in Coastal Forces history – Lt-Cdr Robert Hichens.

Hichens joined the 6th MGB Flotilla when it was being formed at Fowey in November 1940. At 30 years of age he was one of the more mature RNV(S)R officers. Educated at Marlborough and then Oxford, he was, at the outbreak of war, a partner in a firm of solicitors in the West Country. He had always had an interest in small boats and had raced his home-built 14ft International in the Prince of Wales Cup; one of the other competitors was another name to become famous in Coastal Forces – Peter Scott, who would serve as Senior Officer of the Steam Gunboat Flotilla.

In March 1941, with the expectation of more E-boat activity off the East Coast, the 6th MGB Flotilla moved round from Fowey to Felixstowe. Here, the flotilla was frequently called out on air/sea rescue duties, which meant going out in all weathers. The boats were simply not built for going out in the North Sea in gale-force winds, and it was not unusual for half the flotilla to be out of the water at Brightlingsea under repair. Robert Hichens became Senior Officer in August, and just a few weeks later three boats from the flotilla, led by Hichens in *MGB 64*, set out from Felixstowe on an operation that would take its place in the history of Coastal Forces as the first confirmed E-boat loss.

E-boats had been sighted close to one of the East Coast convoy routes but the three MGBs made an inauspicious start; barely clear of the boom off Felixstowe, *MGB 63*'s engines failed and she had to be left behind. Then Hichens' boat was reduced to one working engine and a consequent maximum speed of just 18kt. The original plan, to make for the Hook of Holland and lie in wait for the returning E-boats, had to be abandoned. Although warned that the *Schnellboote* were out in large numbers, Lt-Cdr Hichens decided to persevere and attempt to intercept them 20 miles off the East Coast.

In the early hours of 20 November, the two boats were in position and had stopped engines. They had a long wait before, out to the west, they heard the unmistakable sound of high-speed diesel engines. After much stopping, listening and looking, they saw something ahead. A challenge was flashed in the direction of what appeared to be the outline of a hull. Receiving a garbled reply, the two MTBs surged forward towards what turned out to be no fewer than five E-boats which must have just assembled preparatory to returning to their base at Ijmuiden. Although hopelessly outnumbered and with limited fire-power, Hichens gave the order to attack. The E-boats were taken by surprise, shooting wildly in all directions before they hastily disengaged with no stomach for a fight at such close quarters. *MGB 67* had suffered no damage, but on Hichens' boat one of his guns had been hit. Following at the reduced speed which was all they could muster, the MGBs came across a single E-boat on a parallel course. Hichens then discovered that his starboard gun had now jammed. One can imagine his frustration when, with an E-boat in his sights, he had only one engine to attempt a chase and just a 0.303in Lewis machine gun with which to do battle. Without realizing it, the E-boat commander had the perfect opportunity of claiming an MGB, but then *MGB 67* raced up, with all her guns blazing. The E-boat quickly disappeared into the night, heading back for Holland.

The two MGBs, motoring at 18kt, continued on the course they believed the E-boats would be steering. Confident that they must have inflicted some damage to the enemy boats, they stopped occasionally to listen for the sound of engines. Hichens was just about to turn back for home when his coxswain thought he heard something to the south-west. Conscious that he might be endangering the boats if they remained at sea for much longer in daylight, Hichens decided to investigate. Ahead they spotted an E-boat, motionless and apparently abandoned. It appeared that she had been involved in a collision in the fray and had also sustained damage from the MGBs' guns. The noise picked up by the coxswain must have been one of the other E-boats taking off the crew. Hichens first reaction was to attempt to tow the prize back to Felixstowe, but it became apparent that she had been scuttled by opening the seacocks. She was already settling low in the water, as some of the MGBs' crews boarded her to remove souvenirs. They witnessed *Schnellboot 41* finally disappear beneath the waves, and then returned to Felixstowe, with Hichens' boat proudly flying the German flag beneath the White Ensign.

During the whole of 1941, there were 21 actions in which Coastal Forces were involved. The majority of these were MTB attacks on enemy shipping in the Straits of Dover. The MGBs and MLs were involved in eight actions against E-boats, with only the one confirmed E-boat loss described above. One ML was sunk by enemy action. For the most part, the boats on the East Coast were used as convoy escorts and minelayers during this period.

The experience of the RN officers in Coastal Forces, particularly those who had served in the 1st MTB Flotilla, and the new breed of RNVR officers like Robert Hichens, was invaluable. Their leadership was a source of inspiration to those young officers who would soon be pouring out of the Coastal Forces Training Establishment at Fort William. The name 'Coastal Forces' only came into

British Power Boats of Lt-Cdr Robert Hichens'
6th MGB Flotilla. *IWM 7619*

being towards the end of 1940, by which time the Royal Navy's 'Little Ships' had gained recognition as a fighting unit in their own right. Coastal Forces then came under the single administrative command of Rear Admiral Coastal Forces (RACF). The flag officer selected for this new appointment was Piers K. Kekewich; his chief staff officer was Capt A.W.S. Agar of First World War fame – Agar had been awarded the Victoria Cross after launching a successful torpedo attack in his CMB against a Russian cruiser off Kronstadt.

Rear Admiral Kekewich was initially based at Fort William, then moved his HQ to Portland, and finally finished up in a block of flats in Golders Green. The Admiral's office had responsibility for all Coastal Forces personnel, training, development, supplies, and maintenance, the building programme for the new boats, and the setting up of bases all round the British Isles and further afield. In fact it was responsible for virtually everything except operational control, which remained with the individual C-in-Cs. This was not entirely satisfactory, as these were still early days for Coastal Forces, when some of the C-in-Cs had little idea how to make the most effective use of this new branch of the Royal Navy.

When Admiral Kekewich first set up his department in November 1940 there were only five Coastal Forces bases – *Hornet* (Gosport), *Badger* (Harwich), *Beehive* (Felixstowe), *Belfort* (Fowey) and *Wasp* (Dover). HMS *Beehive* had opened in July because of overcrowding at *Badger*. It was also felt that HMS *Vulcan* was too small to serve as the base ship for the three flotillas working out of Felixstowe. Cdr R.H. McBean, DSO, DSC (another First World War CMB veteran), was appointed as *Beehive*'s first CO. The Admiralty acquired part of the RAF station there, using one ex-seaplane hangar for servicing boats, which were lifted out of the water by a massive hammerhead crane.

During his first 12 months, Admiral Kekewich would see the number of Coastal Forces bases increased from five to 20. After the E-boats launched their first raid on an East Coast convoy off Norfolk in September 1940, it was decided to bring Lt-Cdr W.G. Everitt's newly formed 1st ML Flotilla to Great Yarmouth. At the beginning of 1941 a Coastal Forces shore base, HMS *Midge*, was commissioned there. The 5th MTB Flotilla and two more ML flotillas (the 12th and 13th) would be based at Great

Yarmouth. To the south, the 11th ML Flotilla was operating from Lowestoft where the Coastal Forces base *Minos II* was commissioned in July 1940 (renamed HMS *Mantis* two years later). The MLs from Great Yarmouth and Lowestoft were heavily engaged in convoy escort duties, covering to seaward of the East Coast routes between the Humber and Harwich. The first flotilla of HDMLs was meanwhile forming at Sheerness to patrol the Thames Estuary. Bases were also commissioned in some of the more remote parts of the British Isles, at Blyth, Stornoway, Ardrossan, Larne, Peterhead, Pembroke Dock, and Holyhead. The anti-submarine training base was opened at Ardrishaig. On the South Coast, new bases were established at Newhaven, Cowes, Portland, Dartmouth, and Falmouth, with Immingham being added on the East Coast.

Boats in commission when Kekewich was appointed in October 1940 amounted to 81, comprising 30 MTBs, 29 MA/SBs, and 22 MLs. The building programme between October 1940 and October 1941 increased the overall total to 291. Mostly this was accounted for by the mass-produced MLs, which then numbered 174. There were only nine MTBs launched over this period and the purpose-built MGB was still on the drawing board.

During 1941 crews for the new boats were being rushed through their Coastal Forces training at *St Christopher*. Several near collisions on operations and missed opportunities of launching successful torpedo attacks highlighted the urgent need for a 'working up' base for both crews and boats. It was on the initiative of Rear Admiral Kekewich that HMS *Bee* was set up at Weymouth for this purpose.

The appointment of Rear Admiral Coastal Forces lapsed early in 1943, when the administration of Coastal Forces was merged into the Admiralty, by the institution of a CF Staff Division and a CF Material Department. The contribution of Admiral Kekewich and his hard-working staff should not be underestimated. They laid the foundations for the new boats and newly trained crews arriving on the scene in 1942, which was to prove a momentous year for Coastal Forces. The fortunes of war in the 'Narrow Seas' would at last swing in favour of the Royal Navy, and Coastal Forces would play an important role in bringing about this change.

Chapter Eight

A Fine Balance

February 1942 was marked by a battle with some of the most powerful ships in the German Navy. Only the limited resources of Coastal Forces, a Fleet Air Arm squadron of Swordfish torpedo bombers, and six First World War destroyers would emerge with an enhanced reputation, from a sequence of serious operational blunders and an appalling lack of inter-service co-operation.

After a successful period in the North Atlantic, during which they had sunk 22 Allied merchant ships, the German battlecruisers *Scharnhorst* and *Gneisenau* entered Brest for repairs. This was in March 1941. The battlecruisers would remain here for nearly eleven months before Hitler made the decision to bring them back to Germany. *Scharnhorst* and *Gneisenau* were then among the finest ships in the German Navy, capable of 31kt and each carrying nine 11in guns. On 1 June 1941, these two giants were joined at Brest by the formidable heavy cruiser *Prinz Eugen*, which was less than half the displacement of the battlecruisers but still bristled with heavy armament, and was slightly faster. The German Navy now became increasingly concerned about the three warships remaining at Brest, unable to contribute to the war at sea in either the Atlantic or the Channel and North Sea. They were also well within the range of RAF bombers, which were mounting raids on Brest with increasing frequency.

Back in Britain, the Admiralty and Air Ministry had worked out a joint plan to attack the three cruisers as they made their anticipated dash for home waters. There would be a huge deployment of 250 bombers (including several squadrons of torpedo-bombers), along with hundreds of fighters providing cover. The RN contribution would be

whatever Admiral Ramsay (Flag Officer Dover) and the C-in-C Nore had at their disposal. This was limited, at that time, to six ancient destroyers from Harwich and a dozen lightly-armed MTBs and MGBs.

The Admiralty and Air Ministry had concluded from frequent and reliable intelligence reports and photo-reconnaissance sorties that the German squadron was assembling, and that the break-out would take place during the moonless period between 10 and 15 February 1942. This turned out to be an accurate assessment, but there was one major miscalculation – no one believed the German warships would attempt to pass through the Dover Straits in broad daylight. The RAF stepped up its surveillance, using radar by night, and the Navy deployed the submarine HMS *Sealion* to keep watch outside the Rade de Brest. However, things started to go wrong during a vital three-hour period in which both air reconnaissance and the submarine failed to notice that the German squadron was at last on the move.

There was a certain irony in the fact that this was the direct result of a raid launched on Brest by Bomber Command on 10 February. The Wellington bombers had hit no targets, and did not see the assembling German fleet beneath them. However, their activities delayed its departure by an hour; if the German ships had left as per their original schedule, they would almost certainly have been spotted both by routine RAF reconnaissance flights and by *Sealion*. As it was, the situation of both had been compromised. The RAF's Hudsons, which should have carried out routine night-time radar surveillance of the Western Approaches to the Channel, were prevented from giving early warning of the German squadron's movements because of

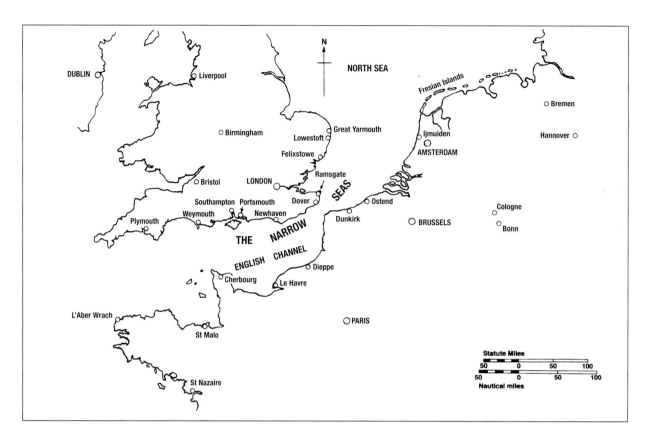

The Channel and the southern North Sea, focus of Coastal Forces action.

faulty radar equipment and the recall of the most easterly of the patrols because of a fog warning over its airfield. The crew of the *Sealion*, meanwhile, had been stood down off Brest, in the belief that any German ships planning to sail through the Dover Straits at night would have had to have left before 2100hrs to pass the Dover Straits while still under cover of darkness.

Back at his headquarters in Dover Castle, Admiral Ramsay stayed up until midnight, and then, with no news, retired to bed. The German squadron, meanwhile, under the overall command of Admiral Ciliax, steamed at full speed through the night. By dawn it was off Barfleur, and still undetected. Here it was joined by more destroyer escorts (making 20 in all), a large number of E-boats, and extensive air cover.

The first report that the German squadron was on the move was radioed back by an RAF patrol at around 1100hrs – more than 12 hours after the German ships had slipped out of the Rade de Brest. An hour later they were in range of the Dover

batteries. The MTBs in Dover had been alerted, along with the Swordfish torpedo-bombers of 825 Naval Air Squadron (NAS) at Manston.

The MTBs initially involved were part of the 6th MTB Flotilla. They included *221* (Lt-Cdr Pumphrey), *219* (Sub-Lt Mark Arnold-Forster), *48* (Canadian Lt C.A. Law), *45* (Lt L.J.H. Gamble) and *44* (Australian Sub-Lt R.F. Saunders). MTBs *221* and *219*, built by Vosper, were designed to be powered by the Italian Isotta-Fraschini engines which were no longer available; they had to make do with the US Hall Scotts, which were a supercharged version of the standard Fairmile B engine. Barely able to notch up 27kt, and mechanically unreliable, these boats could hardly hope to achieve any significant strikes in broad daylight against the might of the German Navy. The other boats, built by Samuel White to a Vosper design, were only marginally better, also fitted with supercharged Hall Scott engines.

A young seaman in Arnold-Forster's boat recorded that, although fired with enthusiasm, the crews never thought their small boats would survive the daylight offensive without air cover. Apart from the torpedoes, his boat's armament consisted of two 0.5in machine guns and three rifles, as the Lewis guns were ashore for maintenance. The high point in the battle for him was the sight of Lt R.E.S. Gould's 63ft *MGB 43*, with her two 20mm Oerlikon guns blazing, single-handedly taking on the German destroyer *Friedrich Ihn* and making her turn away by raining bullets down on her bridge.

The SO of the 6th MTB Flotilla was Lt-Cdr Nigel Pumphrey. Years later, he recalled his flotilla's involvement for BBC Radio. He had just finished a telephone conversation with the naval stores officer about some trivial matter. The phone rang. The message was that German battlecruisers were in the Straits, and concluded with the terse command, 'Get cracking!' And this is what his flotilla did, clearing harbour in record time, everyone strapping on tin hats, with huge grins and giving the thumbs-up. Lt-Cdr Pumphrey described the conditions outside the harbour as rough, but not impossible. They made the best possible speed to intercept the enemy, as the torpedomen struggled to prepare their 'fish' for firing. Their first sight of the enemy was almost as soon as they had put their noses out of Dover, when dozens of Me 109s screamed down on them. A smoke-screen appeared to starboard, and then they saw the E-boats that were laying it. There were twelve of them, on a course converging with his flotilla. At half a mile, the MTBs and E-boats opened fire at one another, and then, through the spray, Pumphrey made out the amazing and unforgettable sight of the three huge German warships, flanked by two long lines of destroyers and E-boats.

Enemy aircraft were by then wheeling about in great numbers; all round the MTBs, water spat up as cannon shells from the E-boats and aircraft fell all around them. Then came the 11in shells of the battlecruisers. The MTBs failed to penetrate the outer shield of E-boats and destroyers, and were forced to fire their torpedoes at a range which made a hit extremely unlikely. In the spray and with the distraction of the continually shifting targets and the E-boats and enemy aircraft, it was difficult to confirm whether any of the torpedoes had found a target.

As the MTBs withdrew, they saw the handful of British fighters escorting the slow, low-flying Swordfish biplanes as the latter tried to get as close as possible before releasing their own torpedoes.

The *Friedrich Ihn*, handled, according to Pumphrey, with great spirit, was laying another smoke-screen between the MTBs and the battlecruisers. The destroyer then showed signs of giving chase to the retiring MTBs, which had re-formed with no casualties and only slight damage. Two MGBs, which had not been ready to leave Dover with the MTBs, now appeared on the scene. MGBs *43* and *41* were converted MA/SBs with little armament. The German destroyer, however, must have thought that the rapidly approaching MGBs were reinforcements, still armed with torpedoes, and turned away to rejoin the main force. On the way back, Lt Gamble's boat picked up two Swordfish airmen.

What Pumphrey's account did not mention was that when the *Scharnhorst*, *Gneisenau*, and *Prinz Eugen* had first been sighted from his MTB, he had radioed back their position and an accurate estimate of the speed and course. This information was relayed to the MTBs at Ramsgate and to the waiting Swordfish. These brave naval pilots, with their torpedo-laden aircraft, had been assured of three squadrons of fighter escort, but as Lt-Cdr Esmonde sat in the cockpit of his Swordfish there was no sign of the RAF. The Swordfish took off, and were eventually joined by a single squadron of just eleven Spitfires. Out of eighteen men in 825 NAS, only five survived. Lt-Cdr Esmonde was posthumously awarded the Victoria Cross. Despite being an easy target for the German fighters, the Swordfish all managed to drop their torpedoes before plunging into the sea. The MTB flotilla from Ramsgate had been in action the previous night and was reduced to only three boats. These could make no impression on the outer shield of E-boats, and lacked the speed to give chase.

The grandiose plans of the RAF to provide 250 bombers with a huge fighter cover force had not materialised. Many of the crews had been either stood down or placed on four hours' notice. The Air Ministry had been reluctant to tie down its resources in a permanent state of readiness, believing that they would have several hours' warning to prepare for their bombing attacks on the approaching battlecruisers.

The blunders seemed to multiply as the German fleet raced through the Straits and into the North Sea. RAF Beaufighters at Thorney Island, armed

MTB 74 under way at speed in coastal waters, as converted for the St Nazaire raid. *IWM FL25732*

with torpedoes, had been on standby, but the call to action stations was for some reason delayed, and when it was eventually received their pilots were hopelessly briefed about the speed and nature of their targets. There was also a muddle about their rendezvous with their fighter escort waiting at Manston. Many of the RAF heavy bombers were ill-prepared for the low cloud, being loaded-up with armour-piercing bombs, effective only if released from 7,000ft. Few of the crews had been trained in bombing moving targets.

Admiral Ramsay's destroyers, which had been on stand-by for a week, were despatched from Harwich to intercept the German fleet. Led by Capt Pizey in HMS *Campell*, the destroyers would soon be reduced to five, HMS *Walpole*, with engine trouble, being unable to keep up. On her way back to Harwich, she was bombed by two RAF Wellingtons. Fortunately for *Walpole*, German fighters chased these off before they could inflict any serious damage.

Although HMS *Campbell* was an old ship, she had the latest in radar equipment, and skilfully led the destroyers through the outer screen of E-boats, achieving some element of surprise, as Pizey deployed his destroyers against the battlecruisers. All managed to fire their torpedoes at reasonably close range, but no hits were recorded. HMS *Worcester* was severely damaged, and most of her crew abandoned ship. The rescue operation mounted by HMS *Campbell* to pick up the wounded and other survivors had to be halted when RAF Beaufighters mistakenly attacked her. As well as managing to put out all the fires, HMS *Worcester*'s valiant skeleton crew kept the ship afloat and raised steam, enabling her to limp back to Harwich at 8kt.

Eventually the RAF arrived in three waves of bombers and fighters. Because of the low cloud, only about 40 of the 240 bombers managed to drop their bombs, many failing to locate any target. Only the Beaufighter torpedo-bombers were able to close the targets and release their torpedoes. They were unlucky not to score any hits. The German ships did not escape totally unscathed, however. Earlier in the afternoon, *Scharnhorst* had struck a mine, and

was forced to drop behind the fleet. Both battlecruisers struck more mines, laid off the Frisian Islands by Bomber Command, but they were still able to reach their home port. This begged the question as to why both the Admiralty and the Air

Ministry declined to act on Bomber Command's suggestion that intensive minelaying, ahead of the German squadron, should be carried out by their bombers as an alternative to trying to stop the squadron with bombs in poor visibility.

From a strategic viewpoint, the Allies preferred the battlecruisers away from the Atlantic war, where they had been so successful. There was, however, no disputing Germany's success and the humiliating failure of the British forces on their own doorstep.

ML 268 took part in the St Nazaire raid.

There had been another truly remarkable plan to attempt to inflict serious damage to the *Scharnhorst* and *Gneisenau* with a surface raid while they were on their moorings in the Rade de Brest. This had evolved from an earlier proposal to the Admiralty for a single-handed assault on these great ships, which had originated from R.C.M.V. Wynn.

After Dunkirk, Wynn and another civilian had volunteered to take 18ft Norfolk fishing boats over to Normandy each night for a week, unsuccessfully trying to locate a large contingent of Welsh Guards believed to have been marooned on a beach. At the end of the week they were asked to go and see Admiral Ramsay, who thanked them and then asked whether they would prefer a decoration or a commission in the RNVR. Both chose the latter, and were offered commissions with immediate effect, subject only to a satisfactory medical in London. Wynn then had to admit that he had been invalided

out of the Army. The Admiral queried what was wrong with him, to which Wynn replied that there was nothing wrong with him, but he had never wanted to be in the Army. The Admiral scribbled Wynn a note, and in no time he had sailed through the medical and was an RNVR sub-lieutenant, intent on serving in MTBs. Still operating with private boats, Sub-Lt Wynn continued carrying out landings in occupied France. Never one to rest on his laurels, and looking for more action, he had submitted to the Admiralty an idea for attacking the *Scharnhorst* and *Gneisenau*, which were then still in Brest. To his surprise, he was summoned to the Admiralty to discuss his proposal, which involved being taken over in a submarine, from which a rowing dinghy would be launched carrying a depth-charge.

The Naval Staff (who considered the operation rather hazardous) sent Sub-Lt Wynn away to have lunch, so that both parties might have the opportunity of contemplating what had been put forward. After lunch, Wynn was told that if he still wanted to go ahead they would advise the C-in-C

Plymouth to give him every assistance possible. They then wished him good luck. Perhaps not surprisingly, C-in-C Plymouth felt that Sub-Lt Wynn needed more than a dinghy and a depth-charge. The idea of slipping into Brest on the surface appealed to the Admiralty, but clearly a bigger boat with a bigger charge was needed. A speed-boat was suggested, then a larger speed-boat, and then an experimental stepped-hydroplane. This was the 45ft Thornycroft *MTB 105*, which was subsequently considered unsuitable as it only had a single, trainable torpedo tube.

The Admiralty finally allocated *MTB 74*, a 71ft Vosper, modified for special operations and capable of 45kt. Aerial reconnaissance had shown that the *Scharnhorst* and *Gneisenau* were ringed with three protective booms and netting. *MTB 74* was equipped to cut, lift or jump the booms, and was fitted with 18in torpedo tubes mounted right up on the bow. Torpedoes would be fired by means of compressed air so that they would be projected 150ft through the air, landing inside the innermost protective boom. They would each be charged with 1,200lb of Aminol high explosive, as they were stripped of all internal motive power.

After a great deal of practice, *MTB 74* made a dummy run over to Brest. As the crew were returning home, they heard on the eight o'clock news that *Scharnhorst* and *Gneisenau* had already escaped. The feelings of disappointment must have been acute, but then at that time they did not realise they would soon be involved in the historic raid on St Nazaire, for, just six weeks after Germany's success in the Channel, Combined Operations and Coastal Forces were to take part in Operation *Chariot*. This was to be one of the most daring raids of the Second World War, and would have serious consequences for Germany, affecting the balance of sea power in the Atlantic.

The prime objective of Operation *Chariot* was to breach the caisson or gate in the entrance to a huge dock which was part of the port of St Nazaire, on the west coast of Brittany. Simultaneously, commandos would be landed to demolish the submarine base, which was housed in almost impenetrable concrete shelters, of which more were under construction. Other targets for the commandos were the heavily protected tanks of diesel for the submarines, the hydraulic plant that operated the lock gates, the pumping house, and more locks and bridges. The operation was to prove a spectacular success, but at a devastating cost. Of the 630 officers and men involved (naval and military), 144 were killed and many more taken prisoner. Of the 18 Coastal Forces' craft involved, one had to turn back with engine trouble, ten were sunk or severely damaged by the enemy, four were scuttled, and only three made it back home. In recognition of the bravery on the night of 28/29 March 1942, no fewer than seven Victoria Crosses were awarded. A posthumous VC was received by the family of Able Seaman Savage, for his gallantry, skill and devotion to duty; but the citation went further, adding that this VC was also 'in recognition of the valour shown by many others unnamed in MLs, MGB and MTB, who gallantly carried out their duty in extremely exposed positions against enemy fire at close range'.

It was the sinking, in May 1941, of the 42,000-ton German battleship *Bismarck* that first focussed the attention of Combined Operations Command on St Nazaire. Naval Intelligence thought Germany might have planned to move its battleships to the only French port with a dock large enough to receive either *Bismarck* or her sister ship *Tirpitz*. With much of the German Navy based at St Nazaire, including several squadrons of submarines, the vital Allied transatlantic convoys would be put at considerable risk.

The dock at St Nazaire had been originally built for the *Normandie* which, when she was launched in 1934, was the world's largest liner. In addition to its function as a dry dock, the gates provided large ships access to St Nazaire's inner basins. Several plans to destroy it were discussed in the weeks before Operation *Chariot*. Cdr R.E.D. Ryder, RN, and Lt-Col A.C. Newman, the appointed commanders of the Navy and Army forces respectively, both argued that surprise was crucial to the success of the raid. They believed that this could only be achieved by a force of coastal craft, which might be able to slip through undetected by the known heavy defences on both sides of the Loire estuary. They would then land the assault and demolition commandos, and re-embark them on completion of the raid. Shallow-draught Coastal Forces craft would be able to cross the sandbanks in the approaches to St Nazaire at almost any state of the tide, apart from low water.

MTB 48 (Canadian Lt C.A. Law) was one of the 6th MTB Flotilla craft involved in the attack on the German warships *Scharnhorst*, *Gneisenau* and *Prinz Eugen*.

This would give the force commanders greater flexibility to choose a night when the weather conditions were most favourable.

Those at Combined Operations, however, felt that the main objective of the St Nazaire raid was of such vital importance that an expendable destroyer should be used to breach the outer dock gate. The plan was that, with fused explosives in her bows, the destroyer would approach the gate at sufficient speed to cut through the steel mesh torpedo net protecting the entrance to the dock. With the bows pushed into the lock gate, Special Service troops would then scramble ashore to demolish the dock's hydraulic equipment and pump house.

The Admiralty made available one of the 50 old destroyers, which had been handed over to Britain by the Americans in an exchange for territorial rights, and appointed Lt-Cdr S.H. Beattie, RN, to command her. She had been renamed HMS *Campbeltown*, and work was immediately started to modify her hull for her unique role at St Nazaire. This work would include stripping out much of her interior to lighten ship, armour-plating the bridge, and providing some protection for the commandos on the upper deck. Accompanying the destroyer would be eight MLs, which would carry 150 commandos. The MLs that could be made available at that time were immediately sent to boatyards at Poole, Southampton, and Appledore. Here each would be fitted out with two 20mm Oerlikon guns and additional fuel tanks, mounted on the deck, to give them the necessary range.

Both Cdr Ryder and Lt-Col Newman persuaded Combined Operations Command that more boats and manpower were necessary to achieve the objectives of Operation *Chariot*. With MTBs or MGBs leading the task force, enemy surface craft patrolling the Loire estuary could be rapidly dealt with before they had time to raise the alarm. This posed a problem, because neither gunboats nor torpedo boats could carry sufficient fuel for the

600-mile round-trip passage to and from St Nazaire. In any event, only one of each class could be spared at that time from those craft operating in home waters. To carry the additional commandos, the ML fleet was increased from eight to ten, and then to fourteen by using four MLs then operating out of Dartmouth (these four each carried two 21in torpedoes, and could be fitted with spare petrol-tanks immediately).

MGB 314, commanded by Lt Dunstan Curtis, was a C-Class Fairmile which had been used by Capt Slocum on undercover operations (*see Chapter 10*). With her radar and depth-sounding equipment, *MGB 314* was chosen to lead the attack. On board, in addition to her normal complement, she would carry Cdr Ryder, the war correspondent Gordon Holman, a navigating officer, and a communications officer. When *MTB 74* became available after her preparations for the raid on the Rade de Brest, her selection for Operation *Chariot* was due in part to the persuasive enthusiasm of her commanding officer, Sub-Lt Wynn, or 'Micky' Wynn as he was known to his Coastal Forces' colleagues. *MTB 74* would be at the rear of the task force, when not under tow. Her 'flying' torpedoes, designed for Brest, were unsuitable for St Nazaire, requiring a completely different delayed-action fuse. Unbeknown to Cdr Ryder, because of the time factor the untested fuses were not actually delivered until *MTB 74* had already taken up her tow, and the crew had to half-remove their missiles from the torpedo-tubes to fit the fuses while they were under way.

Sub-Lt Wynn's brief was to provide back-up, and fire his torpedoes at the dry dock caisson if *Campbeltown* failed to clear the sandbanks in the estuary or was stopped by enemy gunfire before reaching the dock. The next option was to fire the torpedoes into the submarine pens, if the commandos were able to open the lock gates into the inner basin. If this was not possible, *MTB 74* would release these charges to destroy the smaller gates near the dry dock.

The fleet assembled at Falmouth on 25 March, leaving the next day with its escort destroyers HMS *Atherstone* and HMS *Tynedale* towing *MGB 314* and *MTB 74*. Just after midnight on 28 March, *MGB 314* had taken up position ahead of *Campbeltown* and two columns of MLs had formed up

behind her, followed by *MTB 74*. A weak signal from the submarine *Sturgeon* had given the navigator of the task force an exact position from which to make his final approach into the Loire estuary. Each boat was flying the German flag to delay recognition of the raiders. Overhead were 35 Whitleys and 25 Wellingtons, taking part in a carefully timed diversionary air raid.

As *Campbeltown* cautiously crept ahead at 5kt across the shoals in the estuary, she touched bottom twice. At 01.20hrs searchlights all the way along the west side of the estuary were switched on, illuminating the entire fleet. Down came their German ensigns, and the white ensign was broken out. They were still two miles from their target.

In 15 minutes of unexpectedly intense shelling from the batteries defending St Nazaire, half the men aboard the MLs were left dead or wounded. The air raid, instead of acting as a diversion, had aroused the suspicions of the commander of the German anti-aircraft batteries, who had closed up all his gun crews. The pilots of the Whitleys and Wellingtons had been briefed to restrict their raid to specific targets, to avoid civilian casualties. Those who located their target bombed singly, which was unusual, while others, failing to locate the target, never released their bombs.

Campbeltown, having cleared the estuary, increased speed to drive her bows through the torpedo barrier and into the dock gate. The scene was by now one of utter devastation, as one by one the MLs were stopped by the shelling. The surface of the water was ablaze, as ignited fuel spread from exploding tanks. Only *ML 177* and *ML 457* succeeded in landing their full complement of commandos. Other MLs had approached the old mole, only to have to re-embark their commandos in the face of heavy fire from 20mm cannon. One boat, on fire and with many casualties, still managed to come alongside to land her three surviving commandos.

An ASDIC operator on *ML 457*, Ordinary Seaman Dyer, later gave a factual account of his own experiences of this night of horror. *457* was the only ML from the port column to land all her commandos. As they disappeared into the night to carry out their demolition assignments, Germans in the pillbox above the mole started to attack the ML by throwing hand-grenades. One grenade exploded on the bridge, seriously wounding the CO and killing one of the crew. Another landed on the foredeck, taking the lives of the First Lieutenant and gun crew. The survivors managed to push their boat away from the mole, but she was soon seriously ablaze. The CO gave the order to abandon ship, and Dyer was one of the lucky ones, managing to reach their Carley float, along with his CO, their signalman, and a wounded seaman. Most of his colleagues had been either burnt to death or drowned. The Carley raft was swept out to sea by the fierce current until they managed to secure a line to the superstructure of a wreck. Unable to release the line as the tide went down, they could no longer remain in the float. The CO, whom Dyer could see was dying, eventually let go of the Carley float and disappeared beneath the water. The signalman too, although apparently unwounded, decided to give up the struggle, said goodbye, and followed his CO.

Dyer was picked up by a German boat at dawn, and taken with other prisoners to an air raid shelter. Here they at least had the satisfaction of hearing *Campbeltown* explode and knowing that the prime purpose of their mission had been achieved. The wounded were then moved to an hotel to receive medical treatment (Dyer went with them, faking his wounds because he thought it would give him a better chance of escaping). This was not to be, and he spent the rest of the war as a POW.

Sub-Lt Wynn in *MTB 74*, had deliberately held back while *Campbeltown* was being driven into the lock gate and the MLs were attempting their landings. He then raced in at high speed through the burning MLs to find *MGB 314*. She was alongside, to the west of *Campbeltown*, having taken off some of the surviving crew. Cdr Ryder despatched *MTB 74* to deposit her delayed-action torpedoes in the foundations to the lock gates leading into a basin that contained the submarine pens. Wynn reported back to Ryder when he had successfully completed the mission, and was told to make for home after embarking an additional 26 survivors. Lord Newborough (as 'Micky' Wynn became after the war) recalled the dreadful decision he had to make as he increased speed, leaving behind the burning hulls of the MLs. Having reached full speed, he saw straight ahead of him two survivors on a Carley float. Should he stop to

pick them up, or carry on and wash them off the float to a certain death by drowning? He stopped, with tragic consequences. No one had realised that the German shore batteries had been following them all the way out into the estuary, but shooting well astern of the fast-moving target. Immediately *MTB 74* stopped, shells hammered straight into the hull, setting the boat on fire. Wynn was blown from the bridge and through the wheelhouse, finishing up below decks. He owed his life to his chief motor mechanic, Bill Lovegrove, who, before jumping overboard, realised he had not seen his CO. Seeking out the seriously wounded Wynn, he managed to get him on deck and then over to the Carley float. By 1400 hrs the next day, there were only four survivors out of the 36 that had been aboard *MTB 74*. One of them died just before a rescue vessel drew alongside the float.

Sub-Lt Wynn spent the next two years in hospitals and prisoner-of-war camps, including the infamous Colditz Castle, during which time he was promoted to lieutenant. He got back home six months before the end of the war, and after two weeks returned to Germany to help in the relief of a naval POW camp, where he found Bill Lovegrove, who was sick, and brought him home.

Two days after *Campbeltown*'s charges had so effectively exploded, the delay fuses were activated in the charges left by *MTB 74* outside the entrance to the inner basin. Operation *Chariot* had been a brilliant success. What came to be known as 'the greatest raid of all' had permanently destroyed the largest dry dock in Europe and damaged much else of a port that, with its commanding position on the Atlantic seaboard, the German Navy had valued highly. After uninterrupted German domination of the war in Europe, Britain had at last been able to demonstrate, to both the enemy and occupied Europe, that its courage and determination to succeed remained undiminished.

Four months later, no amount of censored news coverage could dispel the belief that all the euphoria after St Nazaire had been somewhat premature, when Coastal Forces were involved in the infamous Dieppe raid. Though it is now recognised to have been a tragic error of judgement, which served only to restore some of Hitler's complacency regarding the defences of 'Fortress Europe', some historians nevertheless still

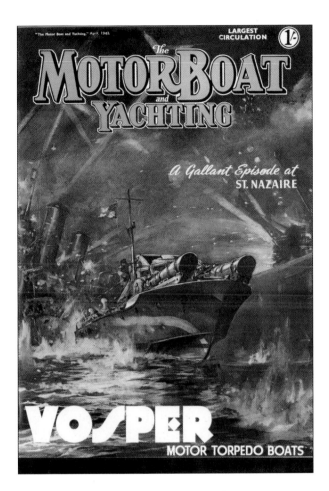

An artist's impression of *MTB 74* in battle at St Nazaire. *Motor Boat and Yachting*

spring to the defence of Churchill and his head of Combined Operations, Admiral Lord Mountbatten, who authorised the operation, claiming that the large-scale attempt to land troops at Dieppe was an invaluable test of the enemy's defences. The lessons learned on 19 August 1942 would certainly influence plans already being considered for the 1944 invasion of Normandy, but the cost of the Dieppe raid was tragic. A little over 2,000 troops returned from the 5,000 that took part, the fatalities totalling almost 900. The Royal Navy lost a destroyer and 34 landing craft.

Twenty-six Coastal Forces craft, consisting of MLs, MGBs, SGBs, and French *chasseurs*, were involved in Operation *Jubilee*, as the Dieppe raid was code-named. Rescue Motor Launches (RMLs) were from the 61st ML Flotilla, which worked closely with the RAF's 11 Group Fighter Command to provide extensive cover for the large number of

bombers and fighters involved. Coastal Forces would be deployed to lead the assault craft in to the beaches. Of necessity, they were also used to lay protective smoke-screens. They marked the entrances to swept channels, and attempted to attack shore defences with their limited firepower. Several MLs were damaged by the shore batteries and by air attacks, but MLs *292* and *190* both succeeded in shooting down enemy aircraft. A German trawler sank many of the landing craft in one of the flotillas, which was being escorted by a steam gunboat. Having become separated from a flotilla of landing craft, *ML 346* distinguished herself by attacking a 200-ton armed German tanker and driving her onto the beach.

The raid was thus faced with very much stronger resistance than had been anticipated and, with a large number of Canadian troops pinned down on the beaches, the decision was made before noon to start withdrawing as many men as possible. Operation *Jubilee* had failed.

No account of wartime Coastal Forces in home waters would be complete without the stories of Dieppe, St Nazaire, and the battle in the Dover Straits against *Scharnhorst*, *Gneisenau* and *Prinz Eugen*; but these were not typical of the war that was fought by the 'Little Ships'. Perhaps one of the attractions for those who served in Coastal Forces was that, until towards the end of the war, they mostly worked independently of other ships in the Royal Navy, and most of their operations were by night.

Officers destined for Coastal Forces were now pouring out of HMS *King Alfred*. The training establishment at Fort William, HMS *St Christopher*, had 24 MLs, together with some MTBs, and was turning out crews every week for new boats being launched all around the British Isles. HMS *Bee*, the Coastal Forces' working-up base at Weymouth and, later, at Holyhead, had built up effective training programmes to bring together ship and crew to form single fighting units. In addition new tactics were being developed to fight the German convoys and their escorts, and with ever-increasing frequency boats were returning to their bases to report successful engagements. Almost imperceptibly at first, superiority in the North Sea and English Channel was being wrested from the German E-boats, convoy escorts, and patrols.

Chapter Nine

E-boats on the Run

One wit suggested that in the earlier part of the war in the North Sea, all the E-boats had to do was to position themselves off Ijmuiden and fire their torpedoes down 'E-boat Alley' towards Lowestoft and Great Yarmouth, and they would almost certainly hit something. Although this suggestion was far-fetched, it highlighted the vulnerability of the East Coast convoys.

Approximately three nights in every week, for much of the war, there would be a convoy of about 50 ships heading north and another heading south. Because of the sandbanks off the East Coast, these convoys could only be two columns wide, resulting in two lines of ships, eight or nine miles long. A

Hichens briefs COs in the Ops Room at HMS *Beehive* in 1943.

Lt Peter Dickens on the bridge of an MTB.
IWM 12526

convoy would rarely have more than about ten escorts, which might be made up of two or three old V and W Class destroyers and some poorly armed MLs. One veteran remembers his Fairmile B being fitted with an old semi-automatic 3pdr forward, with a firing rate of about ten rounds a minute, which might well have been acquired from a museum or barracks; the ML also had a machine gun or two, and an 'awful' 2pdr automatic aft, which jammed so often that they usually never even bothered to uncover it at sea.

In response to the appalling losses of ships and men in the convoys, a new concept of offshore patrolling was introduced in 1942 by C-in-C Nore, to provide a protective outer shield. This was known as the Z-line, which was an imaginary line

about 30 miles off the East Coast, running for a distance of approximately 100 miles between Cromer and Harwich. MGBs, MLs, and the occasional RML, from Felixstowe, Lowestoft, and Great Yarmouth would position themselves at regular intervals along the line, to provide the first line of defence for the convoys. Occasionally these defences might be reinforced by a patrolling destroyer or armed trawler.

The gaps in the Z-line were certainly large enough for an E-boat to slip through undetected, but it provided something of a deterrent. Once on station, the boats cut their engines and prepared for

Coastal Forces craft in the dock at Felixstowe with the crews and shore-based staff of engine room artificers and shipwrights carrying out routine work on board. *IWM A20516*

Robert Hichens (left) and Peter Dickens.

a night spent wallowing uncomfortably in the swell. They would start up only to move back if they had drifted off station with the wind and tide. A hydrophone would be lowered over the side. This was a crude but effective listening device, consisting of a 12ft steel pole, with a receiver on one end in the water, and a pair of headphones at the other end. This equipment could pick up the sound of propeller noises within a range of about two miles, or more in the case of a big ship or a fast-moving one. The deck-watch would take turns to listen, while others kept a look-out for the phosphorescent wake of moving surface craft.

The Z-patrols were the less glamorous side of Coastal Forces. Often operating in cold and wet conditions, in boats particularly prone to rolling, many of the crews would spend night after night, without ever seeing friend or foe. Z-patrols were not, however, entirely without incident. The crew of one boat, picking up propeller noises on the

hydrophone, alerted the look-out that there might be an E-boat in the vicinity. Night glasses scanned the sea for the tell-tale phosphorescence, but nothing was to be seen. The hydrophone operator was by then reporting regularly that the propeller sound was growing louder and louder. The final report, that the propeller must now be very close, was immediately followed by a crash and violent rocking motion. A German mini-submarine had collided with them. The two-man crew managed to scuttle their submarine before surrendering.

There was a famous encounter with E-boats by two MLs out on Z-patrol. It serves as a good example of the hand-to-hand fighting with which Coastal Forces was associated, more so than any other branch of the Royal Navy. The MLs had received a signal directing them to a position where E-boats were believed to be operating. *ML 150* (Lt J.O. Thomas, RNVR) and *ML 145* (Lt R.F. Seddon, RNVR) turned off to the south, making top speed into the heavy seas, with the gun crews closed up. E-boats, on the starboard bow, and travelling at high speed, were spotted by the leading boat. Lt Thomas immediately challenged them to identify themselves, and then opened fire, hitting the second E-boat, which was approaching on an ideal course for ramming amidships. As the two craft met, there was a terrific crash, with metal and wood flying everywhere. The E-boat (*S96*) bounced clear, and then attempted to withdraw, with smoke pouring out of her. *ML 145* went after the maimed E-boat, and succeeded in ramming her in the bows. A third E-boat then appeared, but both MLs were able to keep her at a distance with their gunfire, and she withdrew behind a smoke-screen. There was no opportunity to land a boarding party on *S96*, her crew jumping into the water just before she exploded, scuttled by detonating explosives in the bilges (standard equipment on an E-boat). It took the MLs about an hour to pick up all the survivors. Thirteen of the E-boat crew were rescued by *ML 145*, including the Senior Officer of the 4th Schnellboot Flotilla, who had been aboard as a passenger. He told Lt Seddon that when *ML 145* was virtually alongside after the ramming, he had reached for grenades which he normally carried on the bridge of his boat. There were none – if there had been, he would have had no hesitation in lobbing them into the ML's bridge. Three prisoners had also been taken aboard *ML 150*. Lt Thomas recalled that he went to check on them in the wardroom to find them comfortably wrapped in his blankets, and listening, with their armed guard, to his records, on his record player. The MLs were badly damaged in the encounter; *145* managed to limp back under her own steam, but *150* had to be towed back, stern first, by a passing MGB.

About 10 miles behind the Z-line was an inner line, with boats on station at much wider intervals, but available to come to the assistance of craft on the Z-line. The effect of this defensive deployment of Coastal Forces was a gradual reduction in the merchant ship tonnage claimed by E-boats. By the end of 1943 it had even become noticeable that E-boats were reluctant to adopt their previous offensive strategy, of lying in wait for a target to come within range. By this time they were more inclined to launch a swift torpedo attack against a substantial target, and only when they could make an equally rapid withdrawal. They were also finding it much harder to slip through the Z-line to lay mines in the East Coast convoy routes.

In its offensive role, Coastal Forces was undergoing change. Many of the young RNVR officers assigned to boats in the early part of the war would admit that they attacked largely on instinct, making up their tactics as they went along. There was no HMS *Bee* at this stage (the working-up base was not established until mid-1942), and a general lack of experience in Coastal Forces warfare. Robert Hichens was proving to be a fine leader and teacher in MGBs, with a natural flair for combat. He had many ideas of how to improve both the performance of the craft in his MGB flotilla, and the young officers who served in them. He could have taken a shore job with promotion, training the new crews. Instead, he chose to stay at sea, participating in 148 operations until, on 13 April 1943, a stray cannon shell killed him instantaneously.

James Shadbolt, an RNVR midshipman at the time, recalls that fateful night off the Dutch coast. After spending the first nine months of his war service in a Hunt-Class destroyer, Shadbolt gained his commission in 1942, and was appointed to Coastal Forces. He joined HMS *Beehive*, the Felixstowe MTB and MGB base, early in the New Year, as spare officer to an MTB flotilla. He was then appointed to *MGB 111* to replace the First

Lieutenant, who had become ill while the boat was working-up at HMS *Bee*. *MGB 111* was one of the British Power Boat purpose-built gunboats, replacing the older converted MA/SBs in Hichens' 8th MGB Flotilla. Her commanding officer was Lt T.J. Mathias. Having completed the work-up, *MGB 111* went round to Felixstowe at a time when boats of the 8th MGB Flotilla were frequently out at sea, hunting E-boats off the Dutch coast or 10–20 miles off Felixstowe.

At 0311hrs on 13 April, MGBs *74*, *75*, *111*, and *112* were patrolling off the Dutch coast when the leading boat picked up a radar echo, bearing Red 10 (10 degrees to port), distance 2,000yd. The echo altered rapidly to Red 20, 1,000yd. At 0318hrs two ships were sighted, 2½ cables away, signalling to each other with blue lights. The visibility was by then down to 3 cables. The MGBs altered course at 0320hrs, but almost immediately lost radar and visual contact. At 0343hrs engines were stopped to use the hydrophone, which picked up the sound of reciprocating engines of a moving vessel. At 0355hrs, radar contact was regained at 1,000yd.

Five minutes later, an armed trawler and a smaller vessel were in sight. Lt-Cdr Hichens, aboard *112* in his capacity as Senior Officer, had taken up his usual position during an action. He would stand on top of the wheelhouse with his arms around the mast, with an extended voice-pipe going down to the coxswain. Directing the flotilla by giving orders to the coxswain and flashing appropriate signals to the boats following, Hichens approached up-wind of the enemy with his boats in line ahead. They closed to within 100yd before the enemy became aware of their presence. The gunboats increased their speed to 20kt and opened fire with all guns, including an experimental weapon called the Blacker Bombard. This was a simple spigot mortar, originally designed for the Home Guard, which literally threw its bomb at the enemy, but was only effective when used at very close range.

However, early in the action, as *112* was rapidly closing the enemy, Hichens was killed. James Shadbolt in *MGB 111* remembers that there was considerable confusion as his boat followed *112*, making her run across the bows of the heavily-armed flak trawler. The MGBs met strong resistance, with heavy return fire from the trawler. With the C.O. and First Lieutenant also wounded, a spare

HMS *Hornet*, Gosport, packed with Coastal Forces craft in 1944. 'Pneumonia Bridge', in the background, open to the elements, was used on shore leave to reach the centre of Gosport and the Portsmouth ferries. *IWM A25146*

officer in *MGB 112* assumed command, disengaging at 30kt. *MGB 111* followed *112*, turning to port to disengage. MGBs *74* and *75* lost touch, as they too withdrew. The armed trawler was seen to be on fire. This was the first occasion the Blacker Bombard had been used in action, and it was thought this was perhaps a major cause of the damage to the trawler. Nevertheless, its experimental use aboard MGBs was not considered a great success and was shortly thereafter discontinued.

Three miles away from the action, but still under fire, *111* had reached the rendezvous where she found *112* stopped. Hailing her commanding officer, Lt Sidebottom, Mathias received no reply, and decided to manoeuvre alongside so that his First Lieutenant could establish what was happening. James Shadbolt remembers climbing up to the bridge of *112*, where an RAF officer, who had come for the ride as a passenger, told him that his foot was bleeding profusely into his boot. He said that 'Hitch' had been killed, and was lying in the chartroom. Shadbolt quickly examined his Senior Officer, and then went down below and found Lt Sidebottom seriously wounded. After administering two ampoules of morphia, Shadbolt reported the situation to Lt Mathias, and suggested he should remain on board *112* and keep station astern of *111*. Lt Mathias, however, told him to return to *111* as he was required to navigate the boats (now also including *74* and *75*) back to Felixstowe.

As the boats motored towards the English coast, a routine action report was radioed back to *Beehive*. The report included details of the casualties. James Shadbolt recalls that just after dawn the whole of *Beehive* turned out to witness the return of the much-loved and admired Hichens.

HMS *Beehive* was devasted by the news of Hichens' death. A fortnight afterwards, Peter Scott made a BBC broadcast in which he referred to Hichens as a man whose name had become a byword in Coastal Forces, and whose leadership, dash, and determination had been inspirational. He went on to say that Hichens left a rich legacy - the fruits of his

MA/SB 31 and MTBs in the train-ferry dock at Dover, with camouflage netting above.
Dover Express

energy in the development of the boats, and his experience in the way they should be handled, 'and then that other thing – an example of courage that makes people think as they go into action, "This would have been a mere nothing to Hitch."'

A new name in MTBs had emerged in 1942 – Lt Peter Dickens, RN. Hichens and Dickens had actually met, albeit briefly, in the early part of the war. Dickens, son of an admiral and great-grandson of the novelist Charles Dickens, was serving as First Lieutenant of the Hunt-Class destroyer *Cotswold*. On 20 April 1942, on convoy escort duties off the East Coast, *Cotswold* was seriously mined along with another destroyer and two merchant ships. One of the boats involved in rescuing her crew was an MGB commanded by Robert Hichens.

Lt Dickens was appointed Senior Officer of the 21st MTB Flotilla in the early summer of 1942, based initially at Portsmouth, then Dartmouth, before finally moving round to the East Coast and establishing his flotilla at HMS *Beehive*. The Dutch coast became his main hunting-ground, and it was here that Hichens and Dickens, as Senior Officer MGBs and MTBs respectively, would develop what proved to be a highly successful strategy. Time and time again, MTBs would leave their base with information about enemy shipping on the move. They would be joined by MGBs. While the MTBs were held back, the MGBs would engage the convoy escorts, giving the MTBs the opportunity of a close-range torpedo attack. As the numbers of short MTBs increased, it was Lt Dickens who worked out and practised the tactic of splitting up his flotilla to make simultaneous torpedo attacks from different directions.

The arrival of the D-Class Fairmile provided a new permutation of the already well-established and successful battle strategy. The first D-Class MTB was launched towards the end of 1941, and by the end of 1943 there were nine D-Class flotillas operating in home waters. The 'Dog-boat' would ultimately be built to combine the roles of MTB and MGB; 228 were commissioned in home waters. Armament and crew strength changed considerably as the boats were developed to carry out their dual-purpose role, the last Dog-boat design boasting formidable firepower, with two 6pdrs, a twin 20mm Oerlikon, two twin 0.5in machine guns, and two twin 0.303in machine guns. With their four 18in torpedoes, displacement had increased from 90 tons to 105. The crews of the later boats were doubled to 30, and the speed was reduced to about 30kt maximum.

One of many famous names associated with Dog-boats was Lt-Cdr Donald Gould Bradford, RNR, who was awarded his first of three DSCs for ramming a German E-boat and then turning his boat's guns on more E-boats. He had been a third mate in the Merchant Navy, but jumped ship in Argentina to work on a cattle ranch. He joined logging gangs in Brazil, served in the Bolivian Army in the war against Paraguay, then enlisted in the cavalry of the Spanish Republican Army during the Spanish Civil War, being wounded twice. He returned to Britain at the outbreak of the Second World War, only to be turned down by both the Army and the RAF because of the unorthodox nature of his previous military career. However, because of the time he had served in the Merchant Navy he was eligible to join the RNR. He was in his early thirties when he took command of *MTB 617*, from which he flew a pennant depicting a dagger in blood, which was also painted on her side. His most famous exploits were in the 55th MTB Flotilla, which operated in the North Sea and the Channel in 1943–4. This flotilla of Dog-boats was easily recognised by the red shark's mouth painted on the bows of each boat.

Dog-boats could operate in weather that would keep the short MTBs and MGBs in harbour. With their heavier displacement, they provided much more steady gun platforms. The 'Shorts', however, given reasonable sea conditions, were much faster, some with top speeds of over 40kt. By the end of 1943 there was officially no longer any distinction between MGBs and MTBs, long or short – all were classified as MTBs.

Numerically, the highly popular Dog-boats represented only a small proportion of the 'Little Ships'. On the German side, the same could be said of E-boats. Although it was the E-boats and their dashing commanders that usually grabbed the headlines, the total wartime output of these fine craft, right up to the last launching in April 1945, was only 217. These had to be assigned to many different areas, and there were never more than, at most, six flotillas available for operations in the 'Narrow Seas'. There were, of course, many other small ships in the German Navy, carrying out duties similar to those undertaken by British Coastal Forces. Germany's shipyards built around 300 R-boats (*Raumboote*), which were similar to the MLs except that they were more heavily armed, and with a much greater displacement and crew. They were used for minesweeping, minelaying, and as escorts for coastal convoys. By comparison, approximately 350 B-Class Fairmiles were built in the British Isles, along with 250 HDMLs. Germany's large fleet of M-Class sweepers (*Minensuchboote*), often used as patrols and escorts, were another formidable opponent, more heavily armed and faster than the Royal Navy's J-Class fleet sweepers. They also had flak trawlers, or VP (*Vorposten*) boats, which were difficult, in fact well nigh impossible, adversaries for British Coastal Forces to cope with. Big trawlers designed for Icelandic waters, they were exceptionally well armed, heavily armour-plated, and had their hulls strengthened with concrete. In addition they had a tall mast that gave them a radar range much greater than an MTB's. Coastal Forces gunfire alone could make little impression on them. There were several VP flotillas working out of North Sea and Channel ports, each with 12 boats. Those based at Ijmuiden were nicknamed the 'Four Horsemen of the Apocalypse', because they operated in packs of four.

For much of the war, the prize of capturing one of the much-admired E-boats intact would elude Coastal Forces. MGBs led by Hichens were responsible for the only E-boat casualty (*S41*) of 1941, and throughout the whole of 1942 Germany lost only two in the 'Narrow Seas' – *S53*, mined off Dover, and *S111*, sunk by HMS *Guillemot*. However, 1943 marked a great change in the E-boats' fortunes. As many as 19 were lost that year, some in engagements with Coastal Forces, some to mines, and others to the RAF. With so many commitments elsewhere, the German Navy found itself struggling to maintain a reasonable strength of E-boats operating in the Channel and the North Sea. Their 6th Flotilla had left Ijmuiden for the Baltic, and some of the remaining E-boats were frequently required in a defensive role, to protect the increasing number of coastal convoys necessitated by the RAF's dislocation of Germany's road and rail transport systems. Unlike the British coastal convoys, Germany's merchant ships would travel in twos and threes, mostly by day and making only short passages between ports, encircled by as many as a dozen heavily-armed escorts.

Those in Coastal Forces had a certain admiration for the German *Schnellboote*. Until purpose-built gunboats were introduced and the D-Class Fairmiles, E-boats were superior in virtually every department. With their round-bilge hulls, they were able to operate in almost any weather. In addition,

Landing blindfolded German personnel who were captured from an E-boat after it was rammed and set ablaze by *ML 145* on the morning of 25 September 1943. *IWM AX55A*

their lightweight Mercedes-Benz diesel engines were not only highly reliable but were much less of a fire risk than the high-octane petrol engines used in Coastal Forces. However, diesel was liable to explode on receiving a direct hit, whereas petrol (except when tanks were empty but for vapour) was of too rich a mixture to explode. In addition E-boats were dreadful in a following sea and, of course, rolled much more; this made them notoriously poor gun-platforms, and it was often noticed that much of their gunfire went high overhead. It was when advancing into head seas that they were best able to demonstrate their superiority.

E-boat commanders frequently gave the impression that they wished to avoid head-on confrontation with their British counterparts. With their numbers dwindling, they had to observe strict guidelines on the size of vessel they would attack with their torpedoes. The E-boats were too valuable to risk in a battle against something their own size; this explains the numerous reported sightings of *Schnellboote* making a high-speed withdrawal.

German *Schnellboote* in line-ahead.

There were similar restraints operating in Coastal Forces. Ian Trelawny recalls an incident in October 1943. He had taken over the 11th MTB Flotilla to continue the run of success achieved by Peter Dickens, who had left *Beehive* to join the training staff at HMS *Bee*. Trelawny was out in *MTB 356*, in company with two more *Beehive* MTBs. As usual, at the bottom of his operating orders was 'patrols to be avoided' and, as they were carrying the new Mk 8 torpedoes, they were under strict instructions not to fire them at any target less than 12,000 tons, which reserved these treasured missiles for use against a big cruiser or an equivalent-sized merchant ship. Due to poor visibility, the three MTBs found themselves inside a protective screen of heavily armed enemy trawlers. They were soon spotted by one of the *Vorpostenboote*, which challenged the MTBs and received from *MTB 356*'s telegraphist a reply which seemed to satisfy her.

The MTBs then took up positions as though they were a part of the protective escort. The trawler became suspicious, and flashed an alternative challenge for which the MTBs had no reply, and they were soon under a heavy bombardment. Ian Trelawny described the sinking of his boat as 'like something out of the Keystone Cops'. One moment his boat was making 40kt, and the next she had been abruptly stopped by two shells, one through the stern and the other through a petrol tank. Seeing his SO's boat sinking fast, Lt Peter Magnus, in *MTB 349*, quickly closed to take off the crew, while the other MTB made smoke. However, the trawler, keen to finish the job, was approaching at speed and still firing into the wreckage of *MTB 356*. She presented a perfect target to Lt Magnus in *349*. He fired a torpedo and sank the vessel. When they returned to base, Lt Trelawny had much explaining to do. Why had he failed to avoid a patrol, and why had a Mk 8 torpedo been fired at a target of less than 12,000 tons? The incidents were considered serious enough to be the subject of a report in writing that found its way up to the C-in-C Nore. Trelawny survived these tribulations, and is a name long associated with Felixstowe, both for his service during the war and subsequently for his

Peter Dickens briefs his MTB COs at HMS *Beehive*, Felixstowe. *IWM D12517*

association with the docks where he took over the virtually derelict quays and buildings and changed the place into Britain's largest container port.

In spite of the tendency for E-boat commanders to avoid confrontation, many in Coastal Forces had considerable respect for their opposite numbers. There was an unusual familiarity between some of the E-boats and COs and SOs of some of the British flotillas. The enemy became known by the names they used to communicate with each other over the radio. Curiously, the E-boat officers were not very security-minded in the use of radio, and there was useful information to be gleaned from this source.

In some Coastal Forces flotillas the Senior Officer's boat might carry a 'headache' operator – a German speaking civilian, dressed up as an RNVR officer – who could immediately translate messages picked up on the RT. Occasionally these operators transmitted a message in German to confuse the enemy, and if they were very fortunate they might succeed in diverting enemy escorts in a totally different direction.

Ian Trelawny recalled one unfortunate E-boat commander who was always getting lost, and breaking radio silence with a plea for directions to rejoin his flotilla. In 1944, Peter Scott, then on the staff of Captain Coastal Forces (Channel), introduced a book at *Hornet*, in which any information about E-boat personnel could be entered, to build up an impression of the various personalities ranged against them.

It would be wrong, though, to suggest that this flow of information was all in one direction. Many of the Senior Officers and their boats were well known to the Germans, and were sometimes mentioned by name on news bulletins.

There was also much useful intelligence to be gleaned from prisoners, some willing to give much more information than name, rank, and number. A famous Coastal Forces story is told by Christopher Dreyer. In September 1944, two Dog-boats –

MTB 724 (Lt J.F. Humphreys, RNVR) and *MTB 728* (Lt F.N. Thomson, RNVR) – in the company of the frigate *Stayner*, reduced the enemy's ever-dwindling number of E-boats by three. All were sunk, two as a result of colliding with each other. Sixty prisoners were taken, including the legendary, and much-decorated Kapitänleutnant Karl Müller, commander of the 10th Schnellboot Flotilla. 'Charlie' Müller, as the British nicknamed him, was well known to Coastal Forces for his numerous daring exploits.

It was customary for all prisoners to be interrogated. In view of his rank and reputation, 'Charlie' Müller was first interviewed at a POW camp by Lt-Cdr Peter Scott, who spent about three hours with him, talking mostly about the technical aspects of E-boats. Müller had indicated that he was ready to talk about anything, as long as he did not endanger the lives of his E-boat colleagues still afloat. A week later, Scott invited Christopher Dreyer to join him for a further visit to the POW camp. Naval Intelligence had confirmed they required no more information from Müller and that

both Scott and Dreyer were free to talk with him on any topic they chose. This was, of course, after D-Day, with the war in the North Sea in its last throes. Dreyer remembered him as a pleasant man, perhaps in his late twenties, who showed great charm and spoke English fluently. Their discussions were both wide-ranging and detailed, and in 10 hours much had been learned about the operation of each other's Coastal Forces. Müller then returned to his POW camp, where Scott sent him a first draft of his classic account of Coastal Forces, *Battle of the Narrow Seas*. A stickler for accuracy, Scott asked 'Charlie' Müller to check through the text from the German viewpoint. This publication had been commissioned by the Admiralty, which had yet to have it read for any contents that might have to be censored. One can only imagine the colour of the faces of some of those in Naval Intelligence when, within a matter of weeks, Kapitänleutnant

Kapitänleutnant Helmut Dross and the crew of *S220*, which was sunk north-east of Ostend on 2 March 1945.

Müller was back in the war, on the staff of the Führer der Schnellbooten, for the few remaining E-boat actions in the North Sea. According to Peter Scott he had been on the point of being shipped to a POW camp in the United States when a volunteer had been requested for repatriation to Germany in exchange for an important politician. Karl Müller had been only too pleased to volunteer.

In mid-November 1943, Christopher Dreyer had returned to the UK after eventful and distinguished service in the Mediterranean. He was invalided home, and after sick leave was posted to the Admiralty to write the Confidential Book on the operation of Coastal Forces craft. When he had completed the first draft, at the end of February, he joined the C-in-C Portsmouth's staff. The Admiralty had created a new appointment – Captain Coastal Forces (Channel), and Dreyer was to join as his Staff

Officer. For about 18 months there had been a Captain Coastal Forces (Nore), with responsibility for the East Coast. The new appointment was created to prepare Coastal Forces for the invasion.

They moved into the C-in C's headquarters in a maze of underground tunnels and rooms beneath Fort Southwick, high up on the South Downs over-looking Portsmouth harbour. When Dreyer took up the appointment he had no idea that they would have just three months to prepare Coastal Forces for their role in Operation *Overlord* – the invasion of France.

The responsibility of Captain Coastal Forces (Channel) was to control from shore all Coastal Forces' operations in the Portsmouth Command, and co-ordinate Coastal Forces in the Dover and Plymouth Commands. He would also have responsibility for the co-ordination of all the shore

Vorpostenboot – one of the heavily armed and strengthened Icelandic trawlers used so effectively by the Germans. *Bundesarchiv MW 5077/34*

those who manned the plot 'round the clock', together with liaison officers of Allied navies and communications experts. Christopher Dreyer invited Peter Scott to join the team, which also included Lt-Cdr F.H. Dunlop, RN, who co-ordinated the communications, and Lt-Cdr R.S. Bickerton, RN, an engineer with responsibility for the logistics of gathering and maintaining the largest-ever assembly of Coastal Forces craft. A hundred MTBs had to be accommodated. At *Hornet* in Haslar Creek every foot of space was used, and the boats were soon overflowing down the creek, berthing in their dozens in space normally occupied by submarines at HMS *Dolphin*. More were assembling across the water at the torpedo school, HMS *Vernon*. Another hundred MTBs would be available from Dover, Newhaven, Portland, and Plymouth, along with 200 MLs and HDMLs, 50 US PT boats, and 50 newly arrived US Coastguard cutters.

Christopher Dreyer remembered the three months' planning before D-Day as being an awe-inspiring period, as he became more conscious every day of the enormity of the invasion plans. As the planning reached an ever greater level of intensity, more and more people both at Fort Southwick and at General Eisenhower's head-quarters at nearby Southwick House became aware of both the place and the planned timing of D-Day. It is remarkable that, with so many in the know, the plans for Operation *Overlord* were never discovered by the Germans.

On the first night of the invasion, 96 of the 100 MTBs in Portsmouth Command were out, protecting the west flank of the five mine-swept channels (known as the 'Spout') over to the Normandy beaches. The MTBs and destroyers attached to the actual task forces involved in the landings would take care of the E-boats at Le Havre. The eastern flank of the 'Spout' would be the responsibility of MTBs and MLs in the Dover Command, which were deployed with frigates (a tactic in Coastal Forces' warfare that had been successfully introduced in the months before D-Day). The MTBs would be controlled by Coastal Forces officers on board patrolling frigates fitted

plots, which would show every ship operating in the Channel. This was a new concept in naval warfare, made possible by the considerable improvements in communications and radar, both ashore and at sea. Similar plots would be maintained at Dover and Plymouth, as well as the sub-commands at Newhaven and Portland. The radar was a joint-service network, with the RAF supplying much of the information. The plotting room in each command and sub-command consisted of a huge table chart, surrounded by plot operators from the WRNS, with some WAAFs and ATS. They would be fed the information from the radar stations by land line, which then had to be plotted, interpreted and, when necessary, passed on to patrols in the Channel.

The Captain Coastal Forces (Channel) built up an operational team of about ten. There were also

Coastal Forces craft of the 55th Flotilla assembled in Haslar Creek, Portsmouth Harbour, in June 1944. *IWM A23968*

with the latest and best radar. Lt-Cdr D.G. Bradford, with his 55th Flotilla, was particularly successful in protecting this eastern flank in the assault area, fighting off E-boats and minelayers in a ferocious battle that actually extended into a German minefield, where the MTBs inadvertently triggered off 23 mines, but none close enough to do any serious damage. In subsequent combat off Cap d'Antifer, his flotilla sank two E-boats and a frigate.

Routinely, during Operation *Overlord*, all relevant naval information from the previous 24 hours, together with the latest intelligence reports, would be incorporated into the plans for the next 24-hour period. SOs and COs of the Coastal Forces craft, and of destroyers and frigates working with them, would attend daily briefings at HMS *Dolphin*.

In *Battle of the Narrow Seas*, Peter Scott pays tribute to Christopher Dreyer:

> As Senior Staff Officer to CCF, it was Lt Dreyer who usually carried out this briefing. When I was at Portsmouth he and I took it in turns, but while I had been in France he had done it almost without a break day after day, taking up his station on the plot in the tunnel later each night. It was hard work and a heavy responsibility, but none realised better than the officers who assembled daily in that little room at *Dolphin*, to carry out the operations he had planned, how much of their success depended on the work of Christopher Dreyer. It was during this last and most active week of all that his work showed its most spectacular results, although the planning which led to the successful defence of the invasion convoys, and in which Dreyer played so important a part, had no doubt a greater influence on the war.

Operation *Neptune*, which was the code-name for the naval involvement in Operation *Overlord*, included the provision of the two artificial Mulberry Harbours, and spanned a period of around three weeks. During this time, Coastal Forces were constantly on the alert for enemy shipping on both flanks. The total number of E-boats operating in the Channel was 34, with five being repaired. To the east of the invasion beaches, Germany was

Boats of Lt-Cdr Bradford's 55th Flotilla, with their distinctive shark's teeth decoration, worked with the Canadian 29th Flotilla to protect the eastern flank of the British assault area during the D-Day landings. *IWM A23969*

assembling as many ships as possible in Le Havre, where the 4th E-boat Flotilla was based. To the west, the 5th Flotilla (Korvettenkapitän Johannsen) and 9th Flotilla (Korvettenkapitän Berndt Klug) were operating out of Cherbourg, and there was always the possibility of the German Navy bringing submarines and destroyers round from the west coast of France. Considering the huge armada of ships assembled for the landings, it was remarkable in the event that the German Navy achieved so few successful strikes. Coastal Forces were duly recognised as having provided highly effective protection on both flanks of the landing area.

The E-boats were soon to be dealt a terrible blow at Le Havre. With the Americans driving on,

overland to surround Cherbourg, the 5th and 9th E-Boat Flotillas were transferred to Le Havre. Shortly after their arrival, Air Chief Marshal Sir Arthur 'Bomber' Harris authorised a highly controversial air raid on Le Havre, carried out by 325 Lancasters on the night of 14/15 June. The town and port were very badly damaged, together with much of the shipping in harbour, including 15 E-boats.

By the last days of August, there was no enemy left in the Channel. Many MTBs were moved back to the East Coast, from where operated until the end of the war. The few remaining E-boats were still launching spirited attacks on the East Coast convoy route, and carrying out minelaying operations. In January 1945 there were just 27 boats in the North Sea, making up five flotillas based at Den Helder, Ijmuiden, and Rotterdam. By April, their number had been reduced to 15. Throughout the last months of fighting, their use was severely restricted by a scarcity of both fuel and torpedoes. The war in the 'Narrow Seas' was over.

Chapter Ten

Undercover Operations

Anyone listening to the radio during the Second World War might have been intrigued by the coded messages which followed the World News. The BBC was used extensively to pass on information to the Resistance in enemy-occupied France. A cryptic phrase might indicate that an agent was to be landed under cover of darkness or it might be confirmation that an MGB would be anchored close inshore off North Brittany to embark a party of escaping airmen.

Coastal Forces were much used for such clandestine operations, which were almost always carried out at night. Though their objectives varied, their execution was invariably dangerous. The boats were used to land or take off agents, and to bring arms and other supplies to Resistance groups operating behind enemy lines. A motor gunboat invariably formed the last link in one of the highly successful escape routes organised by the French Resistance to repatriate literally hundreds of RAF and USAAF aircrew who had bailed out over France.

Specially trained commandos were also ferried across the Channel by MTB, and then landed in occupied France. Sometimes their raids were designed for the sole purpose of unsettling the enemy and restoring the morale of the local population; at other times the objective would be to demolish strategic targets such as radio stations and, if possible, to take prisoners, who once back in England would be pumped for information about local defences.

Prior to the Allied invasion of France, it was essential to discover the suitability of the proposed landing beaches, and it was once again the 'Little Ships' which were used to land shore-parties on the beaches of Normandy, clutching spades and jars with which to obtain samples of the sand for analysis. Only with this vital information could the planners be certain that proposed landing sites were suitable for heavy vehicles at all states of the tide.

One particular MTB was involved in many such trips across the Channel and the North Sea. She would close the enemy coastline and, with specially installed radio equipment, the signals emitted by shore radar stations could be used to plot their positions. Invariably there would be a heavy gun emplacement nearby, which could be subsequently confirmed by aerial reconnaissance. With this information, the RAF bombers had clearly defined targets. Wiping out some of the shore batteries would prove invaluable in the British sectors of the D-Day landings. Curiously, the Americans declined the offer of the services of the same MTB to establish enemy radar and heavy gun positions in their sectors, with tragic consequences.

All the Coastal Forces craft that took part in these secret operations had one thing in common – once clear of the land they were on their own, until they were heading for home, when, with dawn breaking, air cover might arrive. If one of the 15th MGB Flotilla was involved, this air cover might be two Spitfires from St Eval RAF Station in Cornwall. The Spitfires would dip their wings, raising a cheer amongst the homeward-bound crew, and one of the pilots would radio back to base that they had the MGB in sight.

In the first year of the war, various intelligence departments were being formed – some were part of the Admiralty, others were attached to Combined Operations, while yet more managed to maintain their anonymity, with no apparent ties with any of the armed services. In these early days there were no MGBs or MTBs working exclusively for any of them.

Like the rest of his colleagues on the boats moored alongside the paddle-steamer on the River Dart, Peter Williams became involved in undercover operations quite by chance. He was a peacetime solicitor who had joined the RNV(S)R in October 1939. After serving in *MA/SB 10* at Dunkirk he took over *ML 118*. His next command was a Fairmile C, *MGB 325*, building at Brixham.

Once she had been commissioned, the plan was that she should proceed to Great Yarmouth to join the 16th MGB Flotilla, which was primarily involved in offshore patrols and providing an outer screen for the convoys. However, instead of making for the East Coast, Lt Williams was ordered to put into Portland, where the boat was to be used for testing a new gun being developed by

MGBs *502* and *503. Camper & Nicholsons*

Later in the evening, when he was ashore, Williams was summoned to report back to *MGB 325* immediately. Lt Hodder's boat, which was to have been used that night for collecting a British agent from the north coast of Brittany, was non-operational with an engine problem. *MGB 325* had been suggested as a replacement. She would undertake the trip with two additional officers on board, Lts Davis and Letty - one as navigation specialist, the other taking charge of the landing party collecting the agent from a pre-arranged pick-up point. Their destination was a particularly rugged 40-mile stretch of coastline on the north coast of Brittany known, these days, as the Côte de Granit Rose, between Paimpol and the Baie de Lannion. The foreshore here is dramatic, with great slabs of pink granite piled on top of each other, like a huge jumble of children's building bricks. There are many hazards: the rocky outcrops of Les Sept Îles and Plateau des Triagoz, although sometimes useful guides for the navigator, have to be given a reasonably wide berth, and a 3-knot current sweeps round the coastline. There are beaches either side of the Pointe de Bihit, but, curiously, the Pointe itself - where there was no obvious landing place for a small boat, and any reception party would find it difficult to climb across the rocky foreshore - had been chosen as the pick-up point.

This was to be Lt Williams' first experience of taking a boat close inshore and letting go the anchor off a hostile coastline. They waited for a shielded torch signal from the French Resistance, to confirm they had the agent, and that it was safe to lower the MGB's tender and row ashore in the direction of the light. An hour later *MGB 325* had still received no signal. The operation was abandoned. Perhaps there had been a mistake somewhere down the line in conveying the exact position of the landing-place. On this trip, it was not revealed to Peter Williams that his two colleagues belonged to a secret Naval Intelligence section under the command of DDOD(I) - Deputy Director Operations Division (Irregular). This was the legendary Capt Frank Slocum, RN.

Related to Joshua Slocum, who was the first man to sail single-handed around the world, Frank Slocum had served with great courage and

Rolls-Royce. This proved unsuitable for an MGB, but while *MGB 325* was berthed in Portland awaiting the removal of the gun Williams met up with a friend of his, Lt John Hodder, who commanded another MGB berthed nearby. Williams discovered that the neighbouring MGB was being used for undercover operations, but Hodder would divulge nothing more.

distinction in Coastal Forces in the First World War. In 1940 he joined the Naval Intelligence Division at the Admiralty with the prime purpose of organizing the landing and taking-off of agents in occupied Europe, and bringing back aircrews who had bailed out over enemy territory and, with the help of the local Resistance, had evaded capture. Peter Williams, who later in the war would join Slocum's staff, remembered him as a short, dapper man with a needle-like brain. He was very charming, but someone not to be crossed.

When Slocum was building up his organisation he had to acquire craft from a variety of sources. At the very outset he was successful in making contact with Breton tunny fishermen, whose *thoniers* were still fishing off Brittany's west coast. Several were recruited, and successfully participated in one of the escape routes for bailed-out airmen on the run in France. There was, however, a requirement for fast craft, capable of making the trip to and from enemy coastlines under cover of darkness. To start off with, Slocum had to make do with a mixed bunch of craft, which included two French power boats (with only limited engine spares) and an air/sea rescue craft. Without any more suitable boats immediately at his disposal, he had to borrow from the Coastal Forces flotillas being established on the East Coast.

After his first taste of an undercover operation, Peter Williams had proceeded up to Great Yarmouth to join the 16th MGB Flotilla but in October 1941 Capt Slocum again borrowed *MGB 325* for a night operation. The objective was again to pick up an agent, only this time the beach was on the Dutch coast. Lt Davis joined the boat as navigator once more. *MGB 325* arrived off the Dutch coast in the right place and at the right time but, as in the Pointe de Bihit operation, there was no one on shore waiting for them. When thick fog came down it was decided that the operation had to be abandoned. The journey back to the East Coast was eventful: they almost collided with a fleet of inshore fishing boats and only just avoided a German patrol boat.

Williams again returned to flotilla work off the East Coast until summoned for a third clandestine operation. This time, the plan was to land two agents on the Dutch coast. Again Williams took a specialist navigator from DDOD(I) and they had no trouble in finding the landing beach. The gunboat's dinghy was lowered and, with the two agents on board, her First Lieutenant, Sub-Lt Elwell, set out to row the half-mile to the beach. Neither the dinghy nor Sub-Lt Elwell returned; on the way in, they encountered several shallow shoals over which there were breaking seas. The dinghy capsized and its occupants had to swim for the shore. They were arrested by the Germans at daylight the next morning. Sub-Lt Elwell spent the rest of the war as a POW, but the two agents were recognised as such and shot. One of the salutary lessons learned from this operation was the urgent requirement for a custom-designed boat, able to land and return through steep surf. It was also realised that extensive training was necessary in the use of such boats.

Williams undertook one more clandestine run towards the end of 1942. By this time he had commissioned a new Fairmile D (*MGB 612*) and was back patrolling off the East Coast. In the company of two more MGBs, Operation *Cabaret* would take him across the North Sea to the Skagerrak, between the north coast of Denmark and the south coast of Norway. Beyond lay the neutral Swedish port of Gothenburg, where two Norwegian ships, with much-needed cargoes of war supplies, were waiting to be escorted through the German-blockaded Skagerrak and then to Britain. When the MGBs were off Denmark they received a radio warning of German shipping, with heavily armed escorts and air cover, on passage towards them along the west coast of Norway. This report, coupled with deteriorating weather, made it unwise to continue with the operation. On their way back, all the boats sustained considerable damage as they made slow progress into Force 9 winds in the North Sea.

Operation *Cabaret* did not come under the umbrella of DDOD(I) who, since the department's formation in 1940, had scored many successes with the limited resources at his disposal. With his temporarily-loaned Coastal Forces craft and his Inshore Patrol Flotilla (IPF) of fishing boats, Capt Slocum had been able to demonstrate the value of Naval Intelligence working with the French Resistance. However, towards the end of 1943 it was becoming increasingly difficult to poach craft, even for 24 hours, from operational Coastal Forces flotillas, which were fully occupied all round the British Isles. In isolation the IPF could never hope to achieve all of its objectives. Consequently, on his return from Operation *Cabaret*, after which *MGB 612* had to come out of the water for considerable repairs, Williams was ordered to report to DDOD(I). Capt Slocum wanted him as Senior Officer of a new MGB flotilla he was forming for use exclusively in undercover operations.

DDOD(I) had hardly been inactive before the formation of the 15th MGB Flotilla. The earliest recorded DDOD(I) operation off the Brittany coast, for the Secret Intelligence Service (SIS), was in June 1940. Coded AFB/SLO.1, this involved landing and re-embarking an agent near Brest. One of the two French MTBs taken over by Slocum was used for this operation. Between June 1940 and December 1943 DDOD(I) concentrated on picking up agents for training in Britain and then returning them to France to organise local Resistance. They also landed equipment and stores for the Resistance, reconnoitred the Normandy and Brittany coastlines, and established 'postboxes' which were used by the French Resistance and emptied by DDOD(I). Over this period various craft sailed for the north and west coasts of France to make contact with the French Resistance through DDOD(I). These included the two French MTBs, *ML 107*, MGBs *314, 318, 319, 323, 324, 325, 326,* and *329*, MTBs *673* and *697*, fishing boats, MA/SBs *36* and *40*, an air/sea rescue launch (*RAF 360*), a submarine, and replica tunnymen with the speed of MTBs, which were classified as Motor Fishing Vessels (MFVs) *2020, 2022,* and *2023*.

One of the key figures in building up the organisation was Ted Davis. Peter Williams and Ted Davis had first met when the latter had joined *MGB 325* at Portland as navigator for the un-successful Côte de Granit Rose operation. They were to work closely together, for Ted Davis became Slocum's local operations officer, with an office at the Dartmouth Royal Naval College. By then he had been promoted to commander, and was already a veteran of over 30 undercover operations between the South Coast of England and occupied France and Holland.

The French Resistance operatives organised themselves into individual *reseaux* or cells, providing a particularly strong and well-organised network along the north and west coasts of Brittany. Soon after the fall of France, early contacts had been established between the French Resistance and Naval Intelligence. DDOD(I) was kept busy developing these contacts. During this period the landing places on the Brittany coastline were established. They were called 'pinpoints', and were adopted after extensive deliberations on both sides of the Channel. Between them, the local French Resistance and Naval Intelligence chose places where the Germans would least expect a motor gunboat, which would thread its way through the rocky approaches until close enough to lower a surfboat. Remarkably, some of these sites were overlooked by heavy gun batteries.

The four most used 'pinpoints' on the north coast of Brittany were (east to west): Anse Cochat, also called 'Bonaparte' beach, five miles to the north of Plouha; Île Grande; Beg-an-Fry, near the Baie de Morlaix; and L'Aber Wrach. These particular pinpoints were never discovered by the Germans, and continued to be used until the liberation of Brittany. This reflected great credit on both the local Resistance and on the boats of the 15th MGB Flotilla. Not all the pinpoints survived, however. Operation *Jealous III* involved landing and embarking SOE (Special Operations Executive) agents, using the Pointe de St Cast in the Baie de la Frênaye. After two earlier successes, *MGB 502* set out for St Cast to land six agents and embark up to nine. Although the flotilla only ever operated during moonless periods, there were still times when an MGB would be clearly visible even in the hours of darkness, when, under a brilliant starry sky and in still conditions, the phosphorescence of her bow-wave would betray her. This was one of those occasions. As *MGB 502* approached the coast, the German batteries on the Pointe de St Cast and Fort la Latte opened fire, hitting the top of her mast. The operation had to be abandoned, along with the Pointe de St Cast pinpoint.

A glance at a chart will confirm that the pinpoints were not chosen for their ease of access. Navigation of the highest order was required, which is why, on many operations, a specialist navigator from DDOD(I) joined the crew, along with another officer who knew the actual pinpoint and the local Resistance personnel. The latter would be responsible for the surfboat landing and for making contact with the local Resistance.

Although the navigators attached to the 15th Flotilla had nothing like the sophisticated equipment carried as standard aboard moderately sized yachts today, the gunboats were supplied with QH – a naval version of equipment developed during the war for the RAF. QH gave the navigator an accurate fix based on signals from two land-based radio transmitters. Echo-sounders also proved invaluable aboard these high-speed craft, enabling an accurate position-check as the boat crossed Hurd Deep, a remarkable narrow undersea canyon or cleft in the seabed, nearly 70 miles long. The midpoint of the Deep is about 45 miles south-east of Start Point, where the navigator would be watching the instrument for the sudden drop in depth. The echo-sounder was particularly useful for approaching anchorages, when there might be only a couple of feet of water beneath the keel. The boats also had a built-in Pitometer Log, which clocked up distances covered through the water, and the reading could be double-checked against a Cherub Log streamed astern. Special buoys, transmitting radio signals, were positioned by the flotilla off some of the landing beaches, to guide the boats in, and were particularly useful if the visibility was poor.

Operating by night, the boats were invariably able to use the lighthouses on outlying rocks and islands, which were kept lit for German convoys. In addition, when closing the Brittany coastline there were sometimes landmarks visible in the darkness, such as the high cliffs of Cap Fréhel, seamarks such as a buoy, a stone beacon, or a distinctive rock formation.

However, even with all the equipment they had, the navigators still had to perform with great skill, particularly when approaching the pinpoint at slow speed, perhaps in poor visibility, and with a strong cross-tide. They had to be absolutely certain of their position to within a few yards when anchoring off the pinpoint. From here, the crew of the surfboat would know the way in to meet up with the beach party, and then find their way back to the waiting MGB. The surfboat was able to keep in contact with both the mother ship and the beach party by S-phone, which was a portable wireless set. To safeguard their position, the transmission was made on one frequency, with reception on another. Lt-Cdr Williams had the idea of providing the landing officer with a simple hydrophone, which could be lowered into the water over the side of the surfboat

and used to provide a reasonably accurate bearing on the MGB's sonar echo-sounder signal.

From the mixed bunch of boats at Capt Slocum's disposal in the early days, a flotilla of new Coastal Forces craft gradually emerged. The first he acquired was *MA/SB 36* – one of seven motor anti-submarine boats being built in 1941 by the British Power Boat Co. This had a displacement of 20 tons, with an overall length of 63ft, and was powered by two 1,000bhp Napier petrol engines. Armed with twin 0.303in machine guns, her complement was one officer and eight men. Although not ideal, with a top speed of only 25kt, *MA/SB 36* carried out several operations for DDOD(I). In company with *MGB 319*, for instance, she was used successfully to reconnoitre the north Brittany coastline between Île de Bréhat and Île de Batz. She also landed an agent in Morlaix Baie, and worked with the IPF.

The next boat to be taken over by Slocum was *MGB 314*, which was one of twenty-four 72-ton, 110ft Fairmile Cs. Powered by three supercharged Hall Scott Engines, *MGB 314* had a maximum speed of 27kt, and a range at maximum continuous speed of 300 miles (this could be increased by carrying additional fuel tanks on the upper deck). *MGB 314* had a particularly busy eight weeks between the end of December 1941 and the end of February 1942. Over this period, she completed seven operations, landing seven agents and embarking thirteen, using pinpoints off L'Aber Wrach and around the Baie de Lannion. Her short but highly successful attachment to DDOD(I) came to an end when she was taken over by Combined Operations to play a major role in the raid on St Nazaire. For Operation *Chariot*, she was commanded by Lt Dunstan Curtis RNVR; greatly damaged during the raid, it was decided that *MGB 314* would never reach home, and she was sunk by the Royal Navy.

MGB 318, another C-type Fairmile, replaced *MGB 314*. Initially commanded by Lt Charles Martin, *318* was to take part in many undercover operations, particularly to the secret landing beaches around Île Grande and the L'Aber Wrach estuary on the north coast of Brittany. Harold Pickles served as an able seaman aboard *318* for most of his wartime service, and remembers the discomfort experienced by the crew when she was at sea. She was a wet boat, and whenever the

MA/SB 36 newly commissioned prior to joining Capt Slocum for special duties. *Southampton City Heritage Services*

gunnery crews were closed up their protective clothing proved totally inadequate to keep out the seawater. Unlike for the shorter Vosper boats, whose crews lived ashore, when *318* secured alongside their depot ship at Dartmouth after a night operation there was no reception party of WRNS to service the boat. The crew's first job was invariably to attempt to dry out the messdeck and their clothing before being able to climb into their bunks to catch up on lost sleep. A hot shower involved taking a liberty boat from their depot ship to reach the shore.

Harold Pickles recalled *MGB 318*'s first undercover operation. The objective was to make contact with members of the Dutch Resistance and transport them back to the UK. Believing they had made an accurate landfall, they flashed their identification signal in the direction of the shore. When they received no reply the CO decided to move further in, and immediately ran aground on a dropping tide. Full astern on the silenced centre engine failed to move *318*. Between grounding and the estimated time of floating off at around

daybreak, the crew was kept busy lightening ship and redistributing the load by pumping out the freshwater tank and moving all the ammunition aft. A kedge anchor was loaded into the dinghy and taken out into deeper water.

Through the early morning mist, they could actually see cars and lorries on the move along the seafront in enemy-occupied Holland. They tried kedging off the boat, with all the crew heaving in unison on the anchor rope. Then they produced a rocking motion, with the crew leaping from side to side. The silent engine was then run at full astern with the crew again heaving on the kedge anchor. Now with full daylight, the final desperate measure had to be taken; the two outer engines howled into life, shattering the early morning peace. With the crew heaving on the anchor rope, *318* at last started inching her way astern. To the stifled cheers of the ship's company, the coxswain could soon round her

MGB 315, a C-type Fairmile similar to *MGB 318*.

up, pointing the bows finally into the North Sea, on course for Great Yarmouth. While *318*'s twisted drive shafts were being replaced, the seamen took a week's leave. When they returned, they discovered they were to leave their East Coast flotilla to join Slocum's 15th MGB Flotilla at Dartmouth.

Capt Slocum also had his eye on some MGBs under construction at the Gosport yard of Camper & Nicholsons. The original order had been for the Turkish Navy, but these had been commandeered by the Royal Navy. However, most of the MGBs under construction at Camper & Nicholsons were destroyed in an air raid on 10 March 1941, and it would be another 12 months before the first Camper & Nicholsons MGB (*501*) was commissioned; and then, after only three weeks in service, she exploded and sank off the Scilly Isles (*see Chapter 3*).

The 15th MGB Flotilla was finally established with just four boats – the next two Camper & Nicholsons, together with *MGB 318* and *MA/SB 36*. The First Lieutenant of the wrecked *MGB 501* (Jan T. McQuoid-Mason, a South African naval reservist) took over command of *MGB 318* from Lt Charles Martin, who transferred to the new Camper & Nicholsons *MGB 503*. Lt Peter Williams, now the Senior Officer of the flotilla and soon to be promoted to lieutenant-commander, assumed command of *MGB 502*. The MA/SB was commanded by a Canadian, Johnny Motherwell. It was to be many months and operations later before the strength of the 15th Flotilla would be increased to five.

Like Peter Williams, Lt Ronald Seddon and his First Lieutenant, Sub-Lt Guy Hamilton, became involved in undercover operations quite by chance. Lt Seddon had already made the headlines when commanding B-Class *ML 145* which, along with *ML 150*, had been involved in a successful action against an E-boat (*see Chapter 9*). Both MLs were badly damaged, leaving their COs looking for new commands. Seddon was delighted to be offered the D-type *MTB 747*, under construction at Shoreham. This was then reallocated to the SO of a Fairmile D MTB flotilla, who required an immediate replacement for his damaged Dog-boat. Seddon was then given *MTB 718*, another Dog-boat, which was being built at Sandbank on the Clyde. When he and his First Lieutenant went up to Scotland to collect

the boat, they were surprised to discover that all four torpedo-tubes were being removed (ironically Lt Seddon had just completed a torpedo course). With orders to proceed to Dartmouth, Seddon still had no idea of the secretive role his boat was to play. It was only when he berthed alongside the paddle steamer *Westward Ho!* and had met his Senior Officer, Peter Williams, that it was revealed that *MGB 718* was the latest addition to Capt Slocum's 15th MGB Flotilla.

Although Dartmouth was an important base for Coastal Forces, the crews of the 15th Flotilla kept much to themselves. Their original depot ship was the old yacht *Kiloran*. This was subsequently replaced by the 460-ton paddle steamer *Westward Ho!*, moored in the middle of the Dart River between Dartmouth and Kingswear. The saloon made an excellent wardroom. Some accommodation in the *Kiloran* was retained for use by agents prior to their departure or when they arrived and were waiting to be debriefed. Direct telephone lines were installed in *Westward Ho!* to Cdr Davis at the Royal Naval College, Dartmouth, and to DDOD(I) in London.

Before leaving on an operation, the officers taking part would assemble in the *Westward Ho!* wardroom for a briefing by Cdr Davis. He would have already advised C-in-C Plymouth of the planned operation, and been informed of any shipping movements (both Allied and enemy) expected within the vicinity. He would also have the latest weather forecast and intelligence reports on enemy shore defences; thanks to the ULTRA code-breakers at Bletchley Park, the MGB would usually sail with the German naval recognition signal operating until midnight.

Peter Williams recalled one occasion when he sailed for the pinpoint in the entrance to the Tréguier River when, for some reason, he had been given no information that the Royal Navy cruiser *Black Prince*, with two destroyer escorts, was operating in the area. As he waited in the tricky entrance to the Tréguier River, anchored close inshore off the sixth stave marking a narrow channel, the whole area was suddenly lit up by a series of star shells. Just off the river entrance, those aboard *MGB 502* had a grandstand view of *Black Prince*'s escort destroyers travelling at full speed from east to west in pursuit of a German destroyer, which had come out of her base at neighbouring Lézardrieux.

It was an unusual experience to watch a naval engagement in which they played no part. *MGB 502* was close enough to see German sailors running around the deck of their destroyer, which was already on fire. The excitement was too much for the DDOD(I) landing officer on board, who pulled out his revolver and accidentally fired a shot, which passed within inches of Peter Williams, bounced off the armour-plating on the bridge, and narrowly missed the coxswain and signalman.

They never received a signal from the beach; tragically the agent had been caught by the Germans that afternoon and shot. Realizing that his boat was now fully visible from the shore, Williams decided that a hasty departure was called for. The anchor rope was cut, and then *MGB 502* motored at full power, making smoke, straight through the middle of the sea battle. The cruiser later reported sighting an E-boat, making smoke, approaching them at high speed!

These clandestine passages to and from Brittany took place over the ten-day period in any one month when there would be little or no moon. Much of the remaining time would be spent training the crews, practising anchoring and man-handling the surfboats time and time again, until these operations could be carried out in almost complete silence. The boat officers and crews would become thoroughly familiar with the behaviour of the surfboats in all weather conditions and with a variety of loads. This training contributed significantly to the flotilla's remarkable success rate.

As already mentioned, the tragic consequences of the foundering of *MTB 325*'s standard naval tender on sandbanks off the Dutch coast had highlighted the urgent need for training and for a custom-built surfboat. The responsibility for the design of a suitable craft was vested in Lt-Cdr Nigel Warington-Smyth, a peacetime yacht designer who had been recruited by Capt Slocum to work with the Inshore Patrol Flotilla. In the early days of DDOD(I), Warington-Smyth was based on a large three-masted schooner, *Sunbeam II*, moored in the River Helford, and used by the crews of the assorted vessels that made up the IPF. A dozen different types of boat, of all shapes and sizes, including a Norwegian *praam*,

were acquired by DDOD(I). Extensive trials included filming the crews of these small open boats struggling to control them in the often spectacular wave patterns to be found off the beaches along the south coast of Cornwall. *MGB 503*'s First Lieutenant, Andrew Smith, was involved at an early stage in these trials, becoming one of the flotilla's most experienced surfboat-handling officers. He recalled testing a boat large enough to carry 60 passengers. *MGB 503* went round to Praa Sands, between the Lizard and Penzance, with the crews of *502* and *718* aboard to make up the numbers. The trial was doomed to failure when it was almost immediately discovered that a sweep oar was totally inadequate for steering a boat of this size when fully loaded. All finished in the sea when the boat was overturned by the surf, and at one point Sub-Lt Smith was dangling over the sea, six feet from the boat, on one end of the sweep oar.

At the end of the trials, Warington-Smyth's own design (the 14ft SN1) was found to the most successful. He went back to the drawing board and, with another famous yacht designer (Charles Nicholson of Camper & Nicholsons), produced a 26ft version, the SN6. Clinker-built, the larger of the surfboats would be able to carry 15 passengers, with four men rowing and one in command. Andrew Smith, because of his experience during the trials, became the flotilla's first landing officer, to be joined later by a pool of experienced small-boat handlers from DDOD(I). Sometimes the landing officer would steer the boat, using a sweep oar over the stern but, as had been proved during the trials, the sweep oar was ineffective with a fully laden boat. The preferred method was to issue hushed commands to the oarsmen to achieve an alteration of course.

Some of the surfboats were built by Camper & Nicholsons at its Gosport yard. The design was unusual in that the boats were double-ended, with a pointed stern and bow. This design enabled the crews to cut through the surf, when approaching a shore. If a large wave was coming up from behind, the crew would cease pulling on the oars, and push instead, to meet the approaching wave and prevent the boat being knocked sideways. The technique was perfected only after many days of practice off Praa Sands, after which the crews were able to cope with surf heightened by a strong on-shore wind.

Launching these boats from the deck of the MGB could be carried out almost noiselessly by three men. With one at either end and another in the middle inboard, they would turn the boat over and outside the guardrail, where it could be lowered on the painter and a stern rope. If there were two agents to be picked up or landed, then only two oarsmen and the landing officer would crew the surfboat. With a heavier load, two additional oarsmen were taken. At some of the pinpoints the MGB might have to anchor a mile off, leaving the landing officer to complete the passage to and from the beach, perhaps having to circumnavigate rocks and make allowances for a strong cross-tide. Landing officers became very familiar with the frequently visited pinpoints. There were times when their greatest problem was maintaining

silence on the beach, as aircrews made emotional farewells to members of the French Resistance who had hidden and fed them.

There was enough deck space on MGBs *502, 503,* and *718* for each of them to carry four surfboats, although they mostly sailed with just one or two, depending on the operation. There was certainly one occasion when *MGB 503* loaded all four surfboats to pick up 65 personnel (mostly airmen) from Bonaparte Beach north of Plouha, used extensively by the Shelbourne Resistance *reseau*; on this occasion Andrew Smith had to make two trips in one of the surfboats, in order to transfer all the airmen from the beach.

The crew of the 15th Flotilla's latest addition, *MTB 718,* had to undergo intensive training to familiarise themselves with what was, to them, a totally new form of warfare. Two of Lt Seddon's crew - Leading Seaman Albert Dellow (second

MTB 718 in Flekke Fjord, Norway, after the war.

coxswain) and a young Canadian fisherman, Ordinary Seaman Hayward Rockwood – proved themselves particularly adept at handling a surfboat amongst the breakers off the Cornish coast. Seddon accompanied his Senior Officer on two trips to the Brittany coastline to gain firsthand experience of what the flotilla's dangerous missions involved.

MGB 718's own first operation, with Lt Seddon in command and his Senior Officer coming along as an observer, achieved its objective but ended in near-disaster. The objective of Operation *Reflexion*, as it was code-named, was to carry three French agents and their equipment from Dartmouth to a small beach in the Baie de St Brieuc, near Plouha in eastern Brittany. These agents were being returned to France after extensive training in Britain. Waiting for them, at one o'clock in the morning, would be the local French Resistance. *MTB 718* approached the pinpoint in the Baie de St Brieuc on silenced engines, and anchored 30–40 yards off the beach. The surfboat was lowered, the three agents scrambled aboard and, with Dellow and Rockwood on the oars, Sub-Lt Guy Hamilton guided the small boat towards the beach. After the agents had been

The crew of *MTB 718*, the 'Lone Wolf'.

handed over, the boat's crew disappeared into the night, rowing, they believed, in the direction of the MTB. After an hour, there was considerable alarm on board *MTB 718* that the boat's crew had not returned. They waited until about four in the morning and then, with the first signs of dawn, hauled in the anchor and headed back to Dartmouth, leaving behind the three members of their crew. There was no question of staying until daylight, and thereby running the risk of disclosing a pinpoint which had been used successfully on several operations.

So what had gone wrong? *MTB 718* had been anchored in the agreed position, which had been carefully checked with bearings on two headlands, just visible against the night sky. Possibly she may have dragged her anchor at a critical moment, for the use of an anchor warp could never be as effective as letting down 10 fathoms of chain, with all the attendant noise that involved. Guy Hamilton believed he may have misjudged the tides, or his compass may have been wrong, but whatever the reason he told everyone later that it was no joke trying to catch an MTB in a dinghy! Having failed to locate their mother ship, and with no sign of the French Resistance, Hamilton had been left with no option but to sink the surfboat, get rid of his walkie-talkie, and lead his two seamen inland. Fortunately Hamilton had worked in the French film industry before the war and spoke the language fluently. (After the war he became a film director, with several box-office successes to his name, including four James Bond films.)

The party spent three days trying to make contact with the French Resistance (and in the process wandered into what they later discovered was a minefield). They were told of someone who might be able to help them escape, but Hamilton was not happy with the contact. They were eventually hidden and fed by an established member of the Resistance, and a message was transmitted to London saying that they were safe. Four weeks later *MGB 503* set out for the same pinpoint to land stores and pick up 15 personnel, including Hamilton, Dellow, and Rockwood. On board *503* was an officer from Naval Intelligence, with Ronald Seddon along as passenger. The pick-up went according to plan. Before Seddon and his First Lieutenant could as much as exchange a greeting, they both had to be debriefed separately by the Intelligence Officer to make certain that security had not been breached.

Enormous importance was attached to maintaining the secrecy of established pinpoints around Brittany. Each CO had orders to avoid confrontation with enemy vessels off these beaches, though this was sometimes difficult. A case in point was Operation *Scarf*. Because of the number of personnel – a mixture of airmen and agents – who might be waiting to be picked up at Beg-an-Fry, two boats (*MGB 502* and *MTB 718*) were detailed for this operation. Six SOE agents were successfully landed at the pinpoint. The waiting airmen were taken out to *MTB 718* while the returning agents climbed aboard *MGB 502*. Peter Williams remembered that two of the agents were women, who, having passed through Paris on their way to the Brittany coast, had treated themselves to Parisian hats and Chanel No 5. Unfortunately one of the women had broken her bottle of Chanel while she was travelling across

France; if the Germans had stopped her they would have been highly suspicious of a girl, dressed as a French peasant, drenched in expensive perfume.

Having embarked all their passengers, the boats got under way to make the return passage to Dartmouth. Almost immediately they ran into one of the armed escorts of a German convoy, which challenged them with a recognition signal. Williams told his telegraphist to flash the signal for the previous 24-hour period. This must have confused the enemy for a short time, but then they challenged again. The telegraphist then replied with a deliberately jumbled signal, as the boats increased speed to distance themselves from the enemy as quickly as possible. At this the Germans opened fire, causing one fatal casualty. Williams did not return their fire, which presumably made the Germans think that they might be engaging their own ships, so that they ceased fire, enabling *MGB 502* and *MTB 718* to give them the slip.

Pinpoints on the north Brittany coast became associated with individual boats in the 15th MGB Flotilla. Some of these wartime ties survived the passage of time, and 50th anniversary ceremonies were held in 1994 close to local pinpoints. Veterans of the boat crews met up again with their Resistance colleagues, some of whom had never been more than shadowy figures on a remote beach. In 1995, several veterans of the Resistance and Coastal Forces attended the unveiling of a plaque at Kingswear to commemorate the 15th MGB Flotilla.

Two tiny islands off the rock-encumbered entrance to the River L'Aberbenoit (near to L'Aber Wrach), at the north-west corner of Brittany, were the pinpoints most frequently visited first by *MGB 314* and then her successor, *MGB 318*. The beach at Beg an Fry, 36 miles to the east of L'Aber Wrach, was associated with the Senior Officer's boat, *MGB 502*. Île Grande, another 7 miles north-east, was used by MGBs *503* and *318*. Eastwards again, rounding the rock-strewn approaches to the rivers Tréguier and Trieux, is Bonaparte Beach, where MGBs *502*, *503*, and *718* were involved on several occasions in embarking escaping aircrews.

The landing beach selected for an operation depended on which group of Resistance fighters was involved. For security reasons each group generally worked independently, but formed part of the *Alibi* network of agents spread right across Brittany. The French had formed the *Alibi* group in 1940, which worked closely with British intelligence. The group grew to 450 registered agents, 20 sub-networks, and 15 transmission stations. Much of *Alibi*'s work involved sabotaging enemy resources through its individual *reseaux* or sub-networks. At the beginning of 1944, however, the head of the *Alibi* network decided that sea links with British intelligence were needed as an alternative to the established lines of communication by radio, aeroplane, or overland through Spain. In January, air reconnaisance was carried out along the north Brittany coastline, at all states of the tide, in consequence of which a new pinpoint was selected on Île à Canton, part of several islets and beaches collectively known as Île Grande.

There are several small, uninhabited islands which can be reached by foot at low water from Île Grande, where there are a few houses and a causeway connecting the island with the mainland. To the south is Trébeurden, which is a small holiday resort. There were nine planned operations to Grande Île. *MGB 503* undertook the first, code-named Operation *Glover*, in February 1944, but this had to be abandoned because of the weather. The pinpoint was then switched to another small islet four cables to the east, called Île à Canton, where equipment was successfully landed and an agent embarked. *Glover II* and *Glover III* were also attempted by *MGB 503*, but neither was successful – there was no reception party at Île à Canton for *Glover II*, and on the next operation the French managed to contact the crew of the surfboat by radio to tell them to return as, unusually, there were too many Germans around. The pinpoint landing was then switched again, to Pors Gelen, which is a small beach at the eastern end of Île Grande. *Glover IV* was attempted first by *PT 71*, one of the American PT boats working out of Dartmouth on undercover operations (*see Chapter 11*). There was no beach reception party at Pors Gelen as there had been communication problems with the local Resistance. *PT 72* completed the operation five days later. *Glovers V to IX* were carried out by *MGB 318*, with the final trip to Pors Gelen, Grande Île, taking place in August 1944, shortly before this part of Brittany was liberated.

The approach to Île Grande is tricky because of the current, which rips round this corner of Brittany, reaching nearly 4kt at spring tides. L'Aber Wrach, 44 miles to the west, is no easier, again having a strong cross-tide in the approaches. The small hamlet of L'Aber Wrach is actually two miles upriver from the entrance. The selected landing place was the tiny Île Guenioc, two miles to the south-west of the rock-strewn estuary, and close to the entrance channel to the River L'Aberbenoit. The Resistance had to ferry agents, escaping airmen, and supplies between Île Guenioc and Île Tariec, which could only be reached by foot at low tide.

The coastline here offers no protection from the south-westerlies, and it is an area notorious for its fogs. It is still treated with considerable respect by boat owners, even those with all the latest gadgetry in satellite navigation aids and radar. There were some seamarks to help *MGB 318*'s navigator as they closed this inhospitable stretch of Brittany coastline. The offshore lighthouse was still operating during the war, sometimes illuminating the whole area with its powerful beam. There were also unlit buoys, which had been left in position for the benefit of the local fishermen, who were only permitted to fish by day. Apart from challenging navigational problems, it was well known that the approaches to L'Aber Wrach and the neighbouring L'Aberbenoit were mined, and protected by three gun emplacements on the high ground overlooking the estuaries.

Although Île Guenioc was the furthest of the landing beaches (110 miles from Falmouth) it was used on seven occasions. The village of Lannilis, a few miles inland of L'Aber Wrach, was the end of one of the escape routes for Allied airmen in 1943 and 1944. All the surrounding villages had Resistance contacts and families prepared to risk their lives by accommodating airmen until *MGB 318* arrived to take them back to Britain. Many of the airmen would, under the watchful eye of the Resistance, travel by train from western Brittany and alight at Landernau, where the station staff were sympathetic to the Resistance movement. The leader of the local *reseau* was a man code-named 'Mao', who was assisted by 'Sarol', and his radio-operator 'Jeannot'. All three, along with several of their colleagues, would eventually be betrayed by one of their own members, and only

'Mao' survived the horrors of imprisonment in a concentration camp.

David Birkin, a specialist navigator, took part in several of *MGB 318*'s L'Aber Wrach operations, including Operation *Envious* on 3–4 November 1943. He attended the briefing meeting to discover that *MGB 318* would sail from Falmouth to Île Rosservor, which is a tiny island two miles south-west of the previously established landing on Île Guenioc. The objectives of Operation *Envious* were to reconnoitre the island and collect 15 Allied airmen who had been assembled in and around Lannilis, along with a bag of top secret intelligence reports which included detailed information about the enemy's V1 and V2 rockets. If all was well on the French side for the operation to proceed, 'Jeannot' would, at precisely 1800hrs, transmit: *Les faux-cols de Georges Henri sont prets chez la blanchisseuse* ('The stiff collars of Georges Henri are ready at the laundry'). Shortly after London received the message, *MGB 318* slipped out of Dartmouth on her way to the north coast of Brittany. London confirmed to the Resistance that the operation was on, by repeating the message about Georges Henri's collars after the BBC's Overseas News at 1915hrs.

Before dusk, when it was low water, 'Mao' led the party of 15 airmen across the wet sands between the mainland and Île Tariec. Since this was in full view of the Germans manning the gun emplacements above them the party was made to look as though it was innocently gathering shellfish. A small boat then made several trips, ferrying the airmen from Île Tariec to Île Guenioc. Once they had off-loaded all the airmen to await the arrival of *MGB 318*, the Resistance quickly departed in the boat to reach Île Tariec in time to complete their return journey on foot before the tide rose.

Aboard *318*, however, all was not well. One engine had stopped due to fuel starvation, requiring someone permanently hand-operating a fuel-pump. Then the visibility started to deteriorate. Lt David Birkin, with visibility down to 200yd or less, virtually conned the boat in amongst the rocks from the chartroom. He plotted the one position line registering on the QH equipment while watching the echo sounder. At the critical moment, both instruments failed. The bridge reported down to Birkin that they could see white breakers ahead on the port bow. This was Le Relec, an isolated drying

rock, which the navigator was using as a seamark. He told the CO to stop way when the rock was abeam, and prodded at the echo sounder wiring until it started receiving an intermittent signal. The sounding confirmed the position, and the navigator was able to tell the CO to steer a new course for 12 minutes at slow speed on muffled engines.

At the end of the run, the navigator went up to the bridge to peer into the mist, which momentarily cleared to give them a view of a rocky islet. The surfboat was lowered and rowed towards the black shape, to make certain it was Île Rosservor. The boat crew returned after an hour, reporting there was no sign of life there. Two boats were then lowered and filled with ammunition and wireless equipment for the Resistance. After they had hidden the boxes as best they could, the boats returned to *318* and she upped anchor, setting off back to Falmouth, dropping a position-finding buoy off Le Relec on the way.

Meanwhile, the 15 airmen waited on Île Guenioc. They said afterwards that they thought they had heard engines, and may have seen the vague outline of a motor gunboat. After the airmen had been on Île Guenioc with no food or water for 48 hours, the Resistance, at considerable risk, once again took to pretending to search the foreshore for shellfish and then rowed across to Guenioc with much-needed sustenance. 'Mao' decided they should remain on the island for another 24 hours, just in case London confirmed that another attempt would be made. This confirmation was not forthcoming, so after four nights on the tiny island, the Resistance ferried the airmen back to civilisation, where they went back into hiding.

The next moonless period was towards the end of the month, when *MGB 318* made another attempt to pick up the airmen and land an SOE agent. A boat was landed on Île Guenioc, but the islet was deserted. In poor visibility, *MGB 318* then moved slowly to the Rosservor anchorage, where the boat was lowered to land the agent on the Île du Bec, from which he could scramble ashore at low tide. There had apparently been a communication problem again. Messages were then exchanged to confirm a third attempt, which was planned for the night of 1/2 December. As the number of agents and escaping airmen had now risen to 10, it was decided that another boat, *MGB 329*, should accompany *MGB 318*. The weather was already starting to break as they approached the coastline, and *MGB 329* was nowhere to be seen as David Birkin concentrated on the most difficult part of the navigation. Then someone spotted her, heading straight for the extensive Grande Fourche rocks, a mile to the north of the Île Guenioc. *329* was told by radio to alter course immediately, and take up position astern of *318*.

Three surfboats were launched and, under the command of Lt Uhr-Henry, they made their way to Île Guenioc; one can only imagine their feelings of desperation when, again, the islet was found to be deserted. Then a red light was spotted flashing nearby. Uhr-Henry took his surfboat over to investigate and reported back by radio that 20 people were waiting to be picked up on Île Tariec. He was told to unload the crates of stores and then return to the waiting MGBs without delay, because a severe weather warning had been received from London. Lt Uhr-Henry contacted *318* by radio, advising the CO that the surfboats were leaving the island with all the escapers on board. This was the last radio message to be received from Uhr-Henry.

On board the MGBs, the wind was howling through the rigging and whipping up breaking seas all around them. Anchors started to drag, and at one time *318* and *329* were dangerously close to each other. Engines had to be started to take some of the strain off the anchor warps. At four in the morning Lt Charles Martin, CO of *MGB 318*, took the decision to abandon the operation as both MGBs were in danger of being wrecked. Then, just as they were on the point of leaving, Uhr-Henry's surfboat was spotted, her crew battling stoically against the heavy seas breaking over them. The surfboat was making no progress against the gale-force wind, so Lt Martin dropped *MGB 318* back towards both her and a menacing reef only yards away. Once the surfboat's crew had managed to grab the MGB's scrambling net all hands heaved them inboard, and then struggled to recover the surfboat itself as *MGB 318* extricated herself from her desperate situation amidst reefs and breaking seas.

Their troubles were still not over, as the gale showed no sign of abating and the MGBs were barely making 8kt. They had to steer several degrees off the course for Falmouth to avoid being rolled over by the rising seas. When dawn came they were

still only about 20 miles from the French coast. To add to their worries, they had to conserve fuel by operating on only two engines. The MGBs eventually reached Falmouth just after dusk, having been out for 25 hours. Uhr-Henry had managed to rescue seven airmen, and news had been received that the crews and passengers of the other two surfboats were safe with the French Resistance. Both boats had been wrecked attempting to make it back to the MGBs.

By the time of the next attempt on 23–24 December, the number of personnel to be taken off Île Guennoc had risen to 32, with a large accumulation of secret mail. Yet again, they were to be defeated by the weather, even though the forecast had been reasonable. Almost as soon as *MGB 318*, now under the command of South African, Lt Jan Mason, had anchored off Île Guenioc, the wind had begun to increase. The anchor started to drag, and then the line parted. A second anchor was quickly dropped, and again the anchor rope parted, leaving *318* no option but to maintain her position by using the wing engines. While this was happening, Lt Uhr-Henry had launched one of the surfboats and was attempting to make for the island with another surfboat in tow. He reported over his radio that he was making no headway, and was abandoning the attempt. He was told to sink the boat in tow, and return to *318*. David Birkin recorded that he would never forget those 15 minutes, watching the surfboat crew desperately struggling through seas, which were repeatedly breaking over the small boat. They somehow managed to make it and, utterly exhausted, were pulled aboard by many willing hands. The crew of *MGB 318* then had to endure one of the worst Channel crossings any of them had ever experienced. They arrived back in Falmouth at 1315hrs on Christmas Eve.

How much they enjoyed their traditional Christmas lunch aboard *MGB 318* is not recorded, but incredibly, soon after the plum pudding, there was a telephone call to say the operation was on again for the same evening, with a promising weather forecast. So, at dusk on Christmas Day, they were back at sea, making for the Helford River to pick up an SOE crew with a 21ft surfboat, which was taken in tow. The party of 32 airmen now waiting at L'Aber Wrach, had celebrated Christmas

Day with plenty of wine, food, and singing, perhaps knowing that this time their evacuation would be successful. And so it was. The weather was kind, the passage over to L'Aber Wrach without incident. Contact was quickly established with the shore party. Three return trips were made in the surfboats to ferry all the airmen and secret mail between the pinpoint and *MGB 318*. By 1000hrs on Boxing Day, the airmen had been transferred to an SOE motor launch, which had come out of the Helford River to meet them.

Let David Birkin, DSC, Légion d'Honneur have the last word: 'So ended the activities of a heroic group who, in spite of crushing disappointments, had laboured for the repatriation of British and American airmen against almost overwhelming odds. What a reward for heroism – and what a terrible price was paid by that gallant Resistance group.'

* * *

Although the majority of operations undertaken by the 15th MGB Flotilla were on the north coast of Brittany, *MTB 718* was selected to make a number of trips to Norway. These clandestine operations involved taking *718* up to Aberdeen, or Lerwick in the Shetland Islands, depending on whether their destination was the south of Norway or the more northerly coastline. The Norwegian trips were a marked contrast to *MTB 718*'s previous undercover operations on the north coast of Brittany. Operation *Cygnus* involved a round trip of 2,500 miles from Dartmouth to Batalden Island, off the west coast of Norway, by way of Lerwick. To make these long trips, it was necessary to carry up to 2,000gals of 100-octane petrol in jerricans on the upper deck.

The objective of Operation *Cygnus* was to rescue a number of Norwegian agents and civilians on the run, virtually island-hopping to evade arrest by the Gestapo. *MTB 718* was urgently despatched from Dartmouth towards the end of May 1944. On the way up the west coast, they put into Holyhead, where they had the misfortune to take on fuel contaminated with water.

MTB 718 always used the Caledonian Canal to reach the east coast of Scotland and the departure points of Aberdeen or Lerwick. On the occasion of Operation *Cygnus*, trying to catch up on time lost because of the fuel problem, she covered most of the canal during the hours of darkness, with the crew operating the lock gates. After sunrise, *718* was making 12kt, ignoring the canal's 6kt speed limit. When they came to the last lock, the lock keepers were not prepared for the vast bow wave approaching them, which left them desperately holding hands across the gates, struggling to keep them shut.

On arrival at a fuelling berth, *MTB 718* was met by the local naval officer-in-command – a four-ringed captain, who was looking far from pleased. He was piped aboard, and glowered at Lt Seddon, telling him that he was in dead trouble, and could well be court-martialled. 'Do you realise', he said, 'you nearly sank the town of Inverness?' The urgency of *MTB 718*'s mission was explained, and a bottle of gin – followed by Scotch whisky – later, the captain departed, saying that he would try to keep the local people happy – which he did.

Cygnus was one of *MTB 718*'s most hazardous operations. Since it was taking place in May there would be no cover of darkness whenever they approached the heavily defended enemy-occupied coast. Before leaving Lerwick, they embarked four Norwegian seamen who would act as the surfboat's crew, along with a Norwegian pilot who knew the local landing area, and an interpreter. They also carried a highly experienced RNR navigator, Lt Salmond.

Seddon always felt that his was a lucky ship, and it certainly was at 0200hrs on 29 May, when, 12 miles from the Norwegian coast, they ran into dense fog, which miraculously lifted when they were 500yd from the pinpoint. A small motor boat and dinghy were sighted near the rocks. After identification signals had been exchanged, they embarked seven men, three women, and a child. The small boats were scuttled, and *MTB 718* headed back to Lerwick.

Operation *Aquarius* took place on 2–3 November, and involved bringing four Norwegian agents back to the UK from a pinpoint near Egersund, in the south of Norway. The duration of the operation was 35 hours, slightly longer than had been anticipated because they met enemy convoys on both the outward and return passages. Visibility was all too good, with a full moon. They were spotted and challenged by armed trawlers, then an M-Class minesweeper fired star shells. Inevitably, a Dornier reconnaissance aircraft was soon on the scene, searching for the MTB's telltale wash. There was no option but to lie still, until the convoy had moved away, and the searching Dornier had returned to base. Later in the month, Lt Seddon received a signal from the Admiralty: 'It is desired to congratulate you on your execution of Operation *Aquarius* which appears to be a copybook example of a faultlessly executed operation.'

Operation *Lola* took place between 12 and 15 February 1945, and coincided with some of the worst weather that *MTB 718* had ever experienced. At the outset, while on passage between Lerwick and Aberdeen to collect Norwegian agents, they ran into two full gales, neither of which had been forecast, and sustained considerable damage. The operational objective was to land 1.5 tons of stores and the two agents, who were to set up an observation post and radio station, near Kristiansand in southern Norway. With agents Møller and Larsen on board, together with a Norwegian navigator, *MTB 718* left Aberdeen at 2200hrs on 12 February. She was carrying an additional 13 tons on deck, made up of 2,000 gallons of fuel in jerricans, stores, a boat for the Norwegian agents, and an SN6 surfboat. On the following afternoon the jerricans were emptied into the tanks – a difficult operation which took two and a half hours in rough sea conditions. Each can then had to be holed and jettisoned. Visibility was reduced to nil in heavy snow squalls, which made the approach to the pinpoint hazardous in the extreme.

Odden Island was first sighted and identified just 300yd away. It was then a matter of threading *MTB 718* through tiny islands and rocks, to reach the pinpoint at 0035hrs. Lt Hamilton and one agent, Møller, launched the surfboat to investigate, and then radioed back that heavy swell ruled out the pinpoint as a suitable landing-place. Seddon recalled the surfboat and, using a lead line from the bows, *MTB 718* crept round to the more sheltered side of the island, anchoring there at 0130hrs. This time Møller was happy with the landing place, and the transfer of the stores commenced.

Both agents had been desperately seasick for the previous 24 hours, and gratefully accepted hot food and sandwiches before saying farewell to the crew of *718* to start their lonely vigil. Ronald Seddon recalled1 feelings of admiration and pity for these

Norwegian agents, who were specially trained to survive for months on end on tiny islands or rocks, where they would carry out 24-hour surveillance, reporting by radio to London on the movement of enemy shipping.

After the operation ended, Seddon recorded bluntly in his log: 'Returned Aberdeen 0830 Feb. 15th after 58 hours at sea and with 5 feet of water in the bilges and mess decks.' They had encountered exceptionally foul weather on the way back across the North Sea, having to reduce their speed at times to 6kt. On arrival, salvage pumps were urgently requested, and by 1500hrs the bilges were clear of water. In his more lengthy official report, the list of defects speaks for itself: 'All watertight hatches on upper deck buckled by heavy seas; watertight bulkheads strained, and leaking from one compartment to another; making about two feet of water per day, possibly through shearing or loosening of bolts through sections of scarphing or the false keel; engine room supports to coachroof and Oerlikon bandstand bent; frames and stringers will require inspection throughout; underwater exhaust valves leaking; all doors below decks strained and out of line.'

In the final paragraph of his report to DDOD(I), Seddon wrote: 'I must wholeheartedly commend the spirit, resourcefulness, and conduct of the officers and men under my command, during these two and a half days of appalling conditions – conditions far in excess of the normal requirements of these small craft, and as physically exhausting to the men as to the boat.' A subsequent signal from the Admiralty asked Lt Seddon '. . . to convey to the ship's company most grateful thanks for this splendidly conducted expedition and to tell you that this potentially very important station is now operating and likely to be completely successful.'

MTB 718 undertook more operations to Norway in April 1945, involving landing agents and stores. Her final trip to these parts, however, was made in tragic circumstances that were felt by all those who served in the 15th MGB Flotilla.

8 May 1945 was proclaimed by Churchill and Truman as VE-Day. Crown Prince Olaf and British representatives had accepted the surrender of Norway by the Germans. Charles Milner, the telegraphist in *MTB 718*, picked up the news of VE-Day while the boat was on passage between

Lerwick and Aberdeen. After celebrating 'Victory in Europe' in the traditional Navy manner by 'splicing the mainbrace' (an extra tot of rum), the crew were given 72 hours' leave. When they returned, they learned that *MGB 502* (by then renumbered *2002*) had been mined, with only two survivors.

Just three days after VE-Day, *MGB 2002* had set out on a goodwill mission to Gothenburg in Sweden, as a mark of appreciation to those who had taken part in the blockade-running operations described in Chapter 3. Lt-Cdr Williams had, by this time, taken up an appointment on the staff of Capt Slocum, and handed over command of *2002* to Jan Mason. The CO of *MGB 2003* (ex-*503*) was Lt-Cdr 'Mike' Marshall, a popular officer and an Oxford rugger blue who had also played for England. He became Senior Officer of Slocum's flotilla, which by then included *MGB 2007* (ex-*507*) and *MGB 2009* (ex-*509*), two new MGBs from Camper & Nicholsons.

Jan Mason had been summoned to Buckingham Palace to receive his DSC, so Lt-Cdr Marshall took his place, commanding *2002* for her visit to Gothenburg. She left Aberdeen on 11 May, and nothing was heard of her until 16 May, when the two survivors, Able Seaman Norman Hine and Motor Mechanic Tommy Sheehan, were picked up by a Norwegian ship from a Carley raft. Both wounded, they had been on their float for five days after *MGB 2002* had been mined in the entrance to the Skagerrak. *MGB 2009* and *MTB 718* received orders to carry out a thorough search of the area, but no more survivors were found.

* * *

Yet another CO who became involved in undercover operations quite by chance was Lt Frederick Bourne of *MTB 344*, as a result of which, on the night of 2/3 September 1942, he found himself anchored off the enemy-occupied Casquets Lighthouse, seven miles west of Alderney, which the Germans were using as a radio listening post. A dory was carefully lowered from the MTB, and Majors March-Phillipps and Appleyard, with six commandos, slipped silently away towards the black shapes of the Casquet rocks. They returned later with German codebooks and seven prisoners – the keepers, radio operators, and guards. Most of them had been asleep, including one whose night attire included a hairnet.

March-Phillipps, Appleyard, and the other commandos belonged to the Small Scale Raiding Force (SSRF) based at Anderson Manor near Bere Regis, which had been set up as a joint enterprise by Combined Operations and the Special Operations Executive in consequence of Churchill's enthusiasm to see pinprick raids carried out in enemy-occupied territory. The commandos involved in such raids would number no more than a dozen, and usually less, the purpose of the raids being largely psychological, with limited military objectives. The idea behind the SSRF was to create a climate of insecurity on the other side of the Channel. Certainly its raids irritated the German High Command. Even more significantly, German guards, particularly along the Normandy coastline and in the Channel Islands, had to maintain a high level of vigilance on a permanent basis, and this effectively meant having to commit more resources to a purely defensive role.

Freddie Bourne had been waiting at *Hornet* for his first command when he met Lt Roger Thornycroft of the shipbuilding family. Learning that Bourne was looking for a boat, Thornycroft asked him if he would be interested in an experimental Thornycroft MTB in which the Army was taking a considerable interest. And so it was that Bourne assumed command of *MTB 344*, which the Royal Navy put at the disposal of the SSRF, who christened her 'The Little Pisser' because of her power compared with the MLs, which the Admiralty had initially offered.

MTB 344, a stepped-hydroplane 60ft hull, was launched on 10 February 1942. Her two Thornycroft 600bhp engines gave her a speed of 40kt in ideal conditions. For quiet running, she had a Ford V8 73bhp auxiliary. The two 18in torpedo tubes were removed to make space for the 18ft commando dory, which was fixed to a launching ramp at the stern. Her armament, for defence purposes only, consisted of two 0.303in Vickers machine guns either side of the bridge, Lewis guns aft of the crew's quarters, and two depth-charges. She was crewed by a CO, petty officer coxswain, petty officer motor mechanic, stoker, telegraphist, and three seamen. Conditions on board were cramped in the extreme, with a minute mess deck, which could sleep one or two at the most. The commandos had to huddle on the deck behind the

bridge or in their dory. The radio operator and motor mechanic worked in a noisy, confined space within six feet of the engines. The navigating table was a board placed over the top of one of the engines. Although it would have been extremely useful for the tricky navigation required, particularly around the Channel Islands, the boat was considered too small to carry radar. The advantage of her size, however, was that her low profile also made detection by enemy radar that much more difficult. On *344*'s first few operations, Lt Bourne would have to leave the bridge from time to time, disappearing below into the engine room to have a look at a chart. Later on, he was provided with an expert navigator, Rick Van Riel, who was a Belgian naval reservist.

Five days after the raid on Casquets, *MTB 344* returned to these waters to land commandos on the small island of Burhou, in the tidal race off the west side of Alderney. The purpose of the raid was to check if the Germans had installed a gun battery here. The island was deserted apart from a colony of puffins.

Still in the same moonless period (September 1942), *MTB 344* set out from Portsmouth on Operation *Aquatint*. The destination was, unusually, a long stretch of sandy beach near Port-en-Bessin in the Baie de la Seine to the east of Cherbourg. The commandos were led by Maj March-Phillipps, with Maj Appleyard remaining on board *344* as he had fractured a leg while clambering down to the dory from the Casquets lighthouse. As the commandos' dory was

MTB 344, Lt Bourne's experimental Thornycroft, carried commandos and, astern, their 18ft dory. The commandos would shelter behind the bridge or in the dory. *National Maritime Museum N12346*

approaching the beach it met a German patrol. There was much shooting, at the end of which most of the raiding party, including March-Phillipps, had been killed. The rest were taken prisoner, including Capt Graham Hayes, MC, who later managed to escape to neutral Spain, only to be handed back to the Germans, who shot him. One or two of the commandos did attempt to swim back to *MTB 344*, but could not escape the bullets of the beach party. By then the MTB had also come under fire, with a bullet putting one of her engines out of action. Caught in the beam of a searchlight, Lt Bourne had no option but to cut the anchor warp and leave with as much speed as could be summoned up on a single engine.

The next operation was a raid on Sark. Maj Appleyard would command the raiding party, which also included the legendary and much-decorated Danish commando Anders Lassen, VC, MC**. Rick Van Riel navigated *MTB 344* close into the rocky Sark coastline, to a position a quarter of a mile from Derrible Point, where they anchored. By taking this difficult approach they thought there would be less likelihood of encountering landmines. After evading a German patrol, the commandos broke into the house of a Mrs Pittard, from whom they learned a great deal about the conditions under German occupation. She told the commandos that the island garrison was housed in an annexe to the Dixcart hotel. They bade her farewell, and went in search of prisoners.

The guard outside the annexe was killed, enabling the commandos to storm the sleeping accommodation of the five soldiers billeted here. Pandemonium broke out, and many shots were fired. The German soldiers were screaming for help, and had their hands bound as they started the steep descent into Derrible Bay. In the end one prisoner was taken back to England. The remaining four prisoners continued to struggle hysterically, and had to be shot, still with their hands tied. This was to have serious repercussions; Hitler ordered that the large number of prisoners taken on the Dieppe raid should be manacled; a further decree was issued that any commandos, in or out of uniform, be they regular soldiers or acting as agents, armed or unarmed, would be executed. The locals had mixed feelings about the raid, but Churchill was delighted, personally congratulating Appleyard.

Operation *Fahrenheit* involved a passage from Dartmouth to the Pointe de Plouezec, on the north coast of Brittany. Its objectives were the semaphore station and command post used for directing an adjacent gun battery. Military intelligence had been provided with detailed information about the target by Resistance fighters Claude Robinet and François Menguy who, with three others, had escaped from France in a small, open boat, and, after five days at sea with little food, had been picked up by a British minesweeper. The commandos were partially successful, once again catching the enemy off guard, one sentry being killed and two badly wounded.

Lt Bourne and his crew participated in 17 raids, off the north coast of Brittany, Normandy, and the Channel Islands. The objectives ranged from the gathering of sand samples from beaches, to fixing limpet mines to ships in St Peter Port, Guernsey. After the SSRF had been disbanded in the summer of 1943, Freddie Bourne had occasion to call on Admiral John Hughes-Hallett, who had his headquarters in the Medina River, Isle of Wight. The Admiral made it clear that he viewed the pinprick raids as a total waste of war effort. Clearly he did not share the enthusiastic views of Winston Churchill. Lt Bourne, with restraint, told the

Admiral that this was not how the operations had been viewed in all his months of working with the Army. To register his displeasure, however, an understandably furious Bourne returned to *344*, cast off immediately, and made quite a spectacle by motoring out of Cowes at high speed.

* * *

When he first presented himself at Croydon Recruiting Office, Bob Haggard could hardly have foreseen the unusual circumstances in which he would eventually finish up in Coastal Forces. He had passed all his medicals and been informed that his first choice in the Royal Navy could probably be arranged. Then someone spotted that he was on a list of amateur radio operators, and he was immediately sent home to await further instructions, and told to read up as much as he could about radio.

Sharing his father's enthusiasm for designing and building radios, Bob Haggard had a transmitting licence by the time he was 16. Now he had to forget any ideas he might have had for his war service, for the Admiralty were about to point him in an entirely different direction. He was instead appointed to HMS *Flowerdown* as a civilian scientific officer in Admiralty Signals. *Flowerdown*, a forest of radio masts just outside Winchester, was the biggest Admiralty communications centre for all fleet radio. Haggard joined a small section in the Department of Scientific Development, carrying out top-secret work on radio frequencies.

Much of his time was spent identifying signals from submarines. Then he formed a small unit, equipped with a Commer van, searching for the signals being used to direct enemy bombers on to their targets. Bob Haggard's brief was to discover the nature and frequency of these radio transmissions, so that the beams could be effectively 'bent', rendering the signals unreliable. Having progressed well with this work, intelligence gleaned that the enemy was developing a new system for directing their bombers, which had been given the code-name *Wotan*. *Flowerdown* was both worried and puzzled by this development, and then someone remembered that Wotan was a one-eyed Norse God. The Germans had unwittingly revealed that they had devised signals to direct their bombers by using just one beam instead of two.

The next assignment would take Haggard, now

entitled to wear the uniform of an RNVR lieutenant, further afield. The Ultra centre at Bletchley Park had decoded signals indicating that Germany had developed a radio-controlled bomb, which they intended using on the Malta convoy routes and then at the Anzio beachhead. Haggard's brief was to establish the frequency and filtering system used by the Germans to control the bomb. With this information, it would then be possible to apply jamming to make the bomb considerably less effective. Working with a bomb disposal squad in Italy, Haggard eventually found an example of the radio receiving equipment intact in a deep hole behind the front line at Anzio, and he returned to the UK with the parts that would provide enough data to design a workable jamming system. By now this fearful weapon had already claimed one battleship and two destroyers, and blown the stern off a cruiser.

The authorities were well pleased with their young scientific officer, and sent him on a month's leave. After 10 days, however, he was called back and asked if he would care to volunteer for a series of undercover operations involving trips over to the enemy coast in an MTB. His department at *Flowerdown* was assembling a team that would consist of two officers and two ratings, to work on the identification of enemy radar signals. There were no ratings with this highly specialised skill, and *Flowerdown*'s only other scientific officer with any relevant experience was a family man, and not inclined to accept the invitation.

Haggard suddenly found himself and his work the subject of top-secret memos, emanating from the highest level, and with a similarly impressive distribution. Someone came up with the suggestion that the exercise should be code-named Operation *Hunting*, but Haggard, remembering how the Germans had given themselves away when they had named Operation *Wotan*, suggested this was too descriptive. They settled instead on Operation *Knitting*. The objectives were to establish the exact positions and frequencies of enemy radar sites along the Channel coastline, with particular importance being placed on information about the gun-laying radar stations.

The first operations took place during the months of planning before D-Day. The most obvious reason for requiring the radar frequencies was so that effective jamming equipment could be rapidly assembled. A less obvious but equally vital reason was that, by knowing the location of the enemy's radar stations, elaborate decoys could be deployed to confuse the enemy about the plans for the allied invasion. This deception strategy had been devised to discourage the enemy from moving their ground and air forces from the heavily-defended Pas-de-Calais region miles to the east of the planned Normandy invasion beaches.

The deception involved building dummy landing craft, trucks, guns and aircraft, and positioning them to give the appearance of the build up of an invasion force around the Straits of Dover. There were also transmissions of scripted radio traffic and messages to double-agents to confuse the enemy about the date and timing of the invasion.

Coastal Forces would take part in this highly successful deception. Hours before D-Day, HDMLs towing balloons with reflectors across the Channel, gave the appearance to German radar operators of invasion fleets approaching Cap D'Antifer to the east of Le Havre and the Pas de Calais.

Vital to the success of much of the D-Day deception was this detailed knowledge of the enemy's coastal radar stations. *MTB 255,* belonging to the 14th MTB Flotilla based at HMS *Aggressive,* Newhaven had been selected to collect the data (*Operation Knitting*). Built by J.S. White of Cowes, the Vosper-designed MTB was commanded by Lt Peter Aspinall, RNVR, with a highly skilled navigator, Sub-Lt Mike Day, as his First Lieutenant. She was withdrawn from routine flotilla service to be fitted with some strange-looking radio equipment. This included a funnel-shaped high frequency waveguide antenna which, 4ft long and 3ft wide, had the appearance of a loudspeaker horn. Since it was mounted on the foredeck, it was only possible to take bearings on the signals it picked up by swinging the boat until there was a nul reading, and then noting the ship's head from the steering compass. There was also a lower frequency dipole antenna at the top of the mast, which could be rotated from the wireless cabin, where Lt Haggard was installed. Half-empty fuel tanks, along with the permanent removal of her torpedoes and depth-charges reduced *255*'s draught sufficiently for her to pass over the top of any minefields too close inshore to have been recorded. However, her basic armament – twin 0.5in

MTB 255 was designed and built by J.S. White. She has a funnel-shaped high frequency antenna on the foredeck and a lower frequency dipole antenna on top of the mast. *R.G.R. Haggard*

machine guns in a power-operated turret amidships, pairs of Vickers 0.303in GO machine guns either side of the bridge, and an Oerlikon – were retained, though these were only to be used in defence. Demolition charges were also placed on board to prevent her falling into enemy hands.

Before the first operation, a memo was circulated from the Director of Naval Intelligence, indicating the importance attached to *MTB 255*'s undercover work. Bombing restrictions would be imposed within a five-mile radius of where she would be operating for the duration of each operation. Air cover would be provided, and *MTB 255* would be escorted by two other MTBs, usually from the 14th Flotilla, which would stay 20 miles out at sea (later altered to 10 miles) but would keep in radio contact in case assistance should be required.

The operations would take place when there was little or no moon. Haggard established himself aboard *MTB 255*, which was being viewed with some curiosity by the rest of the flotilla. He felt that he was a *bona fide* member of Coastal Forces, but there was one anomaly. He was not entitled to the 'hard-lying' allowance for roughing it in the MTB, because the Admiralty did not pay him. As a civilian scientific officer he would have been entitled to danger money for participating in these operations; this, too, was not forthcoming, as the Civil Service, although still paying him, insisted that he did not qualify because he was on loan to the Royal Navy.

The first six operations covered the coastline between the Pas de Calais and the Channel Islands. The original intention was to stay a minimum of 10 miles off the enemy coastline to gather the information. However, it was soon discovered that *MTB 255* had to cover too great a distance to get a second bearing on the radar signal, with a good angle between the two. With the navigator working on dead reckoning (estimating the distance covered over the ground between the two points), achieving the position of the radar with pinpoint accuracy was difficult. Being only five miles off the coastline made the calculations much more reliable, and also made it less likely that they would be identified on enemy radar as a fast-moving target. Eventually, after several operations, they usually took bearings on the enemy radar from within two miles of the coastline. Sometimes they nosed in even further, and on one occasion were so close to

Memorial plaque at Kingswear on the River Dart in South Devon to the 15th MGB Flotilla.

Cherbourg's outer breakwater that they could actually hear conversations in German.

There were times when they would be off what they were certain was a radar station, but were unable to pick up signals to confirm this. Working with thermionic valves, with a limited life, the German operators would turn off the sets to conserve the valves if everything looked quiet, and perhaps sleep was beckoning. On one peaceful night in a flat calm, Haggard and one of the crew went up onto the foredeck, where they banged saucepans to try and wake up the operators. At other times one of the MTB's engines was deliberately started up to guarantee that the operators would leap out of bed and rush to switch on their equipment.

A memorial monument on the Île Grande in northern Brittany to the 15th MGB Flotilla and French Resistance fighters in the *Alibi* network. *Michel Guillou collection*

The Admiralty and the RAF were both extremely pleased with the information obtained on the first six operations, and immediately suggested another six. Then came a further four, this time around the enemy-occupied Channel Islands, with the MTB working out of Dartmouth. More operations took place off the Belgian and Dutch coastlines, with the boat based on Ramsgate or Felixstowe. Bob Haggard recalls those occasions when, having arrived back at Newhaven after an operation, the crew would turn in, while he boarded the local train that ran between Newhaven and Brighton, and then joined the commuters travelling up to London. Dishevelled and dozing off in his naval greatcoat, he was convinced by the disapproving looks he received from his fellow passengers that they thought he had been out on a bender the previous night. Once in London, he would take the plots to the Admiralty, who would record the information and then despatch it, with the same urgency, to the RAF.

In all *MTB 255* would carry out 23 operations before her undercover role came to an end in the most tragic circumstances. The last of them, taking place after the D-Day landings, concentrated on areas off the Dutch rivers, particularly the Schelde estuary, where *MTB 255* was used to try to detect the launching of the V2 rockets, which were believed to be radio-controlled. Along with several other Coastal Forces craft, *255* was then based in Ostend. After the operation they were to return to Felixstowe. The CO had announced that they would sail at 1600hrs on 14 February 1945. He then went ashore to the operations room at Ostend. Haggard also went ashore, to visit the Y Service officer, responsible for intercepting enemy radio transmissions. The Y Service officer was, curiously, dealing with an irate Belgian who was convinced that one of the crews of the Coastal Forces craft lying in Ostend had stolen his pig. The heated argument continued, with Lt Haggard looking frequently at his watch, as *MTB 255*'s sailing time got closer. He was eventually able to have a brief discussion with the Y Service officer and then set off, half-running, back to the boat. He saw Peter Aspinall approaching in the other direction. They were both about 100 yards away when there was a colossal explosion. The cause has never been established for certain, but the explosion is believed to have occurred when *MTB 255* started her engines to warm them up. All aboard were killed instantly except for one man, who managed to swim clear of the boat only to die later. Many other boats caught fire and in the end almost all the MTBs belonging to the 29th Canadian MTB Flotilla were destroyed. There were many other fatalities, both amongst the MTB crews and the Belgian fire brigade.

It is difficult to imagine the shock of anyone who was at Ostend on St Valentine's Day, 14 February 1945. Bob Haggard returned to HMS *Flowerdown*, to continue research work on radio signals. A year later he resigned to follow a career in civil engineering.

Chapter Eleven

Allied Coastal Forces

FNFL

In January 1940, following service as an engineer in a number of merchant ships, Marcel Ollivier joined the motor vessel *Jean-Louis Dreyfus*. She was plying between France and the USA carrying vital war supplies, including deck cargoes of warplanes for assembly. At the end of June, his ship made for Liverpool, and it was here that he answered General de Gaulle's call for Frenchmen to take up arms against the Germans. Ollivier left his ship only after a bitter argument with the captain and with the local representative of the shipping company, whose sympathies were not at that time with de Gaulle.

Over the next few months, Ollivier's service with the Free French would take him to many different places in a variety of roles. He served in the artillery, the Foreign Legion (very briefly), and the tank corps, and saw action at Dakar and in the Gabon campaign. While at Duala in Cameroun he decided to return to sea, joining the sloop *Commandant Duboc*. Then, at Cape Town, he responded to a call for volunteers to crew Free French submarines in England, joining the *Surcouf* at Plymouth before eventually transferring to the flotilla of French *chasseurs* based at Cowes on the Isle of Wight,

Many Free French seamen had succeeded in reaching Britain, to join those of their ships which had escaped the Germans. Initially the Royal Navy had shown little enthusiasm for co-operating with the Forces Navales Françaises Libres (FNFL). This widely held mutual distrust was largely the result of Operation *Catapult*, in which, on 3 July 1940, a large squadron of British warships commanded by Vice-Admiral Sir James Somerville had opened fire on the French naval units anchored at Mers el Kebir, near Oran, after they refused to surrender. The

French fleet was crippled, with an appalling loss of over 1,300 lives.

Three French torpedo boats, VTBs *8*, *11*, and *12*, had arrived at Portsmouth in June 1940. Built of riveted plywood, these craft had been designed to outpace the Italian boats in the Mediterranean. They were based at Cowes and HMS *Tormentor* in Warsash, Southampton Water, but, after only limited use, it was decided that they were not suitable for war service because no spares were available to deal with increasing mechanical problems.

The Free French flotilla of heavily armed 38m (125ft) *chasseurs* (or 'chasers' as they were popularly known) was more successful. Operation of the *chasseurs* would soon impress the Royal Navy, and the Admiralty was persuaded by Free French Amiral Émile Muselier to provide four new B-Class MLs to replace the VTBs. MLs *123*, *245*, *246*, and *247* were handed over to the French in May–June 1941 and, after a period of working-up, they formed the 2nd Division of the 20th ML Flotilla based at Portland, providing escorts, defensive patrols and air/sea rescue.

In April–May 1942, after all the British boats in the flotilla had been lost at St Nazaire, the 20th was reformed with all-French crews and with the addition of MLs *182*, *205*, *269*, and *303*. The flotilla was working well by August 1942, when it was decided that the French-manned MLs should be decommissioned and returned to the Royal Navy in exchange for a flotilla of MTBs. The eight new 72ft 6in Vosper boats now formed the all-French 23rd MTB Flotilla. After sea trials at HMS *Hornet* the French crews worked-up at HMS *Bee* (Weymouth), where they received a visit from General de Gaulle. They arrived at Kingswear, on the River Dart, in February 1943. The flotilla's operational area was

French-built *Chasseur 41*, based at Cowes, Isle of Wight.

the French coastline between Brest and Cherbourg, and the Channel Islands.

The French were enthusiastic about their home-base at Kingswear. Their headquarters was Brookhill - a large villa in extensive parkland, overlooking the entrance to the River Dart. Officers were accommodated at Longford, a small hotel from which they could see their boats moored up alongside the old French sloop *Belfort*. The Free French seamen lived at Brookhill or were billeted with local families. The flotilla was controlled locally from the Coastal Forces' base in the Royal Dart Hotel (HMS *Cicala*). Their first SO was Capitaine de Corvette Meurville. Three French-speaking RNVR lieutenants, appointed as liaison officers, contributed to a healthy rapport between the French flotilla and their Royal Navy colleagues. RN telegraphists also served on the French boats. Unable to obtain their daily tot of rum, these telegraphists joined the French crews in a daily ration of a half-litre of *vin ordinaire*.

Like their British counterparts, much of the 23rd Flotilla's time at sea was spent on routine patrols,

from which its boats often returned with nothing to report. However, in an area where there were plenty of enemy convoys and E-boats there were also many skirmishes. Within weeks of their arrival in the West Country, two of the French boats scored their first success. A 2,000-ton merchant ship with an armed escort was sighted. While one MTB diverted the guns of the escort, the other made her torpedo run from the opposite direction, scoring two direct hits and sinking the freighter. Later on four boats patrolling off Jersey, operating in pairs, sank a 3,000-ton merchant ship and set alight one of her eight escorts, for which all four were awarded the Ordre de l'Armée. These - a uniquely French decoration, bestowed on the boat - were presented by General de Gaulle. The general must have been particularly proud of the 23rd Flotilla, because his son, Philippe, was second-in-command of one of its boats.

During the D-Day landings, the flotilla patrolled the western flank of the beaches. They assisted in the Brest blockade, and were the first French boats to enter this port. The 23rd carried out 451 patrols, with confirmed sinkings of five German ships, totalling 7,000 tons. British decorations included one DSO, five DSCs, two DSMs, and six mentions in despatches.

The French-built *chasseurs*, based at Portsmouth and later the Isle of Wight, were under the control of Commandant Kolb-Bernard. Apart from *No. 41*, which had a wooden hull, the 130-ton *chasseurs* operating in the Channel were steel-built. They carried a crew of about 38 made up of the CO, a second-in-command, three petty officers, and 30 ratings. Each boat also carried a British liaison officer (RN or RNVR) and a British telegraphist and radio operator. Powered by two MAN 1,600bhp diesel engines, the *chasseurs* had a maximum speed of 18kt. They were armed with a 75mm gun on the foredeck, two Lewis machine guns amidships, a 37mm gun at the stern (replaced in 1942 by a pom-pom), and an Oerlikon on each side of the bridge. In addition they usually carried six to eight depth charges. They were never equipped with radar, but Kolb-Bernard was successful in persuading the Admiralty to provide the boats with the latest in small craft ASDIC equipment.

In the early months of the war, the *chasseurs* saw action around the Frisian Islands and the River Schelde, and took part in the evacuation of Allied troops from Dunkirk. They arrived in England in groups, the first reaching the South Coast in June 1940. Initially based in Haslar Creek, Portsmouth,

Free French Amiral Lemonnier inspects *chasseurs'* crews at Cowes.

they then moved alongside an old First World War battleship, which was the Portsmouth harbour base for the Free French Navy until 1944, when she was used as one of the blockships sunk off Arromanches. The *chasseurs* moved to Cowes, Isle of Wight, in May 1941, after Kolb-Bernard and Admiral Muselier had persuaded the Admiralty to provide a base exclusively for the French gunboats. They took over Marvin's Yard, on the west side of the Medina River, just upstream of what is today the UK Sailing Academy. For their base ship, the boats used the 130-ton French sloop *La Diligente*, which was in a mud berth next to the chasseur pontoons. Life ashore for the crews centred around the Prince of Wales, the pub opposite Marvin's Yard. They were made to feel particularly welcome by the island's civilian population – which did not always please the Army personnel on the island. Dances and the cinemas in Cowes were well patronised by the French, and many of the crews had local girlfriends, some of whom they married after the war.

In May 1942 Cowes suffered considerable blitz damage. The 'chasers' and a Polish destroyer put up a heavy anti-aircraft barrage, but several French seamen were killed or wounded, and most of the buildings in Marvin's Yard were destroyed. Plans were then drawn up to provide a custom-built workshop with sleeping accommodation above.

The *chasseurs* took it in turns to spend the night on call off St Helen's Fort in the entrance to the Solent. This was at a time when the Admiralty felt that, in spite of the boom defences off the entrance to Portsmouth harbour, there was always the possibility of enemy midget submarines or similar craft slipping through. They also took part in the raids on Bruneval and Dieppe, provided convoy escorts along the Channel, carried out air/sea rescue operations, and escorted Allied submarines returning from Atlantic patrols. During the Normandy landings they were engaged off Juno and Omaha beaches.

Inevitably, they also suffered losses. *Chasseur 8* was sunk on 13 July 1942 with its entire crew except for the British liaison officer, who for a long time had also struggled to keep the badly wounded French captain alive. Their boat had been escorting a convoy from the Isle of Wight to Dartmouth when she was spotted by an isolated German aircraft, which had flown low over the *chasseur* and succeeded in dropping a bomb down her funnel. *Chasseur 5* foundered off St Alban's Head on 23 December 1943 while escorting a French submarine coming up from the Lizard. The weather was appalling and she simply capsized, the *chasseurs*, with their large, high bridges made top-heavy by the Oerlikons and ammunition, being difficult to handle in large seas. Only five members of her crew escaped from the upturned hull.

D-Day, or Jour-J as the French called it, must have been one of the most poignant moments of the Second World War for the many Free French who participated. Two days before D-Day, Chef Mecanicien Ollivier's boat, *Chasseur 41*, was on station for the usual night patrol off the entrance to the Solent. Afterwards it was revealed that Admiral Ramsay believed that German intelligence must have been aware of the invasion force assembling off the South Coast; even at this late stage, it was considered that a surprise attack on the invasion fleet, or a last-minute minelaying operation, should be anticipated. After an uneventful night, *41* returned to her mooring in St Helen's Bay. At around

noon, the CO, Enseigne de Vaisseau Michel Krotoff, was summoned by radio to report to the RN headquarters at Seaview to be given his D-Day briefing. There was a tinge of disappointment at not being amongst the first of the *chasseurs* to sail for Normandy on the night of the 5 June: only *10* and *12* were off the D-Day beaches on 6 June. *41* was the third of the *chasseurs* to arrive off France, 24 hours later.

At 0500hrs on D-Day, *41* received a signal to rendezvous with about 40 barges and lighters and escort them over to the Normandy beaches. Returning briefly to Cowes to take on fuel and supplies, they found the Solent still packed with invasion shipping, ranging from landing craft to huge troop carriers and liners, which would form the second wave of the Normandy landings.

Marcel Ollivier remembers his first sight of France. It was an emotional moment for those aboard *41*. There were hundreds of ships and the noise of battle everywhere, and clouds of smoke filled the skies beyond the beach. After handing over the barges and lighters to other escort boats, Krotoff was ordered to anchor as close as possible off Juno Beach. For hour after hour he watched tanks and other armoured vehicles clatter ashore, his crew permanently closed up at action stations. Around 2200hrs there was an air raid alert; out of the dusk, three Focke-Wulf 190 fighters flew low over the invasion fleet, probably on a reconnaissance mission. They attracted the fire-power of much of the Royal Navy, and also of *Chasseur 41*, her pom-pom and Oerlikons opening up as one of the fighters flew directly overhead and then disappeared with a long black trail of smoke.

At 2300hrs the sounds of bombardment on shore died away, although there was no cessation in the disembarkation of troops and equipment. Krotoff stood down his crew from battle-stations. *41* returned to Cowes a few days later, but not before her crew had set foot on French soil for a few hours. They learned later that *41* had been positioned close inshore off Juno to be on hand if a full-scale evacuation became necessary; it was the role she had already played at Dunkirk and Dieppe. Although *41* was not the first *chasseur* to reach the D-Day beaches, she was to be the first French Navy ship to enter Cherbourg and Dieppe.

Royal Netherlands Navy

Between the world wars, the Royal Netherlands Navy had gained experience in operating light coastal craft with four coastal motorboats (CMBs). These were the popular 55ft Thornycroft wooden boats, ordered by several navies. They saw extensive use in the Dutch East Indies, but were scrapped before the outbreak of the Second World War. Around the time of the Munich Crisis, the Dutch government authorised the building of a wide range of warships, but the programme had been set in motion too late, and the Royal Netherlands Navy would be ill prepared for the outbreak of war.

The Dutch government had wanted a strong force of MTBs to serve overseas, protecting their colonies in the East Indies, and the building programme included twenty 70ft MTBs for the Dutch East Indies, which, subject to satisfactory trials, would be based on the British Power Boat prototype *PV 70*. The Dutch government confirmed the order on the understanding that the first boat (*TM51*) would be built by British Power Boat at its

Hythe Yard, while the balance, it was planned, would be built under licence by the Gusto shipyard at Schiedam in Holland. Only two of these (*TM52* and *TM53*) were under construction when the Germans invaded. The German Navy used them as experimental boats, renumbered *S201* and *S202*.

In addition to the planned 70ft boats, work had also started on building 18 steel-hulled 63ft boats at Sourabaya in Java, while sixteen 70ft British Power Boat MTBs were subsequently constructed in Montreal to compensate the Dutch Navy for the non-delivery of the 70ft boats intended to have been built at the Gusto yard. Eight other MTBs, originally planned for the Royal Netherlands Navy to use in home waters (*TM54–TM61*), were also captured on the stocks at Gusto, and were completed by the Germans in 1940–1. With three Daimler-Benz diesel engines, these boats were over 90ft long and were of a design more along the lines

The Dutch crew of *MGB 46* at Ramsgate in 1942. *Institut voor Maritieme Historie, 's-Gravenhage*

of the German E-boat. These entered the German Navy as *S151–S158*.

Of all the MTBs being built in home waters for the Royal Netherlands Navy in 1940, only one (*TM51*) would actually sail under the Dutch flag. It was to play an important role, which ultimately led to the formation in Britain of two MTB flotillas manned exclusively by the Dutch Navy.

The story of *TM51* is remarkable. Just before the outbreak of war, this 70ft Scott-Paine boat was undergoing trials in Southampton Water before her anticipated hand-over to the Dutch. When war was declared, the situation changed overnight. The British Admiralty commandeered unfulfilled orders for foreign navies, which included *TM51* along with many other craft under construction. The Dutch, however, managed to persuade the Admiralty that the sea trials should be allowed to continue with a representative of the Royal Netherlands Navy on board, so that lessons learned from the trials could be applied to the two identical boats then under construction at Schiedam.

Lt-Cdr Otto de Booy, Royal Netherlands Navy, made certain that *TM51*'s fuel-tanks were full before setting out ostensibly for further trials in the Solent.

MGB 46, the former *TM51*, was the first Dutch MTB to be involved in the 'Narrow Seas' war. *Institut voor Maritieme Historie, 's-Gravenhage*

Once clear of land, she immediately altered course for Rotterdam, bound for the Gusto shipyard. Here she was worked up, and armed with two 20mm Hispano-Suiza turrets (she was already fitted with two 21in torpedo tubes). The Netherlands had, by this time, been mobilised for war.

TM51's first commanding officer was Lt Jan van Staveren. On 10 May 1940 Holland was invaded, German paratroopers dropping in large numbers near Rotterdam. In spite of being under fierce attack both from the air and from paratroops, *TM51* kept up a constant harassment of the enemy for several hours with her AA guns. With the boat damaged, but her engines still running, she finally withdrew and returned to the yard at Schiedam. For this action, Lt van Staveren received Holland's finest decoration for gallantry. Repairs to the boat were undertaken with great urgency, as arrangements were being made to evacuate the Dutch shipyards and make ready for sea all naval vessels being either refitted or in the final stages of construction.

Lt van Staveren was transferred to assist in the relocation of the newly built submarines, which were soon on their way to England (to HMS *Dolphin* at Fort Blockhouse, Gosport). In the CO's absence, it was decided that the civilian chief engineer of the Gusto yard should take charge of *TM51* for her own passage to England, assisted by a Dutch RNR lieutenant, who joined the boat at the Hook of Holland.

Lt Johan Schreuder first set eyes on *TM51* at Dover. During the early months of the war he had been serving in a First World War Dutch torpedo boat (similar to a small destroyer), operating in the English Channel and Irish Sea. He transferred to Coastal Forces in November 1940 and was immediately sent up to Ardrishaig to learn all about ASDIC equipment for fast motorboats. By this time, *TM51* had undergone a number of changes. She had been taken over by the Royal Navy, which had decided, because of the threat of German submarines, that she should be converted into a motor anti-submarine boat (*MA/SB 46*) and then operate as *MGB 46*, leader of the 3rd MGB Flotilla based at Fowey, Cornwall.

The Royal Netherlands Navy headquarters in London had been reluctant to agree to the transfer of *TM51* to the Royal Navy, which proposed, possibly by way of softening the blow, that in its place the Dutch Navy could take over a 63ft MGB (*41*), building in British Power Boat's Hythe yard. This was not to be, as there was a serious explosion which wrecked most of the port side of the hull. After this the Admiralty was again approached by the Royal Netherlands Navy, with a request to operate *MGB 46* (ex-*TM51*) with an all-Dutch crew. The Admiralty agreed and, with Lt van Staveren again in command and Lt Schreuder as First Lieutenant, *MGB 46* joined the British and Polish crews that then comprised the 3rd MGB Flotilla. While based in the West Country, much of the time aboard *MGB 46* was spent working up her new Dutch crew on exercises, and carrying out occasional escort duties.

At the end of August 1941 the flotilla received orders to sail to Dover where, along with three other flotillas and two Hunt-Class destroyers, they would take part in an operation intended to draw the Luftwaffe into combat with the RAF. It was anticipated that the sighting of the Royal Navy off the French coast at daybreak would put up the Luftwaffe, while only a few miles away, at airfields near Dover, 72 Spitfires and Hurricanes were ready for an immediate scramble to intercept them. But the Germans were not to be drawn, either on this occasion or on a subsequent attempt.

The 3rd MGB Flotilla stayed on at Dover. *MGB 46* remained under the command of Lt van Staveren until he was relieved by Lt Willem de Looze, who had arrived from the Dutch East Indies. On 11 September 1941, de Looze and Schreuder had their first experience of action in the Channel. This was followed by a number of successful operations in the Dover Straits, led by Lt Stewart Gould (the pre-war CO of *MTB 16*, in which he had made the trip through the French canals from Malta to the UK).

The performance of the only Dutch boat operating with Coastal Forces did not go unnoticed by the Admiralty, which decided that four Royal Navy MTBs in the 9th MTB Flotilla should be manned by all-Dutch crews. Lt de Looze was appointed to command one of these, and Lt Schreuder assumed command of *MGB 46*. As more UK-trained Dutch officers and men became available, the Admiralty decided to add to the Dutch-crewed boats to create an MTB flotilla (the 9th) operated exclusively by the Royal Netherlands Navy. Lt-Cdr Hans Larive was appointed Senior Officer. With another Dutch naval officer, he had escaped from the infamous Colditz prisoner-of-war camp, making their way through Switzerland, France, and Spain to Gibraltar, where they had been able to board a Dutch submarine for England.

On the night of 14/15 June 1942, *MGB 46*, in company with a combined force of MTBs and MGBs, was involved in her first major offensive. The boats, with Lt G.D.K. Richards, RN, as senior officer, left Dover to intercept a convoy reported to be making its way northwards along the French coast. As usual, heavily armed escorts accompanied the German merchant ships. The gunboats, including *MGB 46*, made the first approach to draw the fire of the escorts, so that the MTBs could close the convoy and fire their torpedoes. Having cut through to the landward side of the convoy and in a position just off Calais, *MGB 46* commenced laying lines of 'R' mines. During this operation she came under heavy fire, her chief motor mechanic being killed instantly as shells hit the engine room and fuel tanks. With the fresh and salt water cooling systems and fuel lines shattered, all power was lost.

Lt Schreuder ordered the gunners to cease fire so as not to draw any more attention to their plight as they drifted off Calais. The minelaying was completed, and the depth charges – now representing a serious hazard – were released. The abandoned engine room, full of petrol fumes, was again manned as the mechanics heroically struggled to restart the engines. One engine had been severely damaged; the second was started up but quickly became overheated; the centre engine, against all the odds, was started and kept going. Schreuder recollects that, to avoid being overcome by petrol fumes, he made the engine room staff consume large quantities of the milk which *46* had fortuitously taken on board.

As they started their slow passage back to Dover, the German convoy was still in sight. They could make out the MGBs engaging the escorts at close quarters, while the torpedo boats concentrated on two large merchant vessels. In this action one of the British MTBs in Hans Larive's formation was also hit by a shell in the engine room, with three killed and several wounded. Before she sank, the crew were taken off by another MTB and returned to Dover.

Later in the war, a second Royal Netherlands Navy MTB flotilla was to be formed with larger (71ft 6in) boats built by British Power Boat. These were powered with Packard petrol engines and more heavily armed. There was no shortage of volunteers, for many Dutch naval personnel had reached Britain after Holland fell to the Germans, coming both from Holland itself and the Dutch East Indies, where there had been a large Dutch fleet. Some underwent training at the Royal Netherlands Naval College in England. It was something of a tribute to de Looze and Schreuder that it was not considered necessary to appoint RN liaison officers to the two Royal Netherlands Navy flotillas, the Admiralty having been impressed with the way *MGB 46* had worked so successfully as part of the 3rd MGB Flotilla.

In September 1944, the two Dutch flotillas were returned to the Royal Navy, with the exception of one MTB and one MGB. With the liberation of the Netherlands came the monumental task of clearing the Dutch ports, which the Germans had demolished before they left. These two boats were employed to assist in this work, and also to establish

an early presence of the Royal Netherlands Navy in its own home waters.

The original *TM51*, built by British Power Boat back in 1939, had been finally handed over to the Royal Navy in mid-November 1942, and ended her useful life as a training boat for motor mechanics at Portland.

Polish Scigacze

Each of the ten Polish MTBs had the prefix 'S' for *scigacz*, which means 'fast hunter', a term that was used to denote an MTB or an MGB. The Poles never had the pick of the boats built in the UK, but they made up for this with a ruthless bravery. Of the Allied naval personnel whose countries had been occupied, those from Poland would have to live with the knowledge that theirs had suffered the most appalling loss of life. Such was Polish hatred for the Germans that they had an understanding, when working with British boats, that in the event of having to pick up enemy survivors after an engagement, this would always be undertaken by the British, as no Polish crew would ever have a German aboard their boat. British Coastal Forces officers witnessed this from Dover's breakwater on one occasion. A German plane had come down near the South Goodwin light vessel. The nearest boat was one of the Polish MGBs, on passage from Ramsgate to Dover, which was diverted to look for survivors. Those on the breakwater could see the wreckage and the Polish boat, which remained on the spot for some time; when the Poles were questioned about survivors on their return to the base, they simply shook their heads.

The London-based Commander-in-Chief Free Polish Forces, General Wladislaw Sikorski, had called for volunteers to join the Free Polish Armed Services. When Polish ships and personnel started to arrive at British ports, the Admiralty agreed to hand back one of two Samuel White 75ft boats which had previously been ordered for Poland (*MA/SB 48*, which became *S.1*). As more crews became available, the Admiralty allocated two more boats to the Free Polish Navy. These were part of a British Power Boat order for Norway for four 63ft MTBs. Finished for the Admiralty as MA/SBs *44* and *45*, these became *S.2* and *S.3*.

Jan Czarnota was motor mechanic on *S.2*. At 21, he had been conscripted into the Polish Air Force.

When Poland was invaded in September 1939, he escaped into Rumania, where, interned in a camp, he endured appalling conditions with other Polish refugees. After three months he managed to escape across the border into Yugoslavia, and thence to Greece, Marseilles, and a French Air Force holding camp at Septfond. He arrived in Britain on 1 April 1940, and was sent to an RAF camp at Eastchurch, where he was promoted to corporal. In June the following year, he decided to transfer to the Polish Navy, joining MGB *S.2* at Fowey in December 1941.

It was in the first three boats – *S.1 Chart* (*Greyhound*), *S.2 Wilczur* (*Alsatian*) and *S.3 Wyzel* (*Pointer*) – that the Poles built up their fearsome reputation. The Polish boats joined the cosmopolitan 3rd MGB Flotilla which was made up of Polish, Dutch, and British boats (one of which was commanded by a celebrated Frenchman, Roger Le Roux, who had changed his name to Roger King). The flotilla was working out of Fowey in autumn 1940, transferring to Ramsgate in August 1941. A fourth boat, *S.4* (commanded by Lt Schuster), originally built by British Power Boat as a

Polish *Scigacze* (*S.2* and *S.3*) at Ramsgate. *Michael Bray*

71ft 6in MGB similar to the new gunboats being taken over by Hichens at the end of 1942, was assigned to the 9th MGB Flotilla (later renamed the 2nd MTB Flotilla). She was returned to the Royal Navy just before D-Day.

The Senior Officer of the 3rd MGB Flotilla's Polish Division was Lt Wcislicki, known in Coastal Forces as Captain Whisky. On the 21 June 1942, *S.2*, with Wcislicki in command, was involved in a remarkable solo action with several E-boats. *S.2* and *S.3* were on night patrol off Dungeness as a convoy steamed through the Dover Straits. *S.3* radioed her operational base at Dover that she was having engine trouble, and the duty staff commander ordered the boats to return to port. At the same time, Dover radar was plotting the movement of E-boats which had left Boulogne to intercept the convoy. *S.2* remained at sea, choosing to misunderstand the signal from C-in-C Dover, and sped off to intercept the E-boats. Captain Whisky

The crew of *S2*, including Lt Wcislicki.

found six of them, making about 15kt in a south-westerly direction. With all guns firing, *S.2* passed right through the E-boats, which were attempting to encircle him. This caused such confusion amongst the E-boats that, at one time, they were actually firing at each other, adding to the damage already handed out by *S.2*. Only when her ammunition ran out did the Polish boat withdraw, returning to base with only superficial damage.

The following day, the duty staff commander had to point out to the Flag Officer Dover, Admiral Ramsay, that the captain of *S.2* had failed to return to Dover with *S.3* as instructed. Ramsay, however, accepted that, following the tradition of Nelson, a blind eye had been turned, and Lt Wcislicki was subsequently awarded the DSC. After the war he joined the Royal Navy, changing his name to Westlake and finishing his service as captain RN.

As more Polish crews became available, they formed the 8th MTB Flotilla, which was based at Felixstowe in 1944. They operated from here after

D-Day, when there were about 60 MTBs packed into the harbour for the last few months of the war in the North Sea. The boats in this Polish flotilla (*S.5–S.10*), were not a great success. They were part of Samuel White's 1943 programme of 71ft 6in MTBs, which were completed in 1944. They had hulls similar to the Vospers, but used the American Stirling Admiral engines, which were heavier than the Packards used in the Vosper boats. The Samuel White designers were reluctant to add to the displacement and lose performance by strengthening the hulls to take the additional weight of the engines together with a 6pdr forward, twin hand-operated Oerlikons aft, and two 18in torpedo tubes. In the end the boats had a number of structural problems. Unsuitable for the North Sea, they were paid off after only a few months in service.

Royal Norwegian Navy

Per Danielsen, an officer in the Royal Norwegian Navy, arrived at Lerwick in the Shetland Islands on 10 May 1940. His country was by then largely under

German occupation. He commissioned one of two new 60ft Vosper MTBs (*5* and *6*), powered by Isotta-Fraschini engines, and the Norwegian boats joined the 11th MTB Flotilla based at Dover. Although the boats had no First Lieutenant, they each carried a British liaison officer. Their crews were easily recognised by their Germanic steel helmets and uniform belts with dagger and scabbard.

This was a busy time for the 11th MTB Flotilla, by night out on E-boat patrol and by day providing a rescue service for crews of ships targeted by the Luftwaffe as they passed through the Dover Straits, and giving air/sea rescue cover. At the same time Dover itself was being subjected to almost continuous air raids (*as described in Chapter 7*).

In December 1940, Danielsen returned to Norway for a few days on an undercover operation for the Norwegian High Command. He then joined a destroyer, returning to Coastal Forces as CO of *MTB 5* in March 1941. His next appointment was *MTB 56*, a 74ft Thornycroft, one of a mixed bunch of boats operating out of Dover under Lt-Cdr Nigel Pumphrey as the 6th MTB Flotilla.

While here, he took temporary command of another Norwegian boat, *MTB 54*, taking part in a particularly daring attack that Lt-Cdr Pumphrey led against a German convoy. On the evening of 8 September 1941, Dover Command had received a signal indicating that a German convoy was leaving Boulogne, and looked likely to be sailing northwards through the Dover Straits. Only three boats in the 6th Flotilla were available – Lt-Cdr Pumphrey in *MTB 35*, Lt Bonnell, a Canadian, in *MTB 218*, and Danielsen in *MTB 54*. They planned to intercept the German convoy off Cap Blanc-Nez. On the point of departure, Danielsen signalled to Pumphrey that he was having engine trouble, and was told to catch up with the other boats as soon as possible. MTBs *35* and *218* raced across the Channel, guided by position reports from Dover, until they were just off the French coast and within close proximity of the approaching convoy.

Just before midnight, two merchant ships were sighted from Pumphrey's boat, followed by their formidable escort made up of E-boats and armed trawlers. The convoy had passed in a moment, and then it was necessary for the MTBs to reveal themselves by starting their wing engines to give chase. The MTBs were instantly illuminated by star

shells, both from the escorts and a shore battery. Several miles away, the sound of gunfire was heard by the crews of *MGB 43* (Lt Gould) and *MGB 52* (Lt Leith) of the 3rd MGB Flotilla, which had left Ramsgate on a routine night patrol and received a report on the position of the enemy convoy from Dover Command.

The scene had been set for the first of Dover Command's many successful combined MTB/MGB operations. After *MTB 35* had successfully torpedoed the rear merchant ship she withdrew, meeting up with Danielsen as he arrived in *MTB 54*. Pumphrey decided they should pursue the convoy, which had by then also been sighted by the gunboats. There followed a classic example of what was to become a standard Coastal Forces stratagem. While the gunboats diverted the attention of the escorts, the MTBs attacked the remaining merchant ship, *MTB 54* scoring two direct hits with its torpedoes. It was a proud night for Coastal Forces, the MGBs and MTBs having driven off several E-boats and destroyed an armed trawler as well as sinking the two merchant ships. Pumphrey, Gould and Danielsen all received DSCs for the action.

Within a matter of months, Danielsen was awarded his second DSC. On this occasion he was in his own boat, *MTB 56*, part of the Norwegian flotilla based at Scapa Flow. Because it lacked the fuel capacity to undertake a passage to and from Norway, it was decided to tow Danielsen's boat to within 30 miles of the coast, using the Norwegian destroyer *Draug*. After slipping the tow, *MTB 56* was able to make a suprise torpedo attack, sinking a tanker and one of her escorts.

The operations of the Norwegian 54th MTB Flotilla, based at Lerwick in the Shetland Islands, are outside the scope of this book. Suffice to say that, with Lt Danielsen as their first SO, their D-Class boats made many trips over to Norway, where they would lie in wait in the entrance to fjords or in the 'Leads'. Working with the British 52nd MTB Flotilla, they participated in many commando raids. Between October 1942 and June 1945, the Norwegian Dog-boats sank a total of 26 ships. From March to October 1944 the flotilla was based at Great Yarmouth, for deployment in the North Sea following the invasion, but subsequently returned to Lerwick before finally leaving for liberated Norway on 3 June 1945.

Norwegian *MTB 5*, later commanded by Per Daneilsen. *Vosper Thornycroft*

Per Danielsen had arrived in Britain by what would become known as the 'Shetland Bus' – undercover fishing boats operating a lifeline between Lerwick and occupied Norway. However, a fellow Norwegian, Finn-Christian Stumoen, took a much more circuitous route. He had joined the Norwegian Navy in April 1938, and was in Oslo at the Nautical School, studying for his mate's certificate, when Germany invaded.

Determined to join the Free Norwegian Navy, and with the Germans seeking him, Stumoen skied into Sweden on 9 April 1941. From Stockholm he flew to Helsinki, and from there travelled by train to Leningrad and Odessa, where he boarded a Russian passenger ship bound for Istanbul. He then crossed Turkey to Iskenderun, where many Norwegians had assembled. They boarded the British freighter *Durenda* for Port Said, arriving there with the holds flooded, after being bombed by a Vichy plane and an Italian Dornier. He then sailed from Suez in a Canadian troop carrier which eventually reached New York. There he signed on as third mate of a Norwegian tanker, which joined a huge Atlantic convoy, and he ended up at Loch Ewe, on the west coast of Scotland, at the end of October 1941.

After reporting to the Norwegian Navy headquarters in London, Stumoen joined *ML 210*, the Norwegian Navy having taken over eight Royal Navy Fairmile B MLs early in 1941. Crewed mainly from Norwegian merchant ships, the 4th ML Flotilla sailed from Portsmouth to Reykjavik, via Weymouth, Oban, Inverness, Scapa Flow, and Vestmanna island. They carried out anti-submarine patrols around Iceland, and then, in the late summer, sailed for Scotland and then Weymouth. Here, four MLs were returned to the Royal Navy and the remaining four reformed as the 52nd ML Flotilla, having been converted to minelayers at Poole. The Fairmile B funnel was removed, and 'dumbflows' were fitted to the exhaust systems for silent running. The flotilla arrived at Dover in July 1942, joining up with the four British minelaying Fairmiles that constituted the 50th ML Flotilla. For the next two years the two flotillas would work together, laying mines along German convoy routes and in the entrances to enemy ports between Zeebrugge and Boulogne.

Minelaying was a particularly exacting operation, and there was remarkable secrecy about the work of the two flotillas. The mines, stored in bombproof shelters built in the cliffs, came on board during the day, with Wrens setting the depth and the safety pins. The boats would go out at dusk, mostly during moonless periods. In a confirmed position, sometimes marked with a temporary buoy, the

boats would measure the distance from the mark by running out a reel of thin wire. Before the mines were dropped, the coxswain would remove the safety pins, which had to be handed in on their return to Dover, along with a note of the exact position of the new minefield. On the way across the Channel, the boats would be diverted by Dover radar to avoid any enemy patrols. Once over the other side, however, there was always the risk of being discovered by inshore patrols, which, along with shore batteries in the vicinity of the minelaying operations, were a constant worry.

Since the war, the Naval Historical Branch has confirmed that the Norwegian 52nd ML Flotilla and the British 50th ML Flotilla carried out 170 operations off the French, Belgian and Dutch

Minelayers of the Norwegian-manned 52nd ML Flotilla ('B' Class) worked from Dover alongside the Royal Navy's 50th ML Flotilla ('A' Class).

coastlines. Between them they laid 4,000–5,000 mines, which were responsible for sinking 53 ships and damaging another 34. Out of the eight boats that formed the combined flotillas, two British and two Norwegian MLs were lost.

On 30 November 1989, for the first time in 45 years, the survivors of the Norwegian 52nd and British 50th ML Flotillas were reunited at Dover, when the Norwegians presented a Christmas tree to the town in appreciation for the kindness and hospitality they had received during the war.

PT Boats

The three American PT (patrol torpedo) boats that arrived at Dartmouth on 24 April 1944 were shipped over to carry out clandestine operations similar to those undertaken by the 15th MGB Flotilla (*see Chapter 10*). The US Office of Strategic

Services had decided that, as a matter of urgency, it required its own agents in France.

Commanded by Lt-Cdr John D. Bulkeley, the American crews of the three early 78ft Higgins PT boats selected for these missions (PTs *71*, *72*, and *199*) underwent rapid training in the use of surfboats, which had been provided by the 15th MGB Flotilla. Their crews had to learn in a matter of days all the skills which the 15th Flotilla had acquired after many weeks of training. Navigation close inshore and off an enemy-occupied coastline was a new experience, and it would be some time before they had mastered the skills of handling a wooden surfboat. Nevertheless, they successfully completed 19 missions, without ever disclosing their landing places to the enemy or endangering the local French Resistance. Halfway through their clandestine work they were redeployed to the American sector of the D-Day landings.

The PT boats had arrived at a time when the nights were at their shortest, and to complete an operation under cover of darkness called for a fast passage to and from Brittany. With more speed than the Camper & Nicholsons and the D-Class Fairmile, the PT boats would occasionally be used for British operations. On these occasions, their crews would benefit from the experience of the accompanying officers from the 15th MGB Flotilla. Andrew Smith recalled Operation *Carpenter*, carried out in one of the PT boats before its American crew had become familiar with undercover operations. Lt Smith went as landing officer, with his CO, Lt-Cdr Marshall, in overall command of the operation. On the way over they passed patrolling British destroyers, and, to the horror of Marshall and Smith, the PT boat captain fired off a Very pistol flare in greeting (the 15th MGB Flotilla were trained to avoid any sort of contact with passing ships). Then, when they were nearer the Brittany coastline, with the attendant likelihood of German patrols being in the vicinity, the American First Lieutenant decided to try out his revolver, shattering the silence of the night and narrowly missing Smith.

The young American CO was unused to manoeuvring his boat amongst rocks and surf,

especially at a difficult slow speed. The PT boat went dangerously close to grounding, necessitating Lt-Cdr Marshall rapidly taking over the boat to move her into deeper water The calamities continued – one of the American surfboat crew fell into the water, and then Lt Smith had to relaunch his surfboat to pull the PT boat's stern round before it could make a fast getaway as the first streaks of dawn lit the sky. The Americans must have been thankful that the two British officers were on board, for the PT boat soon hit trouble again. This time the steering system broke down, but thanks to the ingenuity of Marshall and Smith a jury rig was fixed up aft, and the PT boat was able to resume her passage at 40kt, hand steered by the coxswain and chief motor mechanic. At times these two were

The much decorated Lt-Cdr John Bulkeley, US Navy, who had served with great distinction defending the Philippines after Pearl Harbor, assumed overall command of the PT squadrons that took part in the Normandy landings in June 1944. *US National Archives*

dangling perilously over the water on the end of a lashed up tiller extension, unable to move the rudder until the boat slowed down.

More PT boats were shipped over from the States to participate in Operation *Neptune*, the naval aspect of the Normandy invasion. Squadron 34, made up of 12 Elco PT boats, arrived in May in time to take part in the actual D-Day landings. The squadron was split into four divisions, to protect the minesweepers which would cross the Channel before the main fleet to establish mine-free approaches to the beaches. They nearly arrived 24 hours early off Normandy, information about the

invasion's postponement from 5 to 6 June because of the weather having arrived at the PT boat base at Portland too late to stop them sailing. They were halfway across the Channel before being intercepted by a patrolling destroyer and sent back.

The three boats from Dartmouth were used as despatch boats, each assigned to an admiral's flagship. After its minelaying escort duties, Squadron 34 reassembled and joined the Western Task Force protective screen, which included destroyers, the British steam gunboats, and a D-Class flotilla. The PT boats were responsible for patrolling an area code-named the 'Mason Line',

Inspection of the Normandy beachhead on 14 June 1944: *PT 199* with Admiral Harold R. Stark, US Navy, aboard. *US National Archives*

operations, taking on board over 200 survivors. One of the PT boats, investigating the reported sighting of a submarine, was herself mined, just managing to be kept afloat overnight in the anchorage off the Îles St Marcouf until she could be beached, when temporary repairs could be carried out, sufficient for her to be towed back to Portland.

On D-Day +7 (13 June), in a desperate attempt to disrupt the landing of Allied supplies and equipment, the Luftwaffe bombed the shipping off the invasion beaches at night, first dropping floats filled with long-burning flares in an attempt to illuminate their targets. The German bombers tried this on two subsequent occasions, but each time were foiled by the PT boats, which were quickly on the scene to sink the floats with their machine guns.

One of the boats in Squadron 2, engaged on despatch duties, was given the task of giving the top brass of the American forces a conducted tour of the invasion beaches. Her CO, Lt W.M. Snelling, USNR, believed he achieved a record for the PT boats, carrying no fewer than five generals, including Eisenhower and Bradley, and five admirals.

Twenty-one PT boats remained on station during the four days of atrocious weather (19–22 June) that destroyed the American Mulberry artificial harbour off Omaha Beach, to the west of the British Mulberry at Arromanches. A week after the storm Cherbourg was about to be surrendered to American troops, and the PT boats were moved westwards, hoping to catch E-boats escaping from the port. They approached the outer harbour forts to find out if they were still occupied. The forts were, and *PT 521* just escaped serious damage from their gun batteries. A day later there were white flags floating over the forts, and the PT boats would soon gain access.

In August, Squadron 2 returned to its undercover operations out of Dartmouth, while nine PTs joined the Portsmouth-based MTBs patrolling off Cap d'Antifer, and another 18 were based at Cherbourg, patrolling off the Cotentin peninsula to intercept any enemy shipping sailing between St Malo and the Channel Islands, or between the islands

which extended 6½ miles to seaward of the Îles St Marcouf, on the western flank of Utah Beach. A new squadron, the 35th, consisting of another 12 Elco boats, was on station on the 'Mason Line' on 7–8 June, just three days after arriving in the UK as deck cargo, while Squadron 30, made up of six Higgins PT boats, reached the 'Mason Line' on 10 June. Up until the end of June there were, on average, 19 PT boats on patrol; each boat remained out for at least a week before returning to its Portland base.

No E-boats were ever sighted by the PT boats patrolling the 'Mason Line'. Mines were the greatest menace, and the boats took part in many rescue themselves. Here the US Navy successfully employed the technique, developed by the Royal Navy, of using the radar of a destroyer or frigate to deploy the PT boats. Peter Scott was loaned as a liaison officer, working from a destroyer with the American PT boats, Canadian Dog-boats, and the French 23rd MTB Flotilla. They carried out several successful engagements around the islands, though one PT boat was lost, with several casualties.

Having seen surprisingly little action when they were patrolling the 'Mason Line', the PT boats, along with British MTBs, found plenty off Le Havre, and from Cap d'Antifer eastwards as far as Fécamp. On 6 August, three PT boats were in action against three E-boats, which they damaged and sent scurrying back to Le Havre. At the end of the month, the PT boats were out on four successive nights, helping to blockade Le Havre. Eventually Le Havre and Dieppe surrendered, which marked the end of the PT boat offensives in the 'Narrow Seas'. On 12 May 1945, just three days after Germany had surrendered the Channel Islands, the PT boats escorted the first Allied ships into St Peter Port, Guernsey, and St Helier, Jersey.

The Canadians

The Canadians, like the Americans, only had their own Coastal Forces' flotillas operating in the 'Narrow Seas' towards the end of the war. There were, however, many Canadian reservists who came over to Britain much earlier. One of these was a young painter, Anthony Law, who has already appeared in this narrative as CO of one of Lt-Cdr Pumphrey's flotilla, which went out from Dover to intercept the *Scharnhorst*, *Gneisenau*, and *Prinz Eugen* (*see Chapter 8*). He was one of the first group of Canadian reservists to arrive in England on loan to the Royal Navy, sailing from Canada in early April 1940 aboard the *Duchess of Athlone*. After officer training at HMS *King Alfred*, Hove, Law served in a converted armed merchant cruiser patrolling around Iceland, and then completed an anti-submarine course at Portland. His next appointment was to Coastal Forces.

At the beginning of 1944 there were still no boats with all-Canadian crews, but this changed when Law was selected to form the 29th Canadian MTB Flotilla, which would be made up of eight new Mark VI, 71ft 6in British Power Boats (MTBs

459–466), building at Hythe and Poole. A fellow countryman, Lt J.R.H. Kirkpatrick, would form the 65th Canadian MTB Flotilla with eight, then ten D-Class Fairmiles.

The first of the Canadian 'shorts' was commissioned in late March 1944, and sailed for HMS *Bee*, to work up at Holyhead. The remainder of the flotilla followed at intervals, and was joined at Holyhead by the Dog-boats of the 65th MTB Flotilla. However, during the 29th MTB Flotilla's working-up period, enthusiasm for their boats was somewhat dampened by an Admiralty decision that they should be stripped of their torpedo tubes. Instead, each boat would be provided with 48 small depth charges. This move resulted from concern about reports of a new type of German submarine which would have represented a real threat to the invasion plans. Intelligence reports claimed that the German W-boat, powered by a hydrogen peroxide-fuelled turbine, was capable of a surface speed of 40kt, and an underwater speed of 30kt. The Canadians were incensed, feeling that they would now be far less effective in action. There was a certain irony in the fact that their boats were amongst the first of British Power Boats' Mark VI design, which successfully combined the roles of motor torpedo boat and motor gunboat. The boats would eventually regain their tubes when the W-boat scare was proved to have resulted from two separate pieces of intelligence having been mistakenly combined, but this would not be until well after D-Day.

Based at Ramsgate, four boats in the flotilla had their first taste of enemy action on 22 May 1944. In the company of four MTBs from another flotilla, Canadian boats *459*, *464*, *465*, and *466* were selected to intercept an enemy convoy off the French coast. This was believed to have a strong escort of flak trawlers, together with E-boats or R-boats. The Staff Officer Operations was pleased with the resultant night's work, and reported to the Admiralty that the Canadian boats had successfully engaged the convoy escorts at close quarters in an intense five-minute action, which enabled the four British boats to withdraw safely after their torpedo attack.

The action proved to be a rehearsal for the 29th Flotilla's D-Day role. They left Ramsgate for Portsmouth on 28 May to prepare for the invasion, the 29th Flotilla, along with the D-Class Fairmiles of

Lt-Cdr D. Gould Bradford's 55th MTB Flotilla, having been selected to protect the eastern flank of the British assault area. This would involve intercepting enemy ships based in Le Havre. Their parent control ship would be HMS *Scylla*, flagship of Admiral Philip Vian. Two boats of the 29th Flotilla left Portsmouth on 5 June, to escort the advance party of minesweepers. Four more left on D-Day, to carry out the first of their patrol duties off the eastern flank of the invasion beaches. They would have an immediate foretaste of the fierce fighting in which the flotilla would be involved for the best part of the next two months.

On their first night out, the four boats had a furious battle against six R-boats, during which both forces strayed into a British minefield, laid some distance off Le Havre. They sank one R-boat, but all four MTBs were damaged in the action, and they had several casualties. At first light the boats went in search of medical aid, only to find that the sickbays

Lt-Cdr Law, DSC, RCNVR, and the crew of *MTB 459*, one of the Mk VI 71ft 6in British Power Boats of the 29th Canadian MTB Flotilla (MTBs *459–466*), which played a major role in the D-Day landings. *National Archives of Canada PA108024*

in HMS *Scylla* and a nearby hospital ship were already full, but eventually they managed to find a doctor aboard a destroyer.

The following night the four boats were out again, patrolling the same area. They came across two Möwe-Class German torpedo boats, which they attacked with their limited firepower, wishing all the while that the Admiralty had not deprived them of what could have been a far more effective weapon – their torpedoes.

The four boats returned to Portsmouth for 48 hours during daylight on 8 June, when the base staff at HMS *Vernon* worked round the clock to get the boats operational again. Three of the flotilla's remaining four boats took over the patrol area, being vectored by *Scylla*, and meeting the same Möwe-Class torpedo boats that had been out the previous night. They fought at close range, and the MTBs scored many direct hits, but in the process the flotilla suffered its first fatality, one of the crew on *MTB 464*. After a second night on patrol the three boats returned to Portsmouth. Thereafter the two halves of the flotilla alternated, 48 hours in the British assault area, followed by 48 hours back in Portsmouth. It was during the periods back at HMS *Vernon* that half the boats had their torpedo tubes refitted. The patrols gradually became less eventful, apart from another meeting with the two Möwe-Class ships; HMS *Scylla* used the MTBs as decoys while sending in British destroyers, but the Möwes raced back to Le Havre.

On the night of 14/15 June Le Havre was bombed, and the patrols became less hectic for a few days. Five days later, with the weather deteriorating, Lt-Cdr Law advised *Scylla* that the boats would seek shelter alongside one of the merchant ships sunk offshore to provide protection for the Mulberry Harbour at Arromanches. After an appalling night, with the gale rising to a storm, the three boats were told to seek shelter in Courseulles. Negotiating the shallows and obstructions off the narrow entrance with some trepidation, they spent the next 48 hours secured snugly behind lock gates in the inner harbour while the storm raged outside.

The 29th Flotilla continued its punishing routine for another four weeks. Cherbourg had been captured, but German resistance to the east of the landings grew more intense. E-boats and R-boats were still operating out of Le Havre, the shore batteries along the coast to the north of Cap de la Hève were a real threat, and air attacks were possible. Mines, however, were perhaps the worst menace. They were everywhere, many being dropped from the air. Yet another worry for the MTBs was the carpet of debris, such as heavy baulks of timber, which could easily knock propellers out of alignment. On 1 July Lt-Cdr Law's own *MTB 459* hit some timber, and had to return to Portsmouth to be slipped for new propellers. While he was ashore, Law learned that *MTB 460* had struck a mine. Six survivors and two bodies had been recovered. Two officers and nine ratings were missing.

One of the many famous Coastal Forces' battles took place on the night of 4/5 July. MTBs *459*, *462*, and *464* were lying in wait, close to the cliffs between Cap d'Antifer and Cap de la Hève, and Lt-Cdr Bradford's 55th Flotilla was eight miles to the south. Their control ship (now a frigate, as HMS *Scylla* had been mined) was eight miles offshore. Conditions were ideal for the MTBs. It was calm, and the moon would illuminate German E-boats once they had left Le Havre. Sure enough, at around midnight, nine E-boats were sighted rounding Cap de la Hève. The three Canadian MTBs raced towards them, and in an exchange of fire one of the E-boats was set aflame and seen to be sinking. The eight remaining E-boats then withdrew, only to run straight into Bradford's flotilla. In another hard-fought battle the E-boats were driven back in the direction of MTBs *459*, *462*, and *464*, which resumed the combat. This time Law's boat was badly hit and, once they had disengaged, the three MTBs were dive-bombed and subjected to heavy fire from German shore batteries. A second unit of E-boats now arrived on the scene, coming down the coast from Fécamp, and another furious battle started, but this time, in the confusion, it was the E-boats that were firing at each other. *459*, *462*, and *464* went in again, and the E-boats, not having the stomach for more, turned for Le Havre, only to meet up with the 55th Flotilla once again. Even then the action was not over. *MTB 462* had returned to the control ship with engine trouble, leaving *459* and *464* to do battle with two M-Class minesweepers escorted by two R-boats, which again disengaged, heading off towards Le Havre and Lt-Cdr Bradford's waiting flotilla.

On 8 July *MTB 463* hit a mine and sank, all her crew being taken off by *466*. With losses mounting, the flotilla had to reform its two divisions. On the night of 9 July, MTBs *459*, *461*, and *464* were lying between Le Havre and Cap d'Antifer when they picked up the sounds of battle to the north of them, and on investigation discovered two British MTBs surrounded by 10 R-boats. One (*MTB 434*) was on fire, and the CO of the other called up the Canadian boats and asked them to pick up survivors, as his boat was damaged and taking in water. They made one attempt to close the burning MTB, but had to disengage under heavy gunfire from the R-boats. All the Canadian boats had by now been damaged, and there was one fatality. A second attempt, with one of the boats this time making smoke, was more successful, and survivors were picked up from two Carley floats.

The strain of the war was beginning to tell. On 16 July the SO's boat, illuminated by flares, was seriously hit in the engine room, suffering two fatalities. The flotilla had by then lost three craft and a third of its crews had become casualties. However, from this time, as the enemy were pushed eastwards, part of the flotilla was able to work from the mobile coastal forces base (CFMU No. 1) at Arromanches, where they remained until the beginning of August.

After combat leave and major refits, the flotilla moved up to Ramsgate, where it was able to meet up with Lt Kirkpatrick's 65th Canadian Flotilla, which had stopped off at Dover. By comparison with the 29th, the 65th, patrolling the western sector of the D-Day beaches, had seen little action. Its main offensive action had been against a convoy with a heavily armed escort off St Malo, in which its boats sank two merchant ships, set one escort ablaze and damaged several others.

In October the 29th Flotilla moved round to HMS *Beehive*, Felixstowe, where it had an uneventful time patrolling in the North Sea. At the beginning of the New Year, the flotilla was told that its new base would be CFMU No. 1, which was now operating in Ostend. The flotilla sailed for Ostend on 15 January 1945. Lt-Cdr Law returned to England on 14 February to have his new boat's radar repaired, and on 15 February the SO of HMS *Beehive* asked to see him. The news he then received was devastating. The 29th Flotilla had been involved in the greatest single disaster in the history of Coastal Forces. There had been an explosion on one of the boats lying in the inner basin of Ostend, which had rocked the town. Fire spread quickly across petrol spilled on the water and engulfed the Canadian boats. In just seven minutes, 60 lives had been lost, along with seven British and five Canadian MTBs. The magnificent 29th Canadian MTB Flotilla had been almost wiped out, and 26 of its crewmen, who had fought courageously in so many actions, were dead.

The aftermath of the tragedy at Ostend. *National Archives of Canada PA116784*

Chapter Twelve

Finale

Germany surrendered on 7 May 1945 at General Eisenhower's headquarters at Reims. The ceasefire would come into effect at 2301hrs on 8 May – VE-Day. Five days later, crowds gathered on the quays at Felixstowe to witness the arrival of two German E-boats from Rotterdam. Out at the South Falls buoy, off the Thames estuary, was a reception party consisting of 10 MTBs, with the Senior Officers of most of the flotillas based on the East Coast. In overall command was Lt-Cdr John Hodder in his Fairmile D,

accompanied, as a guest, by Lt-Cdr Peter Scott. The E-boats were sighted at about 1400hrs, both flying the white flag. They were signalled to stop, and Lt-Cdr Hodder manoeuvred alongside the leading E-boat, which had its bridge packed with high-

Rear Admiral Karl Bräuning salutes Cdr D.H.E. McCowan, DSO, DSC, RNVR, commanding officer of HMS *Beehive*, Felixstowe, following the surrender of E-boats *S204* and *S205* on 13 May 1945. *IWM A28560*

Surrendered E-boat crews at Felixstowe.
IWM A28562

ranking German officers, including Rear Admiral Karl Bräuning.

Peter Scott, who spoke adequate German, boarded the E-boat with two other officers and two signalmen. In his autobiography (*The Eye of the Wind*), he wrote that he felt normal formalities should be observed, and that the behaviour of the British should be scrupulously correct. He saluted Admiral Bräuning, who saluted back. Scott said that he understood the admiral had come to surrender. Bräuning, a small, dapper man in a long, grey leather coat, said that this was not the case; Germany had already surrendered. His mission was to hand over personally to the C-in-C Nore charts of the German minefields, and he indicated that he hoped to return to Germany once this task had been completed.

Scott insisted that White Ensigns should be flown on both E-boats, and that their crews should line the deck as they entered Felixstowe to the excited cheers of the assembled crowd. Armed guards then boarded the E-boats to take off the crews. The

German admiral was piped ashore and then piped again when he boarded the C-in-C Nore's barge. Manned by Wrens, the launch sped off in the direction of Harwich. Admiral Bräuning was then taken by car to Chatham, the C-in-C's headquarters, and was interrogated there before being taken off to a prisoner-of-war camp.

Three months after the surrender of the German E-boats, Ronald Seddon's *MTB 718* was on passage from Portland to Portsmouth. She had come down from Aberdeen, stopping off at Portland to off-load stores and equipment prior to decommissioning. With a skeleton crew, she sailed into Portsmouth harbour, stopping off at the King's Stairs in the Dockyard to take on a young, fresh-faced sub-lieutenant who was to pilot *MTB 718* to her final resting place. One of over a hundred Coastal Forces' craft of all shapes and sizes, *MTB 718* was

unceremoniously driven onto the mud in Portchester Creek.

Few of those deserted boats could match *718*'s remarkable history, with her record of undercover operations in the 15th MGB Flotilla. But they had all played a role in Coastal Forces. Anti-E-boat patrols

TOP LEFT: *S221*, a surrendered E-boat, is escorted into Portsmouth Harbour on 22 June 1945. *IWM A29321*

LEFT: German crews leave three surrendered E-boats – *S221*, *S212*, and *S213* – at HMS *Hornet*, Gosport, on 22 June 1945. *IWM A29323*

Fairmile B MLs laid up at Gillingham awaiting disposal.

night after night; vital air/sea rescue work in the Channel; the monotony of the Z-line patrols; mine-spotting off the Thames estuary; minelaying and minesweeping; patrolling harbour entrances; or escorting convoys – all were essential tasks, and all were performed by the 'Little Ships'. The crews of the boats that were now abandoned in Portchester Creek and elsewhere round the British Isles, and those who had served ashore to keep them operational, could be justifiably proud to have served in Coastal Forces.

Bibliography

Armstrong, Warren, *HM Small Ships* (Muller, 1958)

Beardow, Keith, *Sailors in the RAF* (Patrick Stephens, 1993)

Brown, D.K. (ed.), *The Design and Construction of British Warships, 1939-1945*, Volume II (Conway Maritime Press, 1996)

Bulkeley, Capt Robert J., *At Close Quarters* (US Naval History Division, 1962)

Cooper, Bryan, *The Battle of the Torpedo Boats* (Macdonald, 1970)

——, *The E-boat Threat* (Macdonald & Jane's, 1976)

Dickens, Capt Peter, *Night Action* (Peter Davies, 1974)

Foynes, J.P., *The Battle of the East Coast* (privately published, 1995)

Granville, Wilfred, and Kelly, Robin A., *Inshore Heroes* (W.H. Allen, 1961)

Guillou, Michel, *Operation Farenheit* (AERHDGM, 1994)

Hampshire, A. Cecil, *The Secret Navies* (William Kimber, 1981)

Hichens, Robert, *We Fought them in Gunboats* (Michael Joseph, 1944)

Holman, Gordon, *The Little Ships* (Hodder & Stoughton, 1943)

Lambert, John, and Ross, Al, *Allied Coastal Forces of World War II*, Volumes 1 and 2 (Conway Maritime Press, 1990, 1993)

Lambert, John, *The Fairmile 'D' Motor Torpedo Boat* (Conway Maritime Press, 1985)

Law, C. Anthony, *White Plumes Astern* (Nimbus Publishing, 1989)

North, A.J.D., *Royal Naval Coastal Forces 1939-1945* (Almark Publications, 1972)

Pickles, Harold, *Untold Stories of Small Boats at War* (Pentland Press, 1994)

Ranee, Adrian, *Fast Boats and Flying Boats* (Ensign, 1989)

Reynolds, Leonard C., *Dog Boats at War* (Sutton Publishing, 1998)

——, *Home Waters MTBs and MGBs at War* (Sutton Publishing, 2000)

Scott, Peter, *The Eye of the Wind* (Hodder and Stoughton, 1961)

——, *Battle of the Narrow Seas* (Country Life, 1945)

Smith, Peter C., *Hold the Narrow Sea* (Moorland Publishing, 1984)

Appendix 1

Coastal Forces Chronology

By June 1940

Coastal Forces bases established at Gosport (HMS *Hornet*, 20.12.39) and Lowestoft (HMS *Minos II*, 1.5.40, later re-named *Mantis*). Overseas orders for MTBs and MA/SBs requisitioned by Admiralty. First MLs and HDMLs ordered by Admiralty. A few MA/SBs built by British Power Boat Company handed over to the Navy.

1st MTB Flotilla returns to UK from Malta, and the seven boats considered serviceable re-form at Felixstowe with their depot ship HMS *Vulcan*. 4th MTB Flotilla (three newly-commissioned boats) operates off Blyth, Northumberland, and in the New Year moves down to Felixstowe to be joined by the 10th Flotilla (Thornycroft MTBs, known collectively as 'The Wobbly Tenth'). Experimental MTBs *100* and *102* designated as the 3rd Training Flotilla based at HMS *Vernon*, Portsmouth.

Coastal Forces are involved in the Dunkirk evacuation, patrolling the eastern flank and ferrying troops and senior officers. *MTB 107* is the last warship to leave Dunkirk.

July–December 1940

Rear Admiral Coastal Forces appointed, with headquarters at Portland. Coastal Forces bases established at Felixstowe (HMS *Beehive* 1.7.40), Fowey (HMS *Belfort* 7.9.40) and Dover (HMS *Wasp* 2.9.40). Coastal Forces training establishment commissioned at Fort William (HMS *St Christopher* 31.10.40)

30 MA/SBs in service. 56 MLs launched and building started on HDMLs.

Several actions in the North Sea and English Channel. Six enemy coastal vessels sunk by torpedo. RN losses: 5 MTB, 3ML and an MAC (ex-MTB used as a Minesweeper Attendant Craft).

January–June 1941

Coastal Forces bases established at Portland (HMS *Attack* 15.1.41), Immingham (HMS *Beaver III* 1.5.41), Dartmouth (HMS *Britannia III* 1.5.41 – re-named *Dartmouth II* and then *Cicala*), Ardrossan (HMS *Fortitude II* 7.5.41), Stornoway (HMS *Mentor II* 24.6.41), Great Yarmouth (HMS *Midge* 1.1.41) Peterhead (HMS *Sandfly* 5.5.41), Pembroke Dock (HMS *Skirmisher II* 1.5.41) and an anti-submarine school for ML crews at Ardrishaig (HMS *Seahawk* 1.1.41)

9 MTBs and 12 MGBs completed and around 70 MLs and 30 HDMLs built. Most MA/SBs converted to gunboats in January. Two MTB flotillas operate from Felixstowe and a third from Dover. Four MGB Flotillas operate from Felixstowe, Fowey, Weymouth and Immingham. 1 MA/SB flotilla and 11 ML flotillas have been formed.

One MGB is destroyed in an air raid and another mined. Six MTBs are destroyed under construction in an air raid, 1 by fire at *Hornet* and another mined.

July–December 1941

20 Coastal Forces bases now operating in the British Isles with the commissioning of bases at Blyth (HMS *Elfin II* 1.12.41), Falmouth (HMS *Forte IV* 7.8.41), Larne (HMS *Racer II* 1.8.41) and Holyhead (HMS *Torch II* 1.7.41 – later became HMS *Bee*).

Production of boats now intensive. Approximate numbers over the 6-month period are: 20 Short MTB; 8 Short MGB; 23 Long MGB; 44 HDML; 14 MA/SB; 100 ML.

7 Short MTB and 7 Short MGB flotillas have been formed in Home Waters along with 2 flotillas of Fairmile C-Class MGBs. 14 ML flotillas now operate in Home Waters. Steam gunboats will soon be in service and the first D-Class MTBs are undergoing

trials. Short MTBs and MGBs are arriving from the United States.

19 actions are recorded, MTBs mainly engaged in attacking shipping in the Dover Straits and MGBs intercepting E-Boats in the North Sea. The MTBs sink 5 coastal ships over this period, and the MGBs damage several E-Boats and board *S41* before it sinks (see photo p. 128). RN losses are: 3 MGB, 3 ML, 4 HDML, 1 MA/SB.

January–June 1942

Around 40 Short MTBs are launched but only a handful of Short MGBs. 50 MLs are commissioned along with 24 HDMLs. Six of the originally planned 9 SGBs (Steam Gunboats) are completed. The number of MTB flotillas operating has risen to 10 whereas the MGB numbers have remained static.

Of the 24 actions recorded over the period, two have been widely documented. These are the attack by 5 MTBs on 12 February on the German battlecruisers *Scharnhorst* and *Gneisenau* and the heavy cruiser *Prinz Eugen*, and the raid on St Nazaire on 26-27 March. The St Nazaire raid accounts for most of the RN losses over the period (1 MGB, 1 MTB and 12 MLs fail to return). 3 MTBs and an ML are lost elsewhere, and *Steam Gunboat 7* has to be scuttled in the English Channel.

July–December 1942

Coastal Forces bases are commissioned at Invergordon (HMS *Flora II* 1.9.42), Lerwick (HMS *Fox II* 20.7.42) and Newhaven (HMS *Aggressive* 4.11.42, was *Forward II*), and a working-up base established at Weymouth (HMS *Bee* 1.9.42).

The building programme concentrates on MLs and HDMLs (about 150 launched). Around 40 D-Class Fairmile MTBs/MGBs are completed along with a few Short MTBs and MGBs. Fully operational flotillas in Home Waters at the end of 1942 number: 14 MTB, 13 MGB, 22 ML, 5 HDML.

There are some 50 actions, mainly in the English Channel and off the Dutch coast. With the commissioning of HMS *Fox II* at Lerwick in the Shetlands where 2 D-Class MTB flotillas are based (the Norwegian 54th and the British 52nd), passage-making to Norway starts. The boats hide up inshore awaiting targets. In the next two years they succeed in sinking a considerable tonnage of enemy shipping.

26 Coastal Forces craft take part in Operation *Jubilee*, the disastrous raid on Dieppe.

A new tactic is being developed using destroyers and frigates in the English Channel to direct MTBs on to their targets. 18 enemy vessels are sunk or destroyed over the period. RN losses are 7 MTB, 9 MGB and 2 ML.

January–June 1943

Over 150 boats are completed, as follows: 15 D-Class MTB, 16 D-Class MGB, 26 Short MTB, about 50 ML and about 60 HDML.

There is considerable Coastal Forces activity in the Mediterranean and 46 actions in Home Waters where 19 enemy coastal craft are sunk or destroyed and 2 corvettes. RN losses: 3 MGB, 3 MTB, 1 ML.

July–December 1943

HMS *Bee*, the working up base, is transferred from Weymouth to Holyhead (18.10.43).

The building programme maintains the same level as the previous six months with the completion of 30 D-Class MTB, 22 Short MTB, 60 ML and 74 HDML. Additionally many of the existing MGBs are converted to MTBs. This concentration on torpedo boats is reflected in the configuration of flotillas in Home Waters over this period: 9 D-Class MTB flotillas, 14 Short MTB flotillas, 6 MGB flotillas, 32 ML flotillas and 27 HDML flotillas, plus another 2 MGB flotillas used for training.

48 actions are recorded with a greater number in the Mediterranean where Coastal Forces are particularly active. Warfare in the North Sea and English Channel is changing with the conversion of MGBs to MTBs and the provision of more armament for MTBs. In previous years, MTBs tended to patrol with a protective shield of gunboats. During this period, and for the remainder of the war, MTB flotillas invariably patrol independently, relying on their own firepower. Radar is becoming more reliable for detecting enemy shipping.

21 enemy coastal craft are believed sunk or destroyed. RN and Allied losses: 10 MTB, 1 MGB, 1 ML and 2 HDML.

January–June 1944

The Coastal Forces base HMS *Fervent* is established 1.3.44 at Ramsgate (transferred from Dover HMS *Wasp*).

Although the building programme continues (24 D-Class MTB, 7 Short MTB, 42 ML and 41 HDML), the decision is taken that no more personnel will be drafted to Coastal Forces after 31 March. Paying off older boats is to provide crews for newly built boats.

28 MTB flotillas are now operational in Home Waters along with 33 ML and 32 HDML flotillas.

Coastal Forces are heavily involved in Operation *Overlord* – the Allied invasion of France. On D-Day, 96 of 100 MTBs in Portsmouth Command are deployed with more boats from Dover and Plymouth Commands. Coastal Forces patrol the west and east flanks of the swept channels and the waters off the assault area, protecting the invasion force from attacks by E-Boats and minelayers. Preparing for D-Day, Coastal Forces are also used for minelaying off enemy ports in the Channel. The boats undertake much of the minesweeping preparatory to D-Day and on the actual day pilot many of the landing craft to their assigned beaches.

There are over 100 actions in the English Channel and off the Dutch coast. Bomber Command launches a heavy raid on Le Havre on 14/15 June, severely damaging the E-Boat pens, crippling or sinking 14 E-Boats of 5th and 9th E-Boat flotillas and 3 large Möwe-Class torpedo boats. The total enemy losses for the period are: 35 coastal craft plus the 3 Möwe-Class ships; RN and Allied losses are: 14 MTB, 3 MGB, 1 ML.

July–December 1944

Following D-Day, a mobile Coastal Forces base (CFMU 1) is established at Arromanches, moving to Ostend in October.

More of the older boats are paid off and there is a reduction in the building programme with around 40 D-Class MTB, 25 Short MTB, 16 ML and 30 HDML completed. Bases at Falmouth and Dover are paid off and the shore training bases at Ardrishaig and Fort William are closed down. Several flotillas are moved to Nore Command to concentrate on protecting the supply routes to the Low Countries, and in the latter part of the period many of the actions switch from the Channel to Dutch, German, and Norwegian waters. In 101 actions, around 100 enemy coastal vessels are claimed as sunk or destroyed with relatively few RN losses (11 MTB, 1 MGB, 2 ML and 1 HDML).

January–June 1945

The gradual reduction of Coastal Forces both at sea and ashore continues until the end of the war in Europe. After VE-Day, many of the flotillas of MTBs and MGBs are paid off. There remain considerable clearing up operations, including minesweeping, to justify maintaining flotillas of MLs and HDMLs. Some of the remaining operational flotillas are moved across the water to bases previously occupied by German coastal forces.

There are 50 actions over the period, but E-Boat warfare has virtually ceased by April. The period includes the greatest number of Coastal Forces craft lost in a single day with an explosion and fire destroying 12 MTBs in Ostend on 14.2.45. These losses include 5 of the 29th Canadian MTB Flotilla and 7 British MTBs with a tragic loss of lives. In addition to those boats lost at Ostend, 10 MTBs are lost elsewhere along with 2 MGBs, 2 MLs, and an HDML. 13 enemy coastal craft, a cruiser, and 3 corvettes are claimed as sunk or destroyed.

Appendix 2

Coastal Forces Awards

Coastal Forces was one of the most highly decorated branches of the Royal Navy in the Second World War. With their role in close combat warfare together with their deployment on undercover operations and hazardous duties such as minelaying and minesweeping, it is hardly surprising that crew members of MTBs, MGBs, MLs, HDMLs, RMLs, and SGBs made so many appearances in the *London Gazette* which published most of the names of recipients of awards for distinguished service and gallantry and listed the names of hundreds of Coastal Forces personnel 'Mentioned in Despatches'.

'Distinguished service' was recognised with the awards of the Distinguished Service Order (DSO), Distinguished Service Cross (DSC) and Distinguished Service Medal (DSM). There was one Victoria Cross (the highest award for gallantry), six CGMs (Conspicuous Gallantry Medals), and eighteen DSOs (the highest award for distinguished service). There were over 300 DSCs and over 500 DSMs awarded to members of Coastal Forces operating in Home Waters. There were also many more of these awards to those in Coastal Forces who served overseas.

The two names forever associated with Coastal Forces were both highly decorated.

Robert Peverell Hichens had already been awarded a DSC before joining Coastal Forces. When serving in a minesweeper early in the war, he was landed at Dunkirk to work as a beachmaster during the evacuation for which he earned his first DSC. He was awarded his second DSC or 'bar' (highlighted with an asterisk after the award), for an attack on E-boats in the Nore area on 19–20 November 1941 and a third DSC for attacking an enemy convoy, again in the Nore area, on 14

September 1942. He was awarded his first DSO for an action on 21 April 1942 against E-boats off Ostend, his second DSO for attacking an enemy tanker off Alderney in the Channel Islands on 14 July 1942, and he was three times Mentioned in Despatches.

Peter Dickens, in *MTB 234*, was awarded the DSC for several attacks on enemy shipping over September and November 1942, and then a DSO for attacking enemy shipping off the Dutch coast on 13 May 1943. He was twice Mentioned in Despatches for other actions off the Dutch coast.

Many of those who took part in the famous raids in which Coastal Forces were heavily involved received recognition for their courageous devotion to duty. Operation *Chariot*, the daring raid on the docks at St Nazaire involved 1 MGB, 1 MTB, and 15 MLs accompanying HMS *Campbeltown*. The losses were appalling but the purpose of the raid, primarily to destroy the giant dry dock gate, was achieved. The awards were numerous and included a posthumous Victoria Cross to Able Seaman Bill Savage who, although seriously wounded, remained on *MGB 314*'s bow pom-pom, successfully silencing the gun emplacement on the old mole in the approaches to the docks. In the same action, a CGM was awarded to William Henry Lovegrove who, although wounded aboard *MTB 74*, rescued his badly burned CO and then supported him for 12 hours until they were picked up and taken ashore as prisoners. The COs and other members of the crews of almost all the other boats involved received medals or were Mentioned in Despatches. In total, in addition to the VC and CGM, there were 2 DSOs, 14 DSCs, 21 DSMs, and 21 'Mentions' awarded to Coastal Forces personnel in recognition of the valour displayed on the night of 28/29 March 1942.

There were also awards to flotillas in recognition of operations carried out over lengthy periods. These included 24 members of the 15th MGB Flotilla for their many undercover operations along the north coast of Brittany. Several of the personnel serving in the 54th MTB Flotilla, manned by Royal Norwegian Navy crews, were rewarded for their clandestine missions to Norway. Many of those who served aboard destroyers and frigates, directing Coastal Forces, were also listed in the *London Gazette*.

Personnel in Allied Navies received many British decorations. To mention just a few – DSCs were awarded to Johan Schreuder of the Royal Netherlands Navy, to the Polish Eugenjusz Wcislicki and to the Free French Navy Paul de Bigault De Cazanove, with DSC and bar to the Norwegian Per Danielsen and the Dutch Etienne Henri Larive. In recognition of Commonwealth Coastal Forces, the DSC was awarded to Charles Anthony Law of the Royal Canadian Navy Volunteer Reserve, and DSCs presented to three US Navy lieutenants serving in PT Squadron 35 operating off the D-Day coastline.

British Coastal Forces personnel received many foreign decorations including the French Croix de Guerre and appointment as an Officer of the Légion d'Honneur, King Haakon VII of Norway's Liberty Cross/Medal and Norway's Medal of the Order of St Olav and the Norwegian War Medal. Appointments as Officer of the Order of Orange Nassau and the Military Willems-Orde were awarded by the Netherlands to various British naval personnel. US decorations awarded included Officer of the Legion of Honour, Officer of the Legion of Merit and Legionnaire of the Legion of Merit. These awards were mostly promulgated by the *London Gazette* announcing that named individuals had been granted permission to wear the foreign decorations concerned.

There were also civil awards to naval personnel in Coastal Forces and to non-RN personnel who served in the boats. The Royal Humane Society's Bronze Medal was awarded to individuals involved in the rescue from the sea of survivors. Civil awards to non-RN personnel included those to the Merchant Navy crews of the Camper & Nicholsons MGBs converted for blockade running. For their passages to and from Sweden between October 1943 and March 1944 their captains and chief engineers received OBEs, with MBEs to other officers and BEMs to other ranks.

(Source: *Seedie's List of Coastal Forces Awards for World War II*, published by Ripley Registers, Dormer House, Tisbury, Wiltshire SP3 6QQ)

Appendix 3

Coastal Forces Vessels

A: Technical Specifications

Experimental/ Private venture

	Vosper MTB *PV* (1937)	BPB MTB *PV 70* (1938)
Dimensions		
length (overall)	68ft	70ft
beam (max)	14ft 9in	19ft 10in
draught (max)	4ft 10in	4ft 5in
Hull	hard chine	hard chine
Displacement (full load)	31.5 tons	31 tons
Engines	3 x Isotta-Fraschini 1,150bhp	3 x Rolls-Royce Merlin 1,000bhp
Fuel Capacity	1,000gal	1,440gal
Speed		
max (absolute)	43.7kt	44.4kt
max (sustained)	35.5kt	40.5kt
Range		
max sustained speed	240nm @ 35kt	420nm @ 40kt
cruising speed	340nm @ 17.5kt	900nm @ 22kt
Complement	2 officers, 8 ratings	1 officer, 10 ratings

Early MTBs

	Vosper *MTB 20-23, 29, 30* (1938)	BPB *MTB 01-12* (1935-7)
Dimensions		
length (overall)	70ft 3¼in	60ft 4in
beam (max)	16ft 5in	13ft 10in
draught (max)	4ft 9in	3ft 10in
Hull	hard chine	hard chine
Displacement (full load)	36 tons	19.93 tons
Engines	3 x Isotta-Fraschini 1,150bhp	3 x Napier Lion 500bhp
Fuel Capacity	1,500-1,850gal	500-740gal
Speed		
max (absolute)	42kt	36kt
max (sustained)	40kt	29kt
Range		
at max sustained speed	325nm	234nm @ 29kt

at cruising speed	500nm @ 20kt	493nm @ 20kt
Complement	2 officers, 7 ratings	1 officer, 7 ratings

Early MTBs/MA/SBs

	Thornycroft *MTB 49-56* (1939)	BPB *MA/SB 22-39* (1939)
Dimensions		
length (overall)	73ft 9in	63ft
beam (max)	16ft 7in	16ft 6in
draught (max)	5ft 4in	4ft 3in
Hull	hard chine	hard chine
Displacement (full load)	48.4 tons	27.6 tons
Engines	4 x Thornycroft RY12 650bhp	3 x Napier Lion 500bhp
Fuel Capacity	1,000gal	1,083gal
Speed		
max (absolute)	28.9kt	31.6kt
max (sustained)	25.6kt	23.6kt
Range		
at max sustained speed	160nm @ 25.6kt	390nm @ 23.6kt
at cruising speed	N/A	N/A
Complement	2 officers, 8 ratings	2 officers, 8 ratings

1940–41 MTBs & MGBs

	Vosper *MTB 222-245* (1941)	BPB Mk V *MGB 74-81* (1940)
Dimensions		
length (overall)	71ft 0in	71ft 6in
beam (max)	19ft 2in	20ft 7in
draught (max)	6ft	5ft 8in
Hull	hard chine	hard chine
Displacement (full load)	47 tons	46 tons
Engines	3 x Packard 1,250bhp	3 x Packard 1,250bhp
Fuel Capacity	2,543gal	2,733gal
Speed		
max (absolute)	38.5kt	39.8kt
max (sustained)	35.2kt	35kt
Range		
at max sustained speed	375nm @ 35kt	475nm @ 35kt
at cruising speed	400nm @ 20kt	550nm @ 20kt
Complement	2 officers, 8 ratings	2 officers, 12 ratings

1944 MTBs

	Vosper 73ft Type 2 *MTB 523-538*	BPB Mk VI *MTB 519-522*
Dimensions		
length (overall)	73ft	71ft 6in
beam (max)	19ft 4½in	20ft 7in
draught (max)	5ft 7in	5ft 8½in
Hull	hard chine	hard chine

Displacement (full load)	49 tons	51.6 tons
Engines	3 x Packard 1,400bhp	3 x Packard 1,350bhp
Fuel Capacity	2,500gal + 400gal	2,740gal
Speed		
max (absolute)	40kt	39kt
max (sustained)	38kt	31kt
Range		
at max sustained speed	N/A	N/A
at cruising speed	480nm @ 20kt	600nm @ 15kt
Complement	2 officers, 11 ratings	2 officers, 15 ratings

MGBs and SGBs

	Camper & Nicholsons *MGB 511-518*	Steam Gunboats *S 3-9*
Dimensions		
length (overall)	117ft	145ft 8in
beam (max)	22ft 2½in	23ft 4in
draught (max)	5ft 7in	5ft 3in
Hull	round bilge	round bilge
Displacement (full load)	107 tons	202 tons
Engines	3 x Packard 1,400bhp	2 x steam turbines (4,000bhp total)
Fuel Capacity	3,000–5,000 gal	20–50 tons diesel
Speed		
max (absolute)	31.3kt	35kt
max (sustained)	26.3kt	N/A
Range		
at max sustained speed	372nm	200nm
at cruising speed	2,000nm @ 10kt	900nm @ 12kt
Complement	3 officers, 26 ratings	2 officers, 21 ratings

MLs and HDMLs

	Fairmile Type 'A'	Fairmile Type 'B'
Dimensions		
length (overall)	110ft	112ft
beam (max)	17ft 5in	17ft 10in
draught (max)	6ft 6in	4ft 10in
Hull	hard chine	round bilge
Displacement (full load)	60 tons (increased when re-armed)	67 tons
Engines	3 x Hall-Scott Defender 600bhp	2 x Hall-Scott Defender 600bhp
Fuel Capacity	1,200gal	2,305gal
Speed		
max (absolute)	25kt (on reduced displacement)	20kt
max (sustained)	22kt (on reduced displacement)	17.5kt
Range		
at max sustained speed	N/A	600nm @ 20kt
at cruising speed	600nm @ 12kt	1,500 nm @ 12kt
Complement	2 officers, 14 ratings	2 officers, 14 ratings

MLs and HDMLs

	Fairmile Type 'C'	HDMLs
Dimensions		
length (overall)	110ft	72ft
beam (max)	17ft 5in	16ft
draught (max)	6ft 3in	4ft 9in
Hull	hard chine	round bilge
Displacement (full load)	72 tons	54.3 tons
Engines	3 x Hall-Scott 900bhp	2 x diesels – Gardner 300, Glennifer 320 or Thornycroft 260
Fuel Capacity	1,800gal	1,650gal (diesel)
Speed		
max (absolute)	26.6kt	11.5kt
max (sustained)	23.6kt	10kt
Range		
at max sustained speed	305nm	N/A
at cruising speed	500nm @ 12kt	2,000nm @ 10kt
Complement	2 officers, 16 ratings	2 officers, 8 ratings

MTB/MGB

	Fairmile Type 'D (last series)
Dimensions	
length (overall)	115ft
beam (max)	21ft 3in
draught (max)	5ft 2½in
Hull	hard chine
Displacement (full load)	128 tons
Engines	4 x Packard 1,400bhp
Fuel Capacity	3,000–5,000gal
Speed	
max (absolute)	29.5kt
max (sustained)	24.3kt
Range	
at max sustained speed	270nm
at cruising speed	N/A
Complement	3 officers, 20 ratings

B: Armament

Note: armament indicated below is a guide only as weapons were continually reviewed and improved. Photographs of boats listed below may show a different weapons configuration.

Early MTBs

Vosper *MTB 20-23, 29, 30* (1938)
2 x quadruple 0.303in MG
2 x 21in torpedoes

BPB *MTB 01-12* (1935-7)
2 x quadruple 0.303in MG
2 x 18in torpedoes

Early MTBs/MA/SBs

Thornycroft *MTB 49-56* (1939)
1 x twin 0.5in MG
2 x 0.303in rifles
2 x depth charges
2 x 21in torpedoes

BPB *MA/SB 22-39* (1939)
1 x twin 0.303in MG

1940–1 MTBs & MGBs

Vosper *MTB 222-245* (1941)
1 x twin 0.5in MG
2 x 0.303in rifles
2 x depth charges
2 x 21in torpedoes

BPB Mk V *MGB 74-81* (1940)
2pdr pom-pom
1 x twin 20mm Oerlikon
2 x twin 0.303in MG
2 x depth charges

1944 MTBs

Vosper 73ft Type 2 *MTB 523-538*
6pdr in power turret
2 x twin 0.303in MG
1 x twin 20mm Oerlikon
2 x 18in torpedoes

BPB Mk VI *MTB 519-522*
6pdr in power turret
2 x twin 0.303in MG
1 x twin 20mm Oerlikon
2 x 18in torpedoes

MGBs and SGBs

Camper & Nicholsons *MGB 511-518*
2 x 6pdr in power turrets
2 x single Oerlikon
1 x twin Oerlikon
4 x 18in torpedoes

Steam Gunboats *S3-9*
2 x 6pdr in power turrets
1 x 3in
2 x twin Oerlikon
2 x 21in torpedoes

Fairmile MLs

Fairmile Type 'A'
3pdr Mk 1
1 x twin 0.303in MG
12 x depth charges

Fairmile Type 'B'
3pdr Mk 1
1 x twin 0.303in MG
12 x depth charges

MLs and HDMLs

Fairmile Type 'C'
2 x 2pdr pom-pom
3 x twin Oerlikons
4 x depth charges

HDMLSs
1 x 2pdr Mk IX mounting
2 x twin 0.303in MG
8 x depth charges

MGB/MTB

Fairmile Type 'D' (late 1944)
2 x 6pdr in Mk VII mountings
2 x twin 0.5in MG on Mark V mountings
twin 20mm Oerlikon on Mk IX mounting
2 x twin 0.303in MG
4 x 18in torpedoes
2 x depth charges

Guns of Coastal Forces

The offensive role of the 1st MTB Flotilla was primarily to launch torpedo attacks on enemy shipping and then withdraw at high speed. On these early boats, the gunnery was limited to the 0.303in quadruple Lewis guns to provide defensive firepower against enemy aircraft.

Early in the war, the 0.303in Lewis guns were replaced by twin Vickers 0.5in machine guns in the Mk V power-operated mounting. These had a range of about 500yds and a firing rate of 700rpm. In 1941 the Swiss-designed Oerlikon replaced the Vickers machine gun. Single or twin-mounted, with a range of almost 5,000yds and a rate of fire of 450rpm, the popular 20mm Oerlikon was adopted as the main anti-aircraft armament on many Coastal Forces craft.

Armament was considerably increased to provide gunboats and the combined MTB/MGBs with firepower to engage in direct offensive gun action with enemy shipping. The Vickers 2pdr 40mm pom-pom, widely fitted on MLs and MGBs, had a range of 3,500yds and a firing rate of 98rpm. Towards the end of the war the heavy 6pdr was introduced with a range of over 6,000yds and a firing rate of 40rpm.

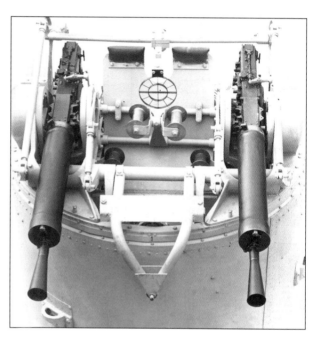

ABOVE RIGHT: Twin Vickers 0.5in machine guns on a Mk V power operated mounting.

RIGHT: A gunner takes up position in his twin Vickers 0.5in machine gun mounting. *IWM D12529*

20mm Oerlikons
mounted forward . . .

. . . and aft on a Vosper
MTB. *Vosper
Thornycroft*

ABOVE: A 6pdr gun on a Mk VII power-operated mounting.

ABOVE RIGHT: Vickers 2pdr 40mm pom-pom on Mk XVI power-operated mounting.

RIGHT: 20mm twin Oerlikon on a Mk V power-operated mounting.

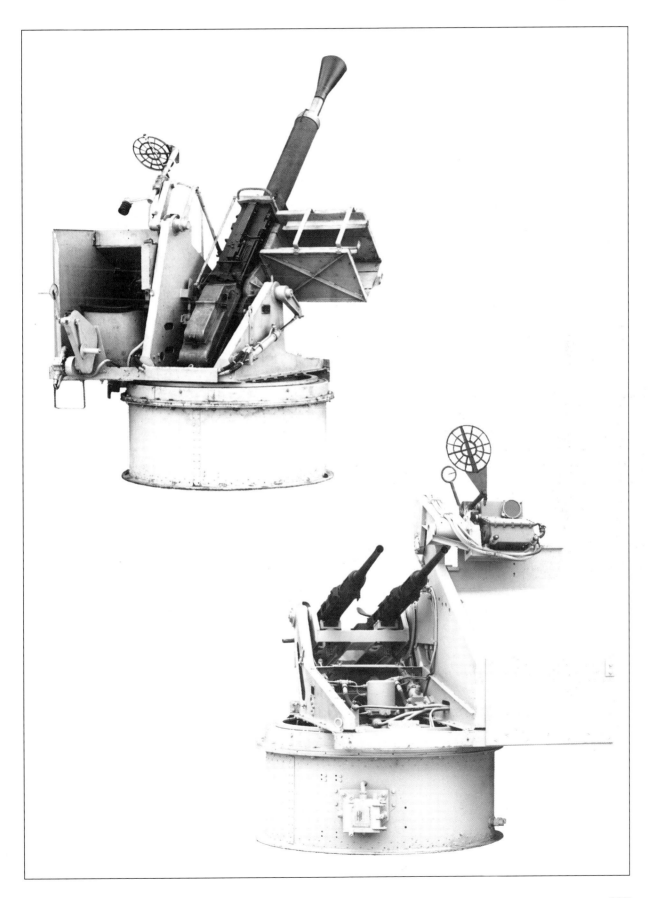

Appendix 5

Schnellboote and Raumboote

Technical Specifications

	1944-5 *Schnellboote S701-709*	1943-4 *Raumboote R130-150*
Dimensions		
length (overall)	114ft 6in	134ft 9in
beam (max)	16ft 9in	19ft
draught (max)	7ft	5ft 3in
Hull	round bilge	round bilge
Displacement (full load)	112 tons	150 tons
Engines	3 x Daimler-Benz 2,500bhp	2 x MAN 900bhp
Fuel Capacity	17 tons	11 tons
Speed		
max (absolute)	42kt	19kt
max (sustained)	38kt	
Range		
at cruising speed	700 miles @ 30kt	1,000 miles @ 15kt
Armament	3 x twin 30mm AA	3 x twin 20mm AA
	4 x 21in torpedoes	
Complement	23	38

Appendix 6

Coastal Forces
Pennant Numbers

Compiled by G. Hudson

MTBs (Short)

	maker	length	programme
	maker	length	programme
1-12	BPB	60ft	1935-37
14-19	BPB	60ft	1937
24-28	Thornycroft	72ft & 55ft	1938
29-40	Vosper	71ft & 70ft	1938-39
41-48	J.S. White	72ft	1939
49-56	Thornycroft	74ft	1939
57-66	Vosper	71ft	1939
67-68	Thornycroft	55ft	oo
69-70	Vosper	70ft	oo
71-72	Vosper	60ft	oo
73-98	Vosper	71ft	1940
100	BPB	60ft	Exp
101	J.S.White	67ft	Exp
102	Vosper	68ft	Exp
103	Vosper	70ft	Exp
104-107	Thornycroft	45ft & 40ft	Exp
108	Vosper	45ft	Exp
109	Denny	43ft	Exp
201-212	Vosper	71ft	1940
213-217	Thornycroft	55ft	oo
218-221	Vosper	71ft	oo
222-245	Vosper	72ft 6in	1941
246-251	Vosper	71ft	1941
252-257	J.S. White	71ft 6in	1942
258	BPB	70ft	Exp
259-268	Elco (BPB)	70ft	US Lend/Lease
269-272	Higgins & Philadelphia	81ft	US Lend/Lease
273-274	Fisher	58ft	US Lend/Lease
275-306	Vosper	71ft	US build 1941
307-326	Elco (BPB)	77ft	US build 1941

	maker	length	programme
327-331	Thornycroft	55ft	oo
332-343	CPB (BPB)	70ft	Canada build
344-346	Thornycroft	60ft, 55ft, 45ft	Exp
347-362	Vosper	71ft	1942
363-378	Vosper	71ft	US build 1942
379-395	Vosper	73ft	1943
396-411	Vosper	71ft	US build 1943
412-418	BPB	71ft 6in	1941-42
419-423	Higgins	78ft	oo
424-429	J.S. White	71ft 6in	1943
430-445	BPB	71ft 6in	1942-43
446	BPB	71ft 6in	1942-43
447-457	BPB	71ft 6in	1942
458-497	BPB	71ft 6in	1943
498-509	BPB	71ft 6in	1944
510	Vosper MTB/MGB		Exp
519-522	BPB	71ft 6in	1944
523-528	Vosper	73ft	1944
539	Saunders Roe	75ft	Exp

oo = overseas order requisitioned by the Admiralty
Exp = experimental
BPB = British Power Boat Company
CPB = Canadian Power Boat Company

239

MA/SBs

	maker	length	programme
1-5	BPB	60ft	1936-8
6-21#	BPB	70ft	1938-9
22-39	BPB	63ft	1939
40-45#	BPB	63ft	oo
46#	BPB	70ft	oo
47-48#	J.S. White	75ft	oo
49	J.S. White	60ft	oo
50-67#	BPB	70ft	oo
68#	Higgins	81ft	oo
69-73#	Higgins	69ft	oo
74-97#	BPB	71ft 6in	1940*
98-99#	Aero Marine	65ft	oo
100-106#	Higgins	69ft	oo

oo overseas order requisitioned by the Admiralty

built as MA/SBs, redesignated MGBs Jan 1941

* surviving 71ft 6in BPB MGBs, redesignated as MTBs Sept 1943

MGBs (Short)

	maker	length	programme
82-93	Elco (BPB)	70ft	ex-US Navy
107-122	BPB	71ft 6in	1941*
123	BPB	71ft 6in	Mk VI prototype*
124-138	BPB	71ft 6in	1942*
139-176	BPB	71ft 6in	1943*
177-192	Higgins	78ft	ex-US Navy

* surviving 71ft 6in BPB MGBs, redesignated MTBs Sept 1943

MLs (Fairmile A, B & C), D-Class MGBs/MTBs, HDMLs, RMLs, Steam Gunboats, Camper & Nicholsons MGBs/MTBs

		length
100-111	Fairmile A	110ft
112-311	Fairmile B	112ft
312-335	Fairmile C (MGBs)	110ft
336-491	Fairmile B	112ft
492-500	Fairmile B (RMLs)	112ft
501	Camper & Nicholsons	117ft
502-509	Camper & Nicholsons	117ft
511-518	Camper & Nicholsons	117ft
511-553	Fairmile B (RMLs)	112ft
554-600	Fairmile B	112ft
601-800	Fairmile D#	115ft
801-933	Fairmile B	112ft
1001-1494	HDML	72ft
2001	Fairmile F Exp MGB	115ft
4001-4004	Fairmile B	112ft
5001-5003	Fairmile D#	115ft
5005	Fairmile D#	115ft
5007-5010	Fairmile D#	115ft
5013	Fairmile D#	115ft
5015	Fairmile D#	115ft
5020	Fairmile D#	115ft

'Dog Boats' - MTB/MGB dual role

S301-309	SGBs (Steam Gunboats)	146ft

Appendix 7

Coastal Forces Losses, UK-based Flotillas

1939

MTB 06	16/11	Swamped off Sardinia in severe weather; sunk by HMS *Dainty*

1940

MTB 15	24/9	Mined, Thames estuary
MTB 33	26/9	Explosion on trials
MTB 106	16/10	Mined, Thames estuary
MTB 17	21/10	Destroyed in action off Ostend
ML 109	30/10	Mined off Humber
MTB 16	31/10	Mined, Thames estuary
ML 127	22/11	Mined, Thames estuary
ML 111	25/11	Believe mined off Humber
MAC 05	26/12	Believe mined off Felixstowe (previously *MTB 05*)

1941

MTB 37	11/1	Fire while under construction at Vosper, Portsmouth
MTB 39	11/1	Fire while under construction at Vosper, Portsmouth
MTB 40	11/1	Fire while under construction at Vosper, Portsmouth
MTB 74 (1st)	11/1	Fire while under construction at Vosper, Portsmouth
MTB 75 (1st)	11/1	Fire while under construction at Vosper, Portsmouth
MTB 108 (2nd)	11/1	Fire while under construction at Vosper, Portsmouth
MGB 12	6/2	Mined, Milford Haven
MTB 41	14/2	Mined, North Sea
MTB 28	7/3	Fire at HMS *Hornet*, Gosport
MGB 98	11/3	Air raid over HMS *Hornet*, Gosport
MGB 90 & 92	16/7	Fire, Portland
MGB 62	9/8	North Sea collision with *MGB 67*
ML 144	22/9	Mined, English Channel
ML 288	11/10	Sunk in severe weather off Hartlepool
ML 219	21/11	Wrecked, Stornoway
MA/SB 30	14/12	Fouled boom, Humber
HDMLs 1092–1095		Bombed under construction, Belfast

1942

MTB 47	17/1	Shelled off Cap Gris-Nez
MGB 314	28/3	St Nazaire raid

MTB 74	28/3	St Nazaire raid
ML 457	28/3	St Nazaire raid
ML 156	28/3	St Nazaire raid
ML 270	28/3	St Nazaire raid
ML 446	28/3	St Nazaire raid
ML 177	28/3	St Nazaire raid
ML 192	28/3	St Nazaire raid
ML 262	28/3	St Nazaire raid
ML 267	28/3	St Nazaire raid
ML 268	28/3	St Nazaire raid
ML 298	28/3	St Nazaire raid
ML 306	28/3	St Nazaire raid (captured by enemy)
ML 447	28/3	St Nazaire raid
ML 160	6/5	Bombed; Brixham
MTB 220	13/5	Sunk by E-Boat off Cap Gris-Nez
MTB 201	15/6	Shelled in Dover Straits, sank under tow
SGB 7	19/6	Scuttled in English Channel after action against R-Boat
MGB 328	21/7	Shelled engaging enemy convoy in Dover Straits
MGB 601	24/7	Shelled in Dover Straits
MGB 501	27/7	Explosion; sank between Lands End and Scilly Isles
MTB 44	7/8	Shelled off Dover
MTB 237	7/8	Shelled off Barfleur
MTB 42	18/8	Shelled off Gravelines
MTB 218	18/8	Shelled and mined, Dover Straits
ML 103	24/8	Mined, Dover Straits
MGB 335	10/9	Damage and fire in North Sea action
MGB 18	30/9	Shelled off Terschelling
MGB 78	3/10	Beached on Dutch coast and abandoned
MTB 29	6/10	Sank after collision during E-Boat action in North Sea
MGB 76	6/10	Sank after action in North Sea with E-Boat
ML 339	7/10	Torpedoed by E-Boat, North Sea
MGB 9	15/10	Beyond repair following action
MTB 87	31/10	Mined, North Sea
MGB 19	6/11	Bombed on slipway
MTB 30	18/12	Mined, North Sea

1943

MGB 109	25/2	Mined off Dover on 7/2; paid off 25/2
MGB 79	28/2	Shelled off Hook of Holland
MTB 80	2/3	Wrecked after grounding off Weymouth
MTB 622	10/3	Shelled attacking convoy off Terschelling
MTB 631 (Norwegian)	14/3	Captured by enemy after grounding in Norwegian fjords
ML 133	11/5	Explosion and fire damage, west coast of Scotland
MGB 110	29/5	Shelled off Dunkirk
MTB 345 (Norwegian)	28/7	Captured by enemy in Norwegian waters
MGB 64	8/8	Foundered in heavy weather between Dover and Ostend
ML 108	5/9	Mined, English Channel
MTB 636	15/10	Sunk by friendly fire
MTB 356	16/10	Shelled off Dutch coast

HDML 1054	23/10	Wrecked off Hartlepool
MTB 669	26/10	Shelled off Norwegian coast
MTB 606	4/11	Action off Dutch coast
MTB 230	9/11	In collision with *MTB 222* off Dutch coast; scuttled
MTB 222	10/11	Severely holed after collision; sunk by RN off Dutch coast
MTB 626 Norwegian	22/11	Fire, Lerwick
MTB 686	22/11	Fire, Lerwick
MTB 357	24/12	Beyond repair after shelling off Dunkirk on 23/12
HDML 1388	24/12	Stranded off Hartlepool

1944

MGB 25	17/1	Wrecked in Thames estuary
MTB 625 Norwegian	8/2	Wrecked in storm in Scottish waters
ML 210	15/2	Mined off Dieppe
MTB 417	16/3	Shelled engaging convoy between Calais and Boulogne
MTB 352	26/3	Collision with *MTB 351* off Holland
MTB 241	31/3	Shelled off Ijmuiden; sank under tow
MTB 707	18/4	Collision with French frigate *L'Escarmouche* off Northern Ireland
MTB 671	24/4	Shelled off Barfleur during torpedo attack on destroyers
MTB 708	5/5	Bombed by friendly aircraft in English Channel
MTB 203	18/5	Mined off Etaples
MTB 732	28/5	Shelled by French frigate in English Channel
MTB 672	29/5	Mined off Berry Head
MTB 248	6/6	Collision with *MTBs 249* and *251* off Normandy in rough seas
MTB 681	10/6	Shelled off Dutch coast attacking convoy
MTB 448	11/6	Damaged in E-Boat attack and then sunk by *MTB 453* off Barfleur
MGB 17	11/6	Mined off Normandy
MTB 734	26/6	Bombed by friendly aircraft off Normandy; sunk by *MTB 612*
MGB 326	28/6	Mined off Normandy
MTB 460	3/7	Mined off Normandy
MTB 666	5/7	Shelled off Ijmuiden
MTB 463	8/7	Mined off Normandy
MTB 434	9/7	Shelled off Le Havre
MTB 430	27/7	Rammed by E-Boat off Normandy
MTB 412	27/7	Collision with wrecked *MTB 430* off Normandy
HDML 1060	7/8	Explosion at Poole
MGB 313	16/8	Believed mined off Normandy
MTB 93	18/8	Collision with *MTB 729* off Harwich
ML 216	28/9	Mined in North Sea (19/9) then foundered in severe weather
MTB 360	1/10	Shelled off Ijmuiden
MTB 347	1/10	Shelled off Ijmuiden, Holland
MTB 441	23/10	Beached after friendly fire
ML 916	8/11	Mined; Walsoorden, Holland
MTB 782	28/12	Mined off River Schelde, North Sea

1945

MTB 690	18/1	Struck wreck off Lowestoft
MTB 712 Norwegian	21/1	Wrecked after grounding, Scapa Flow
ML 183	11/2	Rammed East Pier, Dieppe
MTB 255	14/2	Explosion and fire in Ostend harbour
MTB 438	14/2	Explosion and fire in Ostend harbour
MTB 444	14/2	Explosion and fire in Ostend harbour
MTB 459	14/2	Explosion and fire in Ostend harbour
MTB 461	14/2	Explosion and fire in Ostend harbour
MTB 462	14/2	Explosion and fire in Ostend harbour
MTB 464	14/2	Explosion and fire in Ostend harbour (towed back to UK, paid off)
MTB 465	14/2	Explosion and fire in Ostend harbour
MTB 466	14/2	Explosion and fire in Ostend harbour
MTB 776	14/2	Explosion and fire in Ostend harbour
MTB 789	14/2	Explosion and fire in Ostend harbour
MTB 791	14/2	Explosion and fire in Ostend harbour
MTB 798	14/2	Explosion and fire in Ostend harbour
HDML 1417	15/2	Mined off Flushing
MTB 605	17/2	Struck wreck on passage between Ostend and Dover
ML 466	25/3	Mined off Walcheren
MTB 493	7/4	Damaged ramming E-Boat in North Sea
MTB 494	7/4	Rammed by E-Boat in North Sea
MTB 5001	7/4	Shelled by E-Boat
MGB 2002 (ex-502)	12/5	Mined on passage between Aberdeen and Gothenburg
MTB 709 (Norwegian)	19/5	Explosion; Fosnavaag, Norway
MTB 715 (Norwegian)	19/5	Explosion; Fosnavaag, Norway
MGB 2007 (ex-507)	24/5	Wrecked grounding off Aberdeen
MTB 712	19/7	Aground off Scapa Flow, Scotland; paid off

Appendix 8

Obituaries

The obituaries quoted are the copyright of *The Times*, London, and are published with their permission.

Commander Donald Bradford

COMMANDER DONALD BRADFORD, DSO, DSC and two Bars, Coastal Forces commander, adventurer and businessman, died on 25 June 1995 aged 83.

During the Second World War, the waters of the Channel and North Sea were the scene of many savage sea-fights between the motor torpedo and motor gunboats of the Royal Navy and German coastal convoys with their escorts. In these, Donald Bradford, a Royal Naval Reserve officer, played a notable role, and one totally in character with the dash and verve with which British coastal forces sailed out to battle.

Most of the fighting was done at night when stealth and tactical skill often led to action being joined at very short range. This demanded courage, coolly directed fire and ship-handling skill at high speed amid what was often a chaos of tracer shells, explosions and smoke screens.

Donald Bradford's first DSC was earned in the spring of 1943. While lying on patrol off the Dutch coast, waiting and listening, his small force of two MGBs became aware of the noise of five German E-boats. Seeing their wakes in the darkness, Bradford managed to close to 40 yards before opening fire, sinking one with his guns and sending another to the bottom by ramming it.

In September 1943 Bradford was in command of the 55th Motor Torpedo Boat Flotilla based at Great Yarmouth. A contemporary, generously swallowing his pride in his own flotilla, acknowledged that, under Bradford's leadership, the 55th 'fought more

actions than most and pressed them home more firmly than most'.

His second DSC was awarded as a result of another hot action off the Dutch coast. Manoeuvring among sandbanks, Bradford's force of six MTBs and MGBs sank a large and heavily escorted liner with torpedoes and sank or damaged four of the escorting warships with gunfire.

Later that year, after an aborted Commando raid, Bradford sent his own boat home with the troops and, having transferred to that of a colleague, led an attack against a heavily escorted convoy. Outnumbered, his boat was riddled with holes and had several of its crew killed and wounded. Its petrol engines (always more liable to catch fire when damaged than the diesels of the E-boats) were burning fiercely and the boat was abandoned. Bradford and the commanding officer, both wounded, were among survivors picked up by another boat of the flotilla and Bradford received a mention in despatches.

In April 1944 Bradford's flotilla moved round to the South Coast in anticipation of the D-Day landings. There he was responsible for protecting the flank of the British invasion beaches from interference by German warships in the 'ferocious corner' of the Seine Bay, west of Le Havre. The night after D-Day with four boats, he attacked a force of German torpedo boats and minelayers, sinking one and disrupting their operation. This action was the more hair-raising for being conducted inside a German minefield. The British boats triggered twenty-three mines but survived thanks to their light displacement and speed.

Later, after the fall of Cherbourg, Bradford initiated the close blockade of Le Havre. Again heavily outnumbered, he torpedoed two E-boats and later sank a corvette by gunfire. This and other operations earned Bradford his third DSC and the DSO.

The Times, 6 July 1995

Commander Christopher Dreyer

COMMANDER CHRISTOPHER DREYER, DSO, DSC and Bar, MTB skipper who fought fierce battles against odds in the Channel and sank a U-boat off Sicily, died on 24 June 2003.

A member of the celebrated Dreyer naval family, Christopher Dreyer joined Dartmouth Naval College in 1932 aged 14 and went to sea as a midshipman in the battle cruiser HMS *Revenge* and the cruiser *Sussex* in the Far East. In 1939, he joined Coastal Forces.

In May 1940 all the few available MTBs were heavily involved in the Dunkirk evacuation. Commanding *MTB 102*, Dreyer made no fewer than eight crossings – on his penultimate trip carrying General Alexander. On a previous occasion, the headquarters destroyer HMS *Keith* was bombed off La Panne and Dreyer was called in to pick up Admiral Wake-Walker and his staff and ferry them to Dunkirk to continue organising the evacuation.

German dive-bombers seem to have realised what was going on and gave *MTB 102* their undivided attention. Dreyer wrote 'There were a good few wrecks so twisting and turning were out of the question. I could only go flat out and hope for the best. Luckily everything missed us.' Seeking some morphine for *Keith*'s wounded, he fetched up alongside a mine-recovery drifter whose skipper, eating bread and marmalade and non-chalant among the explosions, also gave him a morning paper and his own tin hat, Dreyer's having been lost overboard. 'Hate the bloody things anyway – they make my head ache.'

On his final trip Dreyer carried Wake-Walker again, directing the recovery of French soldiers. He was always proud of having commanded perhaps the smallest warship to wear an admiral's flag, in this case created from a dishcloth and red paint. He was awarded the DSC.

His second DSC was awarded for his courage and determination in leading a night attack on 6 August 1942, on an important German vessel, the 4,000-ton *Schwabenland*.

In 1943 he was posted to the Mediterranean theatre in command of the 24th MTB Flotilla and took part in the invasion of Sicily, Operation *Husky*. While patrolling at night in the Strait of Messina, he detected two German submarines making passage on the surface. He was so close that he had to back off sharply to allow his torpedoes the minimum range to achieve their set depth, sinking *U561*. He is reputed to have sent a famous signal 'To C-in-C Mediterranean. Sighted two U-boats in position so-and-so. Regret only one sunk.' For this and other actions Dreyer was awarded the DSO.

In March 1944 Dreyer was recalled to assist with the planning and execution of the Allied invasion of Normandy. As Staff Officer (Operations) under Captain, Coastal Forces, he was responsible for briefing commanders on the protection of the invasion convoys and how to prevent German reinforcements reaching their objectives.

After the war, a bout of 'Malta fever' (probably malaria) caused him to be invalided out of the Service. While in hospital he was invited to join Vosper. There he set up the sales department and eventually became its sales director. He assisted in the merger with John I. Thornycroft to create Vosper Thornycroft. He was retained as a consultant until the late 1970s.

He was an active president of the Coastal Forces Veterans' Association and much involved with the *MTB 102* Trust – this vessel having been his command at Dunkirk and which he took there again with the Little Ships for the 50th anniversary celebrations.

The Times, 4 July 2003

Captain Denis Jermain

CAPTAIN DENIS JERMAIN, DSC and Bar, celebrated MTB skipper who later in the war commanded a destroyer escort group in the battle against the U-boats, died on 26 October 2007, aged 89.

Denis Jermain was at sea for almost the entire Second World War, commanding Coastal Forces motor torpedo boats and then anti-submarine destroyers, and winning the DSC and Bar. He was also mentioned in despatches a remarkable five times.

His four years commanding MTBs in the Channel and Mediterranean began in July 1939 in Malta from where he transferred to Felixstowe when war broke out. While commanding *MTB 31*, Jermain made his name by devising a new method of attack against merchant shipping using depth charges instead of torpedoes and gunfire. He credited his father, Captain Henry Jermain, with the original idea, which he studied and practised carefully. Others emulated it.

His first mention in despatches was for the sinking of two armed trawlers north of Calais in October 1940, one by this new method. Fraught with hazard, it required very close quarters manoeuvres under fire. In November 1940 Jermain's boat was the only one of three left to attack a strongly escorted convoy anchored off the Scheldt. The firing apparatus of both his torpedoes failed, so he made two depth charge attacks, breaking the back of the largest merchantman of 6,000 tons. As he scraped past it on the second attack, his gunners fired upwards at anyone putting their heads over the guardrails. For this and other exploits he was awarded the DSC.

In November 1941 he went to America to advise on fitting out ten lease-lend PT boats. Shipped to Suez by May 1942, these became the 10th MTB Flotilla with Jermain in command. His first assignment was to sail to Tobruk to set up a base and prevent a seaborne attack on the beleaguered port. When Axis forces assaulted Tobruk, he sighted tanks approaching and reported by telephone. 'Don't be alarmist,' he was told. 'Look out of your window,' he riposted, to receive a gasp from the other end of the line.

With Rommel's tanks ringing the harbour, evacuation was ordered, and all small craft sailed out under cover of smoke screens. Jermain's flotilla returned to Alexandria, where among a number of impractical operations that was mooted, was a badly planned attack on Tobruk.

He was never allowed to see the reports of the action and deeply resented the staff opinion that the MTBs had lacked 'dash'. Overloaded with soldiers and with deck cargoes of petrol in jerry cans to achieve the required range, they were hardly nimble. The criticism was answered by a highly effective and praised diversionary simulation of a landing behind Rommel's lines before the battle of Alamein. Jermain received a Bar to his DSC and a second mention in despatches.

A shy and private person, Jermain nevertheless had a steely core to his personality and a marked ability to inspire his sailors.

The Times, 14 November 2007

Lord Newborough

LORD NEWBOROUGH, DSC, participant in the St Nazaire raid, died on 11 October 1988 aged 81.

As commander of *MTB 74* during the St Nazaire raid of March 1942, Lord Newborough, then sub-lieutenant Michael Wynn, RNVR, was charged with a crucial role in the operation. Had the main assault by a destroyer against the southern lock gate of the giant Normandie dock failed, Wynn, following up, was to fire two torpedoes at the caisson in an attempt to wreck it. As it was, the old ex-US destroyer HMS *Campbeltown*, packed with explosives, successfully rammed the lock and Wynn was able to use his delayed action torpedoes on a secondary target, the gates to the Old Entrance to the Bassin de St Nazaire. This completely disabled them to provide a doubly satisfactory conclusion to one of the most audacious combined operations of the Second World War.

Robert Charles Michael Vaughan Wynn, the elder son of the 6th Lord Newborough, was educated at Oundle from where he took a Special Reserve commission with the 9th Lancers in 1935. Between then and 1940, when he was invalided out of the Army, he served with several cavalry regiments.

This did not stop him procuring attachment, as a civilian, to the Fleet Air Arm in which he commanded an air-sea rescue vessel and was involved in the Dunkirk evacuation. Though his craft was almost sunk on her fifth trip to the beaches, he found the Navy congenial and next took a commission in the RNVR.

After his capture at St Nazaire he was eventually, as a nuisance prisoner, taken to Colditz. He remained there until January 1945 when he was repatriated to Britain on account of the injuries he had suffered at St Nazaire. He was awarded the DSC for his role in the raid as well as being mentioned in despatches.

In 1965 he succeeded his father as 7th Lord Newborough.

The Times, 20 October 1998

Captain Nigel Pumphrey

CAPTAIN NIGEL PUMPHREY, DSO and two Bars, DSC, wartime Coastal Forces commander, died on 29 September aged 84.

In April 1941, Pumphrey was appointed in command of the 6th Flotilla based at Dover, an early member of a gallant and much decorated band of officers. At that time Dover boasted only six motor torpedo boats, formed in two flotillas, and two motor gunboats. Living in the Lord Warden Hotel, Pumphrey records that the early type of radar that was installed near Dover conferred a valuable tactical advantage. His flotilla was certainly busy and up to March 1942 Pumphrey himself took part in about twenty battles, some successful, some not.

He was mentioned in despatches for the sinking of an escorted tanker in April 1941; this was followed by the award of the DSC for his part in a spirited action when his three boats attacked a heavily escorted convoy, sinking three ships. Pumphrey's boat was badly damaged (it was described by its coxswain as a '****ing colander') and finally sank after reaching Ramsgate, he and two of his sailors suffering wounds. He was again mentioned in despatches in November for the sinking of another enemy ship in the Dover Straits.

On the morning of 12 February 1942, Pumphrey was in his office 'doing a little placid paperwork' and expecting a telephone call from the stores department. But when the telephone did ring it was to convey no such humdrum information, but to tell him, instead, to sail immediately to intercept the battle cruisers *Scharnhorst* and *Gneisenau* which, under the command of Vice-Admiral Ciliax, had broken out of their Atlantic coast lair at Brest and were steaming up-Channel. They were accompanied by the heavy cruiser *Prinz Eugen* and a destroyer escort, not to mention sundry other small craft. Meanwhile, overhead an umbrella of Messerschmitt Me 109s, Me 110s and Focke-Wulf Fw 190s, maintained by patrols flown in rotation from French and Dutch airfields, provided a formidable air defence.

The breakout had been widely expected, but it was not anticipated that Ciliax would attempt the passage of the Straits of Dover in daylight. Furthermore, failures of aerial reconnaissance meant that the Germans had been steaming for more than 12 hours and were well into the Channel before they were spotted.

Despite being at four hours' notice, Pumphrey's five boats were at sea within twenty minutes. His laconic report says that as both aircraft and E-boats were engaging his MTBs, he was unable to get closer than about 4,000 yards to the heavily armed warships which in that weather had a speed advantage. For this and his other actions, Pumphrey was awarded his first DSO.

In March 1942 he was in hospital with his third wound, later remarking with characteristic modesty and wit: 'Can it be coincidence that every wound I suffered in the war was behind!' Having made an acknowledged contribution to the tactical doctrine of coastal forces, he was appointed in April to command the Hunt-Class destroyer HMS *Brocklesby*.

The Times, 8 October 1994

Lieutenant John Perkins

LIEUTENANT JOHN PERKINS, DSC and Bar, Coastal Forces skipper who fought many night actions in the Narrow Seas, died on 1 June 2008, aged 88.

While commanding *MTB 683* and attached to a Norwegian flotilla based at Lerwick in Shetland, John 'Polly' Perkins found himself alongside a jetty up a Norwegian fjord having completed a clandestine operation, landing agents and recovering refugees from the attentions of the Gestapo. As it was a few days before Christmas 1944, he sent one of his sailors ashore to root up some Christmas trees.

The MTB returned to Lerwick with three saplings, which were displayed on the upper deck and in the officers' and ratings' messes. But the Norwegian admiral who had come aboard to be de-briefed on the operation begged for two, which were swiftly flown to London as gifts to King Haakon and the prime minister of the Norwegian government-in-exile. Coastal Forces like to think that this incident is the origin of the annual donation from 1947 of a Norwegian tree to Trafalgar Square each Christmas.

Commanding *MTB 230*, Perkins was awarded his first DSC and a mention in despatches for actions against the enemy in the Nore area in October 1942 and March and June 1943, the first being against a heavily escorted convoy off the Dutch coast where he earned a reputation as an 'eager and aggressive torpedo marksman'. The many difficulties of the MTBs' early days included their un-silenced engines. Lacking star shell, radar and radio navigation aids, they were often unable to find the enemy or achieve the surprise necessary for the decisive close-in torpedo attack – sometimes becoming the hunted, not the hunter. His own lobbying helped to obtain the vital engine mufflers for the flotillas.

His second DSC was awarded for his part in another action off the Dutch coast while commanding *MTB 683* in June 1944. He remembered the campaign after D-Day as being one of 'various bloody actions against flak ships'.

In command of *MTB 766* Perkins was engaged in offensive operations up the Scheldt river with the aim of opening up the port of Antwerp when his seagoing career was brought to an end by 'the Ostend disaster'. Numerous MTBs were berthed at Ostend when a mechanic spilt a bucket of petrol into the water. This caught fire and the subsequent explosions, which included the large compressed-air vessels of torpedoes, caused the loss of twelve boats and the deaths of 68 sailors. Perkins was blown into the water with his navigating officer, who was never seen again. After survivors' leave Perkins was appointed to Coastal Forces staff division of the Admiralty until his retirement.

The Times, 23 June 2008

Commander Derek Wright

COMMANDER DEREK WRIGHT, DSC and two Bars, wartime Coastal Forces skipper who was three times decorated for his skill and courage in sinking German shipping at night, died on 10 May 2008, aged 92.

At the outbreak of the Second World War Derek Wright – always known as Jake – gave up his burgeoning career in the tea business with Brooke Bond and, being a keen yachtsman, swiftly became part of the huge expansion of the Royal Naval Volunteer Reserve which, at least initially, favoured those volunteers having amateur sea experience.

He volunteered for Coastal Forces and for the next four years took part in the bitter fighting in the Channel and North Sea. Fought mainly at night, these battles involved groping for enemy convoys in often poor visibility, keeping as quiet as possible until contact was made, then with all engines at full

power, the dark lit up by explosions and multi-coloured tracer shells, these lightly built craft would close at high speed to the short ranges necessary for a successful torpedo attack.

Wright was awarded his first DSC for his part while commanding *MTB 32* in a spirited action against enemy supply ships and E-boats on the night of 29 July 1942. After he had risen to command a unit of three MTBs, Wright's first success of many occurred in March 1943 with a well-planned attack on a heavily escorted convoy of three merchant ships, Wright stalking his prey for an hour and a half and getting down-moon before the final assault in a dazzle of star shell and tracer. Further actions in 1943 earned him a bar to his DSC.

He became known as one of a handful of MTB commanders who 'knew precisely what they were about', having commanded flotillas of two types of MTB as well as Fairmile 'D' gunboats, and contributed to important material and tactical innovations.

His attacks were brought to a pitch of perfection, as illustrated by an incident to the north of Walcheren during the invasion of Normandy where Wright's team of five Fairmile boats stalked four enemy warships and, apparently unseen, launched torpedoes that sank them all. His third DSC was awarded for outstanding leadership and skill in successful actions during July 1944. Promoted to temporary lieutenant-commander, he was mentioned in despatches for a further action in the North Sea in August.

He was present at the surrender ceremony, where senior German officers commanding their surviving E-boat forces came over to Felixstowe to brief the local C-in-C about the position of German minefields, an event conducted with dignity between brave men. Over five years, manned almost exclusively by RNVRs, Light Coastal Forces had fought 464 battles in home waters, sinking 269 enemy vessels for the loss of 76 of their own.

The Times, 18 June 2008

Sir Noel Macklin

SIR NOEL MACKLIN, builder of the 'Little Warships', died on 10 November 1946.

Sir Noel Macklin, who died suddenly on Sunday, was the creator of the plan that gave Britain over 800 small warships to fight the Battle of the Narrow Seas.

Albert Noel Campbell Macklin was born in 1889 of a family long associated with the law. He was educated at Eton. On leaving school he devoted much time to racing on the track at Brooklands and elsewhere, and also became a successful amateur jockey. He served in France in the 1914–18 war as an officer in the Royal Horse Artillery, and was invalided in 1916, whereupon he joined the RNVR as a lieutenant.

Early in 1938 he evolved a scheme for producing a large number of small warships in the minimum time. Macklin financed the undertaking himself and began the construction of the prototype vessel, originally intended for submarine hunting, but afterwards developed into an all-round small patrol vessel for convoy work, minelaying, minesweeping, troop conveyance, and a hundred other war purposes. When war broke out the organisation became so big that the Admiralty acquired it, and Macklin and the whole of his organisation became Admiralty servants.

Several types of vessel were produced and at the summit of production between twenty and thirty ships were put through their trials and handed to the Admiralty monthly. In brief, the plan was to prefabricate all parts in special factories and deliver them by road transport to small yacht builders in all parts of Great Britain – 45 yards and 87 slips were kept busy. In addition the complete parts were shipped to Egypt, Bermuda, Jamaica, Hong Kong, South Africa, Dar-es-Salaam, Australia, and New Zealand, and plans for identical construction were sent to Canada. When war ended, at the special request of the boat-building trade the Admiralty appointed Macklin director of small craft disposals to dispose, on behalf of the Treasury, of the vast numbers of craft of every description.

He was taken ill in 1941, largely through overwork, and although after six months' illness he recovered sufficiently to carry on with his work as head of a great organisation, physically he was crippled, though his brain remained keen and alert as ever. He received a knighthood in 1944 in recognition of his services in warship production.

The Times, 12 November 1946

Index

Index

Index